Annihilating Noise

Annihilating Noise

Paul Hegarty

BLOOMSBURY ACADEMIC
NEW YORK · LONDON · OXFORD · NEW DELHI · SYDNEY

BLOOMSBURY ACADEMIC
Bloomsbury Publishing Inc
1385 Broadway, New York, NY 10018, USA
50 Bedford Square, London, WC1B 3DP, UK

BLOOMSBURY, BLOOMSBURY ACADEMIC and the Diana logo
are trademarks of Bloomsbury Publishing Plc

First published in the United States of America 2021

Cover design by Louise Dugdale
Cover image © Mlenny / Getty images

Bloomsbury Publishing Inc does not have any control over, or responsibility for,
any third-party websites referred to or in this book. All internet addresses given in
this book were correct at the time of going to press. The author and publisher
regret any inconvenience caused if addresses have changed or sites have
ceased to exist, but can accept no responsibility for any such changes.

A catalog record for this book is available from the Library of Congress.

ISBN: HB: 978-1-5013-3543-3
       PB: 978-1-5013-3544-0
       ePDF: 978-1-5013-3546-4
       eBook: 978-1-5013-3545-7

Typeset by Integra Software Services Pvt. Ltd.
Printed and bound in the United States of America

To find out more about our authors and books visit www.bloomsbury.com
and sign up for our newsletters.

For Sarah, for our listening

Contents

Nothing Is Not the End

This is where the anecdote goes. This is where the personal experience validates the succeeding slew of words. This is the place for Athanasius Kircher, the brazen bull, ancient computers and where one man goes into a quiet room. This is where the universe expands into being, where its sound tails on and on, the ultimate prelude. It is where a key event crystallizes an argument so well its presence alone suffices. Where sound is studied, the prelude harkens, as if signalling that all sound existed before we heard it and wanted to write about it. As if signalling this in so many ways, so many times, would get 'us' over the melancholy of coming too late to hear it. To compensate for that, there is sonic archaeology, an imagining of sound before recording could fix it in place. To further triumph over the great tragedy of there having been sound before 'us', we can look and hear in literature, in documents across many media, and extrapolate back from today's natural phenomena to imagine a soundworld that, in also preceding 'us', salves that precedence and makes of it an always-already-before.

The anecdote can be imaginary, artistic, playful. It can glimpse a future, dream something new, something to the side, to give balm to the worry that so much goes unheard by 'us'. This thing that is not, or is for only a small group of people, or happens somewhere else, including virtually, consolidates all that 'we' miss into one alluring image. The prelude has power, the story is its medium. Its example is the exemplification that lies outside the rest of the system, conveying its power, its force within.[1]

Alternatively, the anecdotal can give way to the conceptual, the rigour of opinion, controversy or an often misleading hint at a theory of everything sonic. Luckily, noise has no such anecdotes, framing devices or exemplary moments of ecstatic access. Or, it is only those things. Noise is nothing, after all. Or everything. I didn't have an anecdote, but had fashioned an intra-anecdotal moment of self-satisfaction, a perfect start in some ways, but far better if it could end everything.

When noise began (if it did, and, although it did, you missed it), it interrupted. When the first noise, or type of noise, was heard *as noise*, it performed an interruption. It did not need a beginning, because it is precisely that act of opening. Many readings and interpretations of noise imagine it in light of a firstness – and this lies either in the belief that noise is a synonym of creativity (and therefore profoundly human, and maybe, therefore, unwittingly, the source of all normativities), or that it is a breach in a saga of human achievement. But noise can also be thought of in terms of lastness, of ending, (en)closure, shutdown, rejection. In the rush to embrace noise, anyone who does otherwise clings through prelude-necrophilia to what is gone, a crunchy dusty set of bones. These relics can be much adored, as Jörg Buttgereit showed in his 1987 film *Nekromantik*, but they are bones nonetheless. If noise has a reality, a fleshy newness, it is a newness that does not live at the beginning but lies in its release of endings.

To take this differently, and without exhuming a tale of listening past, many musicians imagine their new compositions/sounds/eructations to represent a beginning by virtue of being new. But if they in some way contain noise, they are an intrusion (or are defined as such by the unhabituated, unsocialized listeners), and therefore seek to stop something happening even as they fruit in the damp soil of real music. This stopping is an essential part of any type of noise, across all genres. It is why music that comes after the 1960s, after jazz, after rock, after industrial, after hip hop etc.,[2] has the possibility of using rejection as its mode of subversion, or, in a word from another age, transgression. Noise rejects, it does not build or build upon. This is not to say that 'noise musicians' do not listen to, learn from, emulate, respect and try to move on from existing 'noise music'. But the noise is not to be found there. There is no noise in noise music. It is not *in*, it is between noise and music and acts as the process between them.

The idea of noise music has been with us some time, and spawns many micro-avantgardes (or, we could say, the many micro-avant-gardes of contemporary music each offer the possibility of noise as outcrop to the practice of that specific micro-realm). Fans, musicians and critics all often expect a progress toward extremity, that noise is a type of escalation – maybe even an exemplary form of it. If this was the case, that moment has gone and joined the remnants of what was previously noise. This might suggest another model, where noise is only a melancholic sense of incompletion, such that no amount of noise will satisfy, no matter the gateway sound that brought you in. But I think that the failure to match an apparent demand for ever more noise, ever more loudness (the real escalation of loudness happened in digital simplifications of recording pop music) is benign, not tragic. The noise hungry live on in the end. Because once there was noise, identified as such, not out there in the wild, as the wild has no noise (what it has, for prospective receivers, are signals), then the end began. So my origin story is one where the end was introduced, and finally the possibility of making everything stop could take form. At a very basic level, knowing that the end has already happened (or will never happen) doesn't mean the end either has or has not happened – it means there is a living-on as if it had ended while it clearly had not. The presence of noise, a structuring and de-forming process always before or beyond identification, brings absence close to 'us', brings the limit into audition.

Maybe music could just stop. Music was already stopped the moment the potential was there for it to stop (or to have been stopped at some ur-time 'we' all missed), and the same applies to meaning, normative law and morals. That bringing of the end was relatively easy. The real challenge is how to stop noise. Not the proliferating unknown that noise presages (present noise is always a failed future-noise that suffers its failure in sounding, in being heard) but the things that happen in the place of music, in the place of noise music, or all experimental musics that want to latch on to the noise-value of the word noise. This is not the noise to end all noise, but the noise that tells us that noise can never be, can never settle, even relationally, and still be noise.

This seems abstract, but it is just because names, incident, history and time have been excluded. The situation described above is the sorry situation where no amount of not-saying, or of positive-saying can excise the actuality of noise's complexity and resolute resistance to disappearing. When noise stops noise, it is not the same as incorporation, reification, selling out, etc. It is the playing out of the finality of noise, the emptiness of event. And that's why this anecdote is going to be about listening to Vomir's *Black Box* (2019; that title used for convenience, it is untitled). Vomir (Romain Perrot) makes harsh noise wall, a thick, solid noise that some might wish to think relentless. Harsh noise wall eschews variation in the interest of a hearing that through being misled, hears all sorts of artefactual content and change. Vomir writes properly nihilistic manifestos about absence of development, about hiding away from society and about nothing, echoing The New Blockaders's rejectionism first issued in the early 1980s. The 2019 Vomir manifesto begins with

NO ACT
NO POINT
NO REMORSE
NO STRATEGY[3]

And carries on in that vein, a profound refusal to even refuse properly. While the aesthetic around Vomir's releases has varied to some extent, the core is this properly nihilist set of ideas – an ideal illustration of how 'negativity' in noise is both in a relation (to something else) and the creator of new relations. Noise musicians have sought for some time (perhaps less now) to maintain the resolution of 'being against', thus maintaining both an antagonistic relation and not offering a positive solution, or any utopia. But still, there is something – many things, as the pile of Vomir's releases to be found on discogs.com will show. Most of this is the same stuff, that wall of harsh yet static noise, seeming to peak and trough, pulse and thud even as it just sits there, as unchanging as sound moving in time can be. Of course it is not, it is impossible to hear 'unchanging' even if it really was so.

The sound is also not nothing in that it takes effort, choices, machinery, editing, formatting, naming etc. The shape and sound of Vomir's releases and concerts are not like the noise generated by a white noise machine designed either for electronic calibration or for soothing the unsleeping or tinnitized. The combination of multiple devices in sequence means a constant generation of variation, albeit within a sonic morass that threatens to not allow any incident an escape velocity.

The experience of listening is not nothing either. Instead of any sort of overwhelming volume, like at a Sunn O))) concert, the sound is set so that it gradually and stealthily creates an effect of loudness through stasis – which is not nothing as loudness and 'noise' are usually what we think of intrusive, jagged sounds. Responses can range from meditative to amused to a sense of immersiveness, or often, an initial scepticism or simple glee, replaced by an involvement that is not quite listening (listening for detail is being thwarted at every point) or hearing (as it is not just happening, raw, it is heavily contextualized). But it is a nothingness that generates all the not-nothing around it. As Perrot stands still and the hard drive or even phone plays the new 'composition', there is nothing to see, no action, no event. Yet this all requires a something for nothing to happen in, and like all noise, whether at a beginning or middle or somewhere else, it is a sort of end, a living-on in the end. It is tempting to think of exhaustion – a using up of noise, even as the more mundane tiredness sets in as you perhaps switch to CD 2 of *Black Box*. Each CD is more than an hour long and, while nothing really happens, there is a sense of continual change, of permanent involution.

How much more will there be? When will it end? In recorded form, 'we' know, 'we' can see the timer on the CD player or computer, or the progress of the needle, or cassette. It is still hard to imagine an ending, because although each 'piece' of Vomir has a defined length, there is no evident logic, even allowing for material format constraints, as to why it should be a certain length. It would be tempting to take the longer 'works' as reflections on or of the fate of the human: with nothing in front of us, 'we' are forced inward, and with no sense of when the end is coming, just that it is, we are getting close to phenomenology. Step back. If we are that close, we are not close enough, or too close, because what happens in the endless reflectiveness of nothing is that nothingness spreads in each thing reflected, emptying all the time. That is not to say that after all six CDs of *Black Box* we will know anything more, or feel differently. 'We' might have heard something of the emptiness even of nihilism, of the redundancy of searching for meaning (even as noise) that will fail, and in failing is not even absurd, just flat. Forget flat ontologies, the wall is where flatness is thingly, even as things lose definition. Vomir's *Black Box* carries no evidence about what happened, just that something did.

The experience is very pleasurable for all the possible seriousness and indeed 'affect' that 'we' might find there, or for all the smugness of having heard a harsh noise wall once, 'we' (a different 'we' this time, but 'you' feels, as it were, 'harsh') move on to other experimentations. The fullness of sound, the display of lack of choice allows freedom, a freedom that is given parameters and, if experienced with enough volume, not simple enough to become an ear balm. The paradoxes of noise as practice and idea are here in the lavish if sometimes also low-grade object that is a Vomir release. The search for something ultimate, something sublime etc., is both available and thwarted. This failure is not tragic, or to be ignored, instead it is a condition of possibility that is different to living in the realm of the simply positive that states 'this is' or 'this is the right or good thing'. Mostly when encountering noise, 'we' do not want to think about that, and do not need to, but it is there, nonetheless, there as a lingering absence. Vomir (or any other harsh noise wall) is not the endpoint because there is nowhere beyond – it is something like an endpoint because its very form (or formless[ness]) is about there being nothing beyond.

Noise music continues, it does not need to do MORE than Vomir, it just carries on in the specific non-presence of those sounds, i.e. noise music, fully genrified [*sic*], even if still multiple, grows. Noise as a DIY genre is in rude health, noise as part of experimental festivals is still present. Performers like Mattin or Torturing Nurse are spawning micro-avant-gardes continually, harsh noise emanates from The Rita, Prurient, Pharmakon, the returning 1990s noise musicians from Japan, Puce Mary, Werewolf Jerusalem, Moor Mother ... bands and projects rise and fall, but all live on in the end that is noise. Noise is not there, not in experimentation that is established, but in the complex, often contradictory and always paradoxical relation of noise to something that it is not, or seeks not to be, or is not allowed to be.

Black Box is perhaps a bit softer than other Vomir CD releases, where often what distinguishes the 'force' is the production. All the parts are biased toward the higher frequencies and have what I have to describe as noticeable flanging. Each CD starts with a rush, no lead-in, and ends the same way. In between lies 70+ minutes of amorphous sound, with tentacles of certain frequencies reaching out, or seeming to move more than others. Rhythms descend and fall, there is a surprising amount of percussiveness, which is either an artefact of listening or of the machines playing each other (or both). Listening is not sharpened or honed, but lured, betrayed, played with. Are these CDs really any different from each other? They sound different as 'we' proceed through them, but I know that re-playing the same Vomir CD will sound more different than almost all other CDs, which slowly begin to offer what 'we' might think of as their true shape. Or, perhaps this box contains only one work, broken by the 'limits' of the CD, like Morton Feldman compositions that span multiple discs. I think it is better to think of it as one piece that has five breaks, and these are like the banded charts of spectroscopy or genome sequencing. More mundanely, and always lower, always hinting at the pathetic, it is about how much of the rest of the world, in terms of sound, time and events, is allowed to interrupt this interruptive continuum that comes in CD-length bursts. This type of music is about scale not because of its length, but because it addresses the question of scale and extension.

The Vomir CD, like the live performance, is an intrusion of explicit scale (sound, time, change or otherwise) that legitimately summons thoughts of a range of scientific phenomena. The most obvious is the statistical likelihood of emptiness and dispersion identified and developed by nineteenth-century physicist Ludwig Boltzmann. Except – this is the opposite as it summons a sort of structure, a bounding at least (an inside and outside, a before and after), and within the island of stability (as 'we' sense it) that is ordered living where humans are, this is not unusual. What is unusual is the structuring that can at least indicate the more likely possibility of complete equilibrium (the even distribution of all matter such that it conveys no information as each part is too distant from the next) and absence of meaning.

This means that harsh noise wall is a limit condition that is both ending and the impossibility of ending, because its natural (withheld) habitat is flat fullness, a residue and reflux of dynamism. So how literally does it stop and what happens then? As noisemaker Clive Henry points out, there are two ways harsh noise wall can stop: one is the slow fade, the other, more common end is the sudden cut, a cut that performs the break between in and out, and, in the moment it happens, does not quite restore the world of not-noise. Both retain a violence that makes it hard to adjust back to not hearing the harsh noise wall.[4] The reason for this lies in the solidity of the sound and the paradoxically large range of what 'we' can hear as the fatberg of sound inches along in what does not feel like real time. Unlike a rock track, or one with an overt complexity of instrumentation or sound sources, which have multiple ways of ending, there is no way out of the wall whilst retaining its wallness, other than these two options. Anticipating this end is one of the visceral pleasures of doing something like listening to Vomir or others.

One slightly different way of ending is introduced by way of the approach to the machinery, the apparatus that brings the condition where noise is (or maybe is not). Marja-Leena Sillanpää's sound works are often centred on summoning lost voices, notably of women outside the canon of experimental art, and use non-thematic found sounds to that effect. She also engages with highly physical soundwork where the sound is generated from actions. But one genre that I suspect she would reject, and yet approaches, is that of harsh noise wall, which she builds from a radio receiver and other electronics. The sound slowly reaches wall intensity, then holds, and moves as richly dense and layered noise. Her self-awareness as a performer translates into a statement of diffidence as she stands to the side, neither intent nor disengaged, and somehow manages, through this affectless absenting, to make the sound more inhuman than Vomir, even. After some unspecified amount of time, she then moves toward the apparatus and the noise goes away. As an exercise in present-ing, it is exemplary, a type of acceptance of sound that nonetheless does not make presumptions of its audience or allow its audience to make them.

While Vomir to some extent encourages such presumptions about aesthetic, political, desiring choices, he too diminishes those as the wall just keeps on happening. In both cases the physical attitude matters – Vomir stands still, Sillanpää is also still but more curatorial, more as if she is extracting something through her slight distance from the machinery. The stillness of harsh noise wall, or the thick electricity generated by Sillanpää, goes against the increased gesturality of electronic music. This has been enabled by 'intuitive' machines such as the kaossillator, but is already there in musicians' signalling that, even though they are essentially operating complex digital machinery in ways no different to working in traffic flow monitoring, they are present and active, interacting through their bodies. Hence 'we' have seen the spread of the swooshing knob turn, the hammering down on an FX pedal, all kinds of active twiddling, the various shapes of digit-based dexterity needed for craft DIY electronics, the throwing down of stuff, the 'disregard' for the pile of machines on a tabletop etc. The ending too has its own gestures in improvised, experimental, noise or whatever we wish to call music that is odd but not classical, played yet non-virtuosic in skill. How will we know it's over? With harsh noise wall, there might be a sense that this will never end, an infinity of being in 'your' present moment, but it will still end. Perhaps there will be a dramatic twist to zero of the volume switch, or an unplugging, or throwing everything on the floor, or walking out as something pre-recorded comes to a stop. All of these restage the Romantic drama of the end of everything in a way that is certainly satisfying even if it is more rock than noise.

Noise musicians have tried whatever 'we' can think of to vary the experience, but why even bother? With harsh noise wall, there are only those two options. In improvised music in general, the sudden stop is possible, but is hard to do, and potentially disrespectful within the group dynamic (the harsh noise wall is mostly the product of one person, mostly inactive as it plays). So these improvising performers need to tell everyone when the thing is over, complete. The listener can get a sense of this sometimes, if every piece of stuff on a table has been used, but still, has the sound really faded out fully? So what has evolved as a physical marking of the end is the settling back, the release of physical attention and tension that allows the audience to mirror it back to the performer (as I write that sentence, I have a genuinely vertiginous reaction to the end of CD 3 of Vomir's *Black Box*). The performers look up, released from their service, their work is done, their bodies say, and we are ready for the end to be acknowledged. This satiety is not what happens at the end of a harsh noise or harsh noise wall concert, where often, even mostly, there is a pause and everyone recalibrates to the loss of the sound that accompanied them so strongly. Then the box continues, each CD slabbing noise that somehow isn't as settling as a white noise soothing machine, although it can simulate the real world pleasure of external interruption if listened to from far away but still indoors.

CD 4 opens up, just like the last three, and continues for 76 minutes 57 seconds. Then, and still, it ends abruptly, as the knowledge of the end is outweighed by the alteration in what has become habitual over the period of 75 minutes.

CD 5 is 75 minutes 07 seconds of more. Or less

CD 6, 73.43 and the end.

Annihilating Noise is a book about how noise relates to music and beyond. It looks to what is beyond the parameters of recorded or performed noise but never leaves that 'musical' part behind. We can avoid music in conducting sound-based research, but without music as a reference point, it is not clear to me how Western culture at least ever really attended analytically to sound. Perhaps listening to what is not music, or indeed, what is not noise in or as music, is a way out of music, a return to the world, but it feels narrower and impoverished, like sound art telling us to block out all senses and social conditions to just! listen! As the structured form of sound that is the result, location and drive for reflection on the acoustic, and dwelling in it, as opposed to not even hearing it, music is essential, even as that which is excluded, say, from a social study of sound or noise. Noise is also essential, but only if we retain its capacity to be against, to be wrong in some way. Noise is even better, or worse, when it fails to do this, when it attempts to become noise and never quite attains that status – and this is more likely something to be encountered in music, or in social antagonisms toward certain types of music at different historical moments and geographical sites.

The book is divided into four parts, each with their own brief introductory section outlining the key idea or focus of the essay – this book is, after all, a collection of connected essays, and each part follows its own specific thematic. The first part, the most theoretical, focuses on 'nature' and ecologies of noise. This hyperbolic Bataillean ecology permeates the book, along with the word 'etc', the theories of Fred Moten on music, performance and social location of the avant-garde, along with a smattering of entropy, and also the work of Karen Barad on quantum phenomena. Part Two probes at questions of social definitions and positionings in relation to artists making noise in the place of music. In Part Three, the point of attention is the material, in the context of dematerialization and demonetization of music-making except for top-level 'blue chip' performers.

If there was ever a fear about over-commodification of noise or experimental music, the exploitative freeing up of music has fixed that for good. Part Four is all about specific examples of noise, as it appears in the work of musicians across a range of styles. That final part, and the book, closes on a return to the idea of the end, and the consumption of noise by individuals, by the market, by familiarity. Finally, noise is revealed as never enough, always too much, and always in need of emptying out.

Massive thanks to Leah Babb-Rosenfeld and all at Bloomsbury.

Part One

Ungrounding

This section is about an expanded realm of noise. It is not uncommon to posit models for sound, music and noise that exceed direct human experience and presence, and this section works through some of those ideas to remind us of noise as disruption and also of human relation to it, in defining it. For all the attempts to leave the human behind in favour of objects, materiality and so on, there is a broad tendency in contemporary thought to reject deconstructive modes of thought in order to return to a positivistic way of seeing the universe, which means statements about things that exist autonomously, made anew into uncritical categories. In the four chapters that make up this part, I try to reintroduce a nihilistic and deep critical reading of noise that can nonetheless work on scales that are more-than-human, in order to illustrate the value of the less-than. This is the most 'technically' theoretical part of the book.

The first chapter addresses noise on an extravagant scale, a way of rethinking sound in nature as threat, as action, as effect; in short, it is an attempt to fashion a general ecology of a nature that does not exist for our listening pleasure. The second chapter in this part continues on the theme of sound 'in the world' to think about the question of 'field' in field recording. What is the natural world that is presumed in the process of field recording? Where Chapter 1 considers the idea of sound in nature, this looks at how we record it, process it and add to its claims of objective realness. Beyond the sounds to be found in the 'field', how do we hear the field itself? What do we presume when going 'into' the field? Closer inspection reveals that there is no field other than generated through the apparatus of recording. This is not about inadequacy, or dishonesty, but a deep failure connected to the dark ecology of sound that is beyond 'us'. From there, the third chapter looks at noise and coding. Pioneers of information theory have much to tell us about noise, but readers and listeners need to have perspective: information theory is just one of many codings of noise, and it is in its failure to understand noise that it can be useful to compare with the much fuller theorizations available if we adopt a multiple, more open sense of what it means to encode or decode. The perverse uncertainty of Warren Weaver in his use of 'etc.' offers that theory a way back in, as part of a way to understand the recodings [sic] at play in the hearing of noise. Along the way, entropy within mid-twentieth-century telephonics is distinguished from the version developed by nineteenth-century physics. The fourth and closing part of this section is about temporalities and noise, via a heavily sound-based exhibition curated by Philippe Decrauzat and Mathieu Copeland that established a multilayered relation between film and music or sound, and a complex genealogical model of sound as open temporal device. Origins, proper placement of noise and relic-validating are all marshalled on the way to a declaration of the terranormativity of sound.

Earth Apathy: A General Ecology of Sound

'Nothing is more foreign to our way of thinking than the earth in the middle of the silent universe and having neither the meaning that man gives things, nor the meaninglessness of things as soon as we try to imagine them without a consciousness that reflects them … But animal life, halfway distant from *our* consciousness, presents us with a more disconcerting enigma' (Georges Bataille, *Theory of Religion*, 20–21).[1] Such was Bataille's sense of mirroring emptiness.

The isolation of presence in outer space is captured by 'in space no-one can hear you scream', the line that helped sell Ridley Scott's 1979 film *Alien* and that centres on sound, on the sound of the human voice, of that voice in pain, that voice warning. The sound is isolated because it will not be heard – there is no one there to hear, there is no hearing, this not hearing is insurmountable. Just you, your scream, in space. As you scream, the futility of the sound informs, materializes the meaning of the sound even more than if it were heard. Of course, despite several centuries of assertions about the silence of space, it would seem that in fact sound can occur in space, with the potential question being about its reception, as opposed to its occurrence.[2] The universe has its own perma-ambience in the form of the cosmic microwave background, the static that feeds all static, the formless that we hear as a trace of the creation of form from within which we hear. Planets make sounds, and in 2003 a black hole was discovered humming low and slow, oscillating once every 10 million years at a note fifty-seven octaves below human hearing. This is only the start of it, as, again, contrary to vacuum fans or phobics since Blaise Pascal, space is full of stuff, it is the scale of things that has confused humans into thinking it was empty. Sound at any frequency requires something to vibrate, and therefore the wavelength needs to be longer than the distance of molecules one from another. As this situation is not at all frequent, there is plenty of quiet, but also plenty of

Earlier version presented at Kingston University, in 2016.

yet undiscovered sound (given the scale and statistical nature of the presence of the conditions for sound) and, more curiously, lots of local sound. Perhaps we can move from the supposedly silent scream into another kind of silence that emerges after considerations of the vexed place of nature, and of sound beyond the human, a silence of dread apathy.

When a human speaks, they are not only alive, they mark their existence through sound, and, argues Giorgio Agamben in *Language and Death*, the beginning of this human voice lies in animality. The origin of the voice is the scream emitted by the dying animal, as a moment of complete presence.[3] This is there as potential in human existence, but it is suppressed, with language coming into existence as the trace, the supplement of the transitional vibration between human and animal, as seen from a human perspective, at least. When a human is alive, they are still full of cavities with gas and liquid which can vibrate. In space *you* will hear yourself scream, knowing that no one else can hear. You will increasingly hear sounds that are your body creating not just high fidelity but total fidelity, uninterrupted by anything else auditory, or any other receiver. Like an anechoic chamber designed to deaden sound, only a lot more instructive. But, even adrift in your spacesuit, other sounds can filter in, perhaps generated directly by the brain, in an uncanny analogue of digital sound-making. And the chance of switching off radio communications is probably slim. The warmth of others' voices who can still hear your transmission may offer some comforting community but it is likely to be a community based on your death, a perfect expression of the general economy of sacrifice that, for Georges Bataille, grounds human existence, even when it is repressed, forbidden, elided, unheard, routinized into labour, measured activity, normative behaviours.

Radio was the first clue that space was not empty of sonic phenomena, the first aural glimpse into the prospect of sound worlds beyond our own limited apparatus for the sonic. Radio waves travel unhindered through vast distances, if the medium permits. Unlike light, radio is much less directional – the waves expand, spherically and imperfectly, whether initially broadly cast or not.[4] But it is not unbounded, either – it can be blocked, or halted, as the medium runs out. So the screaming astronaut's sound could vibrate outward indefinitely, but its short waveband will more likely result in a bubble of sound, a space in which it is unlikely there will be any one (else) to hear. But between the localized productions of sound and the potentially huge number of sounds unheard by humans or their prostheses, the main reason no one will hear you scream is that there is so much sound occurring in the universe … or so much soundlike stuff, and so many listeners, but so widely separated, that very little is heard, with sound an exemplary human experience of the limits of the human or even existence-centric being, in true Boltzmannian entropy. For physicist Ludwig Boltzmann, the fundamental state of the universe was to be empty. This led him to the idea of a statistical entropy which on the one (massive) hand gives us complete equilibrium and heat death, where 'in the course of time the universe must tend to a state where the average *vis viva* of every atom is the same and all energy is dissipated', whilst on the other (small) hand, local pockets of communication do occur.[5] Listeners will likely be biologically and situationally limited in range of hearing, and will not perhaps be interested in some sonic phenomena, nor pay attention, or hear but not listen. No one will hear you, not because they are not there or your voice has no traction in vacuum, but because, just as if the universe were empty, no one cares to listen. Stephen Hawking regularly expressed his concern that humans are making so much noise and trying so hard to attract alien attention that we risk being contacted and destroyed, but what if 'The Great Silence' out there is not due to any of the many ingenious ways of explaining the Fermi paradox (the probability of intelligent life versus the absence of evidence) but due to a properly cosmic, quasi-sublime apathy?[6]

Those are all sounds 'out there', caught between multiplicity and being inactivated. Earth, though, is a sound-filled place. To us at least, as we (a very broad we, this time) have evolved to be able to process sound waves, our gills remoulded into tapping devices serving as the entry to a complex set of processes by which a brain hears sound. All this attention to sound may in itself be very local, a dying astronaut's gasping as they float at massive speed. But, from within the locality of Earth, sound is not only important in proximity, but at all distances, as the primary use of sound seems to be to spatialize (within a loop where hearing identifies dimensions, and sound structures space and spaces, as suspected and mobilized by sound artist Alvin Lucier in his *I Am Sitting in a Room* from 1969, a work that will appear spectrally several times in this book). Sound is localization, as perceived by listeners, and leaving aside whether a tree falling makes a sound if no one is there to hear it, because obviously, it both makes and doesn't make sound in this scaled-up quantum question. My point is that sound itself is contingent, dependent on capacity (if not necessarily actuality) of hearing and listening. So how should we treat sound as neither factual, 'objective' (it just is), nor as 'subjective' (needing to transmit through perception)? Perhaps we should think about the use of the word 'sound', and stop saying 'sound does this or that' or 'we hear', 'hearing is always open' or 'sound cannot be controlled'. Instead of sound, sounds themselves, as caught within perceptual systems, are needed to do sound studies.[7] Sociology does not talk about light when it thinks about TV or public rallies, nor does art history address visual culture through light. I am suggesting a hyperbolic recalibration, something extravagant and seemingly out of step with the machine pragmatics of technological change and the aesthetic or ethical modes of disruption that seek only to empty existing forms.

This is going to require the return of the 'sublime', and a rethinking of what 'nature' has come to mean in the thought of sound – because addressing nature in terms of its sounds is still new enough to not have developed satisfactory critical approaches, largely, I think, because it turns its back on the value of analytically deconstructive approaches in favour of metaphysical truth claims that are hedged in parts of theory that legitimate a return to unreflective and positivist assertions of what is seemingly 'true'. Theory becomes a statement of 'isness' or 'ipseity' rather than a set of methods. Even Steve Goodman's explosive *Sonic Warfare* rests on the claim of 'an ontology of vibrational force' (xvi), which may be processual, it may be complex and unhuman, but it's still a metaphysical truth claim.[8] That said, I'm going to make another claim, based on the groundless and violent recasting of the sublime by Georges Bataille, and this will be from a position of addressing specific materials, seeing how they work, and ultimately bringing us to the kind of sound that is largely marginalized in sound studies – the sounds of animal death, or more precisely, a sound that does not show the bringing or causing of the death but its very clear 'presence'.

Sound studies looks at nature in a kind of sanitized David Attenborough mode, and this is not because it is 'hindered or tainted by thinking about music', as some writers believe to be a problem in thinking about audio phenomena,[9] but because it tracks an inheritance from field recording, acoustic ecology and the politically managerialist notion that listening is morally good, and in fact IS a moral good in itself. There are attempts to play with ideas of nature, of merging what had been accepted as category borders, between humans, media, animals, deep space etc. Not least among these is Douglas Kahn's *Earth Sound Earth Signal*, wherein Earth is recast as a kind of privileged routing station for cosmic sounds, where humans form part of a system with the planet they mostly (all but six currently) dwell on.[10] Earth exists 'in circuit' (*Earth Sound Earth Signal*, 256–57), as revealed in the discoveries of elemental sound, often in the form of interference, that arose through the development of new media in the nineteenth century. For Kahn, it seems that nature becomes audible as supplement, due to the supplement of those new media – i.e. the original, ever-oscillating threads in nature are brought into being for us, and then located in atemporal pre-existence – what Heidegger or Derrida would refer to as 'always already'. So when Kahn says that 'nature was broadcasting globally before there was a globe' (*Earth Sound Earth Signal*, 2), he is making a claim at several levels: nature does not need human media; humans discover and use natural waveforms, but do not definitively master them; lastly, nature is to be taken knowingly as a human construct. Kahn's model suggests both an autonomous sonic universe and the limitation that humans can only know it through treating humanity itself as medium – he mostly does not directly claim that there is a nature that is 'out there', but he sometimes forgets and then goes on to deal with nature as something true, essential, objectively existing, producing masses of sound which cannot be known or controlled by humans.[11] So what Kahn offers is a step into thinking sound and sonic media beyond the human, whilst illustrating the difficulty in philosophically maintaining that position.

Jacob Smith's *Eco-Sonic Media* also attempts to place human sound production and reception into wider circuits, or more precisely, Latour-inspired networks, with various animal and vegetable actants, in 'biological eco-systems and industrial infrastructures that enable sound reproduction [in order] to assess the eco-cosmopolitan potential of various modes of sound-media communication' (*Eco-Sonic Media*, 3).[12] More than looking at how media process natural phenomena, or how sound itself transmits information of any sort, he is interested in how eco-sonic media arise:

> Sound media become eco-sonic media when they manifest a low-impact sustainable infrastructure; when they foster an appreciation of, or facilitate communication with, nonhuman nature; when they provide both a sense of place and a sense of planet; and when they represent environmental crisis.

(6)

For Smith, human and nature interact through media. Media becomes the interaction, the set of linking activities, as opposed to being simply an enabling tool. We should then build an ecologically friendly set of discourses and practices into our sonic interaction with the world. Eco-sonic media are ideologically consistent with one political position, one philosophical outlook – which is that of acknowledging humanity's reckless waste of planetary resources, while trying to correct that through increasingly proper behaviour. Despite Smith's gestures toward Timothy Morton's 'dark ecology', Arne Naess's massive initial step, in 'deep ecology', toward removing humans from the centre of ecological importance, is sidestepped.[13] Not for the first or last time, humans using tools will know nature better, know nature well enough to save it, if only they care, if only they listen properly.

Such a listening underpins both ecologically aware sound writing and sound recording, and emanates from R. Murray Schafer's concept of acoustic ecology, developed through a series of projects and books in the 1970s, wherein the world's natural sonic balance is constantly under threat from human, industrial and machinic takeover. Sound is indeed a useful and under-used way of directly capturing ecological changes in specific environments. But what I'm interested in is how nature, as sound-producer, has slipped easily into being a new kind of resource, one that is being tapped in parallel to ecotourism and indeed tar sands and subpolar mineral searching. Maybe it's sustainable, but it is increasingly the case that nature can be mined to help its own cause.

Eco-sonic media emphasize the creation of sound as species/material crossovers, and field recordings are part of that, very obviously making nature into a sound artefact, via the artefactuality of recording process, and, at its best, revealing this taut self-deconstruction at the, or as the, core of its activity. Jean-Yves Bosseur is the latest (in *Musique et environnement*) to catalogue the many ways composers, installation artists and architects with sonic interest have attempted to configure sound into an environment suffering from its loss of aural authenticity.[14] At the core of Bosseur's book is Schafer's belief that urban, modern environments experience a lack, are low fidelity, due to the mass of uncontrollable and loud sounds, whereas nature and 'traditional' domains (as also valorized by Smith) offer high fidelity, and therefore a higher level of authentic dwelling with and in nature.[15] For Bosseur, sound artists can have a massive influence on how we think about sound and also affect how such thinking feeds into wider ecological concerns. This rich panoply of species of creators in the soundscape-scape, each with their own niche, will actually improve us all, bringing a greater sense of harmony between nature and culture (*Musique et environnement*, 48).

There is little sense, among the newly global, universally conscious sound thinkers, that nature itself is largely a cultural product (or, as Karen Barad calls it, 'naturalcultural practices'), at least in terms of people approaching it as a single object, there to be used theoretically and acoustically.[16] But, of course, none of Kahn, Smith, Bosseur nor the million and highly diverse sonic creators living in the teeming arts landscape in need of preserving, wish to exploit nature. As one, they call for nature to make its sounds, and in making its sounds, we will begin to hear, and live as one with it, and nature will be able to save itself, due to its variety, novelty and musicality. Dominic Pettman tries to move on from a 'romantic salvage operation' of Nature (*Sonic Intimacy*, 74), yet calls for 'an ethical resonance theory' (ibid.).[17] Bosseur talks of letting sound be, Kahn says now that we've found the electricity of the spheres, it can play out as always, Smith tells us that nature is always making sounds, and making sound in media contexts. Where Smith wants us to imagine a naturally, sonically, active set of objects out in the world, Seth Kim-Cohen provides a note of warning – we need to think of 'sound's expanded situation' (*In the Blink of an Ear*, 217), and this is not just through the diversion of the objects, material conceits and ideological productions that act as carapaces to the sonic.[18] Instead it is to think about what happens, what we do, when we listen, when sound 'happens' and, I would add, when specifically identified sounds happen. Kim-Cohen targets 'acousmatic' listening (i.e. where the sound is isolated and divorced from its source), but it could apply to all art-context sound work, in theory or in practice when he says that 'acousmatic listening involves a naïve, blank reception of the auditory' (13), which is in fact an entirely imaginary access mode. All we can do is recognize the limits of 'sound in itself', at least for we humans, a category of entity that seems too often to be deemed to share an ear.

One way in which we can imagine such recognition is in combining human-made music, or consciously structured sounds, in the context of what we can continue to call natural sounds. Here, then, musical creation could look to nature as collaborator, as material, as inspiration, as source of musicality from which music or musicality can spring, ever more literally. There are two modes to this – one, the almost absurdly literal playing of music with nature, and second, the making of musical or quasi-musical objects through the intervention of recording.

Professional philosopher-musician and Zen improviser David Rothenberg is perhaps an extreme variant on the valorization of nature as inherently good, and of our attention to it as a boon to the world. Nonetheless, there are few involved in sound studies or sound art who do not at least covertly adhere to some of his thoughts, perhaps because of what Smith terms 'springs of hope in sound studies' (*Eco-Sonic Media*, 145). In short, sound studies correctly aims to have a moral compass, political and ethical interests, but at base, it seems to need to share sound art's view that the material of art can somehow improve us when framed correctly, or is 'allowed to be' in some way currently not permitted. Rothenberg is not just a commentator on acoustic ecology, he is very much an embedded practitioner. He attributes his favoured mode of playing music to nature, arguing that it too improvises, that 'the world [is] a confluence of sudden happenings' (Rothenberg, *Sudden Music*, 2).[19] The musicality of the world is total, waiting to be released into human consciousness, through 'hearing nature for what it is: a vast unstoppable music' (89), leading to an 'essential oneness with the unspeakable meaning of the world' (48). Nature itself is open-ended (though as it is discoverable through listening and indeed playing duets with it, it is a thing, available for human perception). Nature features prominently by name, an amorphous container for all that Rosenberg wants to put in to the world: it is the 'ideal listener, or it may be a blank slate' (17). It is also and vitally immanent:

> To be a musician is to know the musicality in all life, to struggle to hear the constantly changing music not of any distant spheres, but of the immediate earth … The struggle is to hear as music a sound world that does not cease, that has no initiation, no conclusion.
>
> (191)

Ultimately, though, despite the mystery and power of natural sound worlds, this sonic realm is something within which dwelling can be achieved: 'if we treat each sound as part of a meaningful sonic world, the natural world might resound more like the home that it is' (92).

Rothenberg is not content to merely wander the world, learning from 'traditional' musicians, each of whom confirms his belief that improvisation is a universal, or playing his clarinet into the wind up a mountain. He also wants to play with whales, which he has done by suspending a speaker under water as he plays, with the humpback whale joining in.[20] We can be thankful that Jacob Smith only constructed an actor network with digital media, himself and his canary, Bing. Despite Rothenberg's ontological goodness model of the sonic world and how we can choose to mingle and merge with it, he has some interesting ideas – the idea of suddenness in natural sound is underexplored, including by him, and his 'nature', while monolithic in many respects, does contain darker sounds (but not physical danger). He also represents the sense that music is not just about the music itself but multiply determined settings in which sound occurs. In fact, his fatuous faith in nature underpins much of the sound studies project: unveiling a reality that was already there, were we only to listen, and no less firmly held by sonic practitioners, who, says Kim-Cohen, continue to find solace in 'the naturalism of sound' (*In the Blink of an Ear*, 87).

The demagogues of acoustic ecology are hardly the worst political scourge of today's world, but their ideas can easily be seen as insisting on problematic bases: returns to lost pasts, on purifying the present, on maintaining tradition and shunning incoming sounds, sound can only be what is acceptable to the setting in which it occurs. Marie Thompson refers to this situation as a 'dualistic "aesthetic moralism", which positions "noise" as "bad" to silence's "good"' (*Beyond Unwanted Sound*, 88), where nature is characterized as harmonious and worth listening to, if only we could hear it free of distraction and disruption.[21] Sound artists are the avant-garde creative wing of acoustic ecology – it is they who will help our ears open and bud, they who will bring us from the bondage of hearing and into freedom of listening, and properly hearing, once our listening has been disciplined sufficiently to reveal the correct wonders of the sound world.[22]

Jean-Yves Bosseur closes his book on music and environment with a demand for more sonic intervention – not for disruption, but to insist that everyone militantly ambience the urban world many live in. One way this can happen is through nature being brought to us, and so an exemplary case is Chris Watson, a leading recorder of 'the natural world', working on many nature programmes, but also his own releases and on installations. In all these formats, he composes through editing, striving to leave the 'real sounds' as they are. For this to happen, the soundworlds are clearly enhanced and sound very pleasingly full. He talks of his location recordings as bringing out the musicality of a place, its 'essence' (Mark McLaren interview, *Binaural*, 4), with this being complete as he edits and changes levels and uncovers the 'musical chord or a series of notes which characterizes any location' (5).[23] Watson's high definition extends R. Murray Schafer's sense of nature as a high-fidelity environment into positing nature as proximate: his sounds are brought relentlessly close, creating a sense of immersion, of place. That this has created a peculiar deconstruction of place (with 'there' being brought 'here' for a different 'there').[24]

Watson praises Francisco López's *La Selva* (1998), which is a sometimes surprising attempt to get to what the rainforest really sounds like – a mass of competing sounds, taking their turns. And although the work sounds very composed, so too is an ecology, to some extent – Bernie Krause has argued that turntaking in natural settings has come into being through evolution, just as have physical or temporal niches (*The Great Animal Orchestra*).[25] The fact remains that López believes he has captured the real, has caught nature and brought it out to human ears.[26] Nature is full of sound – natural sound (not the truism it appears, it is a philosophical claim); sound itself is natural, and can be captured; the sound of nature is good; listening is a good; all of this plays out in the field recording as would-be innocent document, a presumption stripped out by Pierre-Yves Macé, who questions the referentiality of the sound 'document'. The field recording claims to simply grasp the real (this process is the focus of the next chapter), maybe to hear it even better than unassisted human ears (though all human ears come prosthetically enhanced with cultures). This 'phonography' is exactly as Barthes described photography – the activity within which it is supposed that a real has been captured (Macé, *Musique et document sonore*, 77–86).[27]

So, with Macé, I think we can try to look outside of the total musicalization of the world, or its placement into circuits of use value, understanding and even weaponry, and remember sound that exceeds processing capacity. And here, we have a longstanding model – the sublime – that is never far from the words of sound hunters, foragers, boosters, advocates, cautiously critical artists and writers. Too often, especially in the hands of the field recordist, the sublime is misunderstood, mishandled as a synonym for something that merely is. If only it was 'merely' – not just something that really is, something with extra solidity, where the sublimity arises from our previous ignorance, from which we will be brought on sound safari so that we can hear, truly hear what truly is. Analysts also tend in this direction, so those writing on nature are very keen to reduce anthropocentrism in their readings (not critiques) of listening, and emphasize 'sounds in themselves', sound that arrives as excess (as heard in Nancy's booklet on listening).[28] Macé puts it best when he refers to the sonorous as the arising of the unknown ['le surgissement de l'inconnu' (*Musique et document sonore*, 13)]. This refers to the hearing of nature, but also the re-presentation of that hearing in the form of 'real sounds' amid music, or in the place of music, say in a sound art composition.

Kahn appears troubled by the recurrence of the sublime in his own argument in *Earth Sound Earth Signal*, and refers primarily to the conservative eighteenth-century thinker Edmund Burke. Burke noted that sound was part of the sublime, or, as Kahn says, 'sound on its own could invoke the sublime' (133), while Immanuel Kant, surprisingly perhaps, did not refer to sounds of environmental disaster (from a human perspective) such as the Lisbon earthquake of 1755 (*Earth Sound Earth Signal*, 134). There he leaves it, implying that there is a sublime that exists – one that is precisely in the excess of the Earth's own sound-making. For Kant's philosophy, of course, there *is* no sublime, but there is the experience of the sublime as that which exceeds rational processing. It exists in ideas, and in the incommensurability of reason and that which escapes it, when *felt* as that which escapes it (*Critique of Judgement*, 105–06, 124).[29] Kant stresses that experiencing something which escapes our capacity to process it 'elevates' the mind, like the catharsis of violent drama (120–21). But, for this to happen, the sublime necessarily involves fear and a sense of danger. While nothing in nature is inherently 'monstrous' (109), human minds find many phenomena highly affecting and likely to induce a sense of the sublime as danger – a danger that arises from human incapacity faced with the thing that is too big, uncontrollable and/or somehow proximate even though colossal. The sublime creates (is the creation of) 'agitation' (115), 'arous[es] fear' (119) and brings into being 'an abyss in which the imagination is afraid to lose itself' (115). Thus, Kant continues,

> any spectator who beholds massive mountains climbing skyward, deep gorges with raging streams in them, wastelands lying in deep shadow and inviting melancholy meditation, and so on is indeed seized by *amazement* bordering on terror, by horror and a sacred thrill.

> (129, emphasis in original)

Kant then returns to the idea of a retreat into catharsis as the person in thrall to the sublime dwells within it precisely when secure from actually threatening effects. Although Kant does not explicitly refer to the audition of the sublime/ exceeding of rational processing of sound as sublimity, the phenomena, often natural, that he refers to can be noisy, such as the 'raging streams' above. The point is that, like noise, there is no inherently existing sublime, only a negatively defined sublime that is equivalent to noise (by negatively defined, I mean defined 'negatively' as *contrast* to something with which it is in relation, or in nested opposition). For me, the sublime resurfaces, ruined, blackened, in the 1930s work of Georges Bataille, and it is through his low materialist take on the phenomenon that we can make a space for sound in nature that exceeds us, if only to fall below a heroic if depersonalized excess of 'the object', or 'nature'.

Eugene Thacker has been on these tracks already, and to some extent so has Timothy Morton. Sound studies likes the idea that its focus is somehow dirtier, it gives it a sense of what it wouldn't like to think of as Heideggerian authenticity, so Jacob Smith refers to the dark ecology of radio, even David Rothenberg writes that 'nature is more than life. It is death, eternity, calamity, softness and devastation' (*Sudden Music*, 91). But Thacker is fuller still of 'melancology', the trans-Romantic melancholy of black metal, when he writes of mysterious sounds found by NASA in 2009 that 'the sound is so much sound, so much in excess of itself, that it is a sound that paradoxically has never been produced' ('Sound of the Abyss', 184–85).[30] This leads him to muse on the unsound: 'more than the hearing of silence, or the listening to all sounds that compose silence; an unsound is the possibility of sound becoming something other than acoustic or sonic' (191). The emergence of something like unsound is a ruined sublime, from within a 'dark ecology' of sound, and one that enfolds the world of all sound.

Maybe instead of encompassing, it needs to be clearer that in a Bataillean general ecology sound is both within and without understanding, controllable and excessive. In his model of the general economy, Bataille argued that the universe is fundamentally based on expenditure, and the world of objects, material, people, beliefs, even form, all exist only as residue of this primordial residue. This extreme metaphysics continually undoes itself, because the one all-encompassing principle of waste, destruction, excess is all there is. And *that* isn't. Not until and unless we live in a world of matter, beliefs etc., and retrospectively identify 'excess' as having been, always and, if you like, already, there. Bataille was not shy of using very literal examples to demonstrate how this played out for us humans, on this earth, an earth both formed and brought under ruinous human jurisdiction and capable of destroying or just being pleasantly surprising, at any moment. This idea that Bataille had, initially in the 1930s, has yet to be surpassed in its posthumanity, to be anachronistic. Bataille's model of nature is not one that awaits capture, or emerges from being understood or as a result of finally being heard correctly. It does not produce the sound of structure, except as a by-product (as most evolutionary theories tell us, almost every organic phenomenon is a by-product of masses of chance operations, many of which remain harmful). Long before *proper* ecology, with its fear of humanity losing its privileged status in the world, Bataille looked to an ecology of total and pointless violence. In sonic terms, it might be very much what Goodman called 'the acoustic violence of vibration' (*Sonic Warfare*, xiv).

Dark ecology does make its way to this point, in the explicit dark of Chris Beckett's excellent *Dark Eden* books, or Vin Diesel in *Pitch Black*, and some models of a blackened ecology remind us of the possibility of a black sun.[31] Bataille posits a rotten sun, and, in the form of the mouth, the possibility of dark silence, a supersymmetrical part of white noise perhaps. The idea of the rotten sun is that the sun is brought low from its heights as lifegiver, vision enabler, knowledge symbol. Closed- and open-eyed inspection of the sun both lead us away from its productive side, and toward it as destructive and wasteful, like 'refuse or combustion' (Bataille, 'Rotten Sun', 57).[32] This sun is the sun of 'a man who slays a bull (Mithra), ... a vulture that eats the liver (Prometheus)' (ibid.). The blinding sun whose rays are merely waste is paralleled in the bellowing of a bull with its throat cut, its blood dripping on the lucky celebrant. This rethought sun is one way Bataille brings low, removing the exalted attributions to natural phenomena, and through exorbitant exemplification, is exposed as so much less, always lessening. Which in turn renders the attempts to match it even more absurd. The mouth is taken in the same direction – away from speech, and back to animality – Bataille claims that 'for neighbouring animals' it is 'the most terrifying' part ('Mouth', 59).[33] The mouth can become the conduit for sound that is not under human supervision:

> on important occasions human life is still bestially concentrated in the mouth: rage makes men grind their teeth, while terror and atrocious suffering turn the mouth into the organ of rending screams … The overwhelmed individual throws back his head, as if explosive impulses were to spurt directly out of the body in the form of screams.

> (ibid.)

The sonic removal of the mouth from economies of controlled human social activity is the re-emergence of banished animality of which human form is the persistent trace – and Bataille does not refer to a return to animality, but its continued proximate absence in everyday human life. This mouth then becomes a privileged location for rotten silence. Instead of the joyous productivity of nature making its sounds for Adamic humans to find, identify, name and appreciate in service to human improvement (or environmental improvement that helps humanity to cement its control over something it calls nature), Bataille helps us identify silencing in a way that is separate to control, discipline, censorship. This rotten silence, or dark absence of sound, has had its benign side stripped away – so at its most literal this can be heard in the sound of what threatens – or the sound of being threatened, the unsound of the prospect of attack. *This* unsound is terror. Terror (in the context of sound) does not arise from specific sounds, nor does it make particular sounds. Instead, it is a removal of sound from its restricted, normal economy, and relocation in a nature that is not going to help, that is not there for you.

This rotten silence can be heard as the unsound within the horrified listening induced by the sound of predators eating. Without wishing to universalize about what makes humans frightened, the exemplary sound of carnivores such as lions eating, and crunching bones in particular, opens up the abyssal prospect of extreme violence as normal, natural, inevitable and also unconcerned. In the twilight of lions' existence on a planet defined by murderous acquisitiveness, the lion still has to eat. As humans shoot, collect and 'conquer' this rival predator, its sound is perhaps one of the truest forms of acoustic ecology, not because it is real, but because its realness occurs without 'us'. Unlike the 'benevolent' surveillance placed on lions (like that of many non-humans who are now valorized enough to be brought inside a Foucauldian regime of care and control), the sonic capture of this animal puncturing 'the animal' wavers at the edge of co-option into human forms of natureculture.

There's a very literal framing in this topic, and this is matched by the tagline of a video that has been removed from YouTube that showed the bone intervention of a lion – 'the most horrifying sound in the world', plus it's about death and the eating of prey. Both of which were shown as functional in this video, once we hear beyond the catchy title. From a Bataillean perspective, though, it is the eating of the head that takes us out of the realm of utility: the face is brought out in all its meatfulness (for those worried about missing out on the original video, there are plenty more, increasingly more, videos of lions eating).[34] The sound is not one of great danger, or of anything that signifies to other lions in the proximity. It may tell us of the power of lion teeth, and set up a Burkean sublime. But – what is interesting is that this is the sound of apathy – the sonic rotten sun of hearing what has no interest in you. Away from the overexcitement on YouTube about 'terrifying sounds' and mysterious sonic threats, it is the apathy of the animal wave over wave that can occasionally be heard, even at this distance, via networked screens. For Bataille, apathy, not excitement, is the final conclusion, the lowering of heroic overcoming into pathetic sovereignty. Nature is recast as that which does not make sound for you – but nature is not so worthy of elevation that it is above making sound. In the *Theory of Religion*, Bataille talks of animals within nature being like water within water. This is not a Rothenberg-like koan, but occurs in the context of eating – that is where the immanence of the animal is given (17). And this is the sound of that immanence. But lastly, the lion is a higher wave of the water (18–19). This height is not an achievement, or a moment of triumph, but as with the tiger, eating is the moment where animals (including humans) are vectors of the energy of the universe (Bataille, *The Accursed Share*, 38), and here the lion does this in wave form, agitating the water.[35] All the listening in the world cannot control the generation of a sound that does not matter, does not affect matter through the imposition or cloaking of meaning, where 'the apathy that the gaze of the animal expresses after the combat is the sign of an existence that is essentially on a level with the world in which it moves like water in water' (*Theory of Religion*, 25).

Catch and Capture: 'Field' and 'Recording' in Field Recording

The story of field recording is one of discovery, and also of replication. It comes burdened with stories explaining how field recording represents something that 'just is'. The 'whatness' of the sounds is valorized over the 'whatness' of the recording, of what it is that we actually have when we use or listen to field recording. Field recording is the isolation of the process of capturing the sounds of the world in a process of 'phonography' (the sounds of the world, 'caught' in mediated, documented, aural form). It was always already going on in the anthropological research into customs, speech and, above all, music, at the turn of the twentieth century. It then spread into radio, then film, then TV sound. In anthropological research, the capturing of rare sounds likely to pass into the void (songs transmitted orally, the last speakers of a language, informed speakers of languages 'new' to the crypto-scientist) was taken to be transparent, a simple mode of delivering information, no different to writing, photographing, sketching or carrying home. Likewise, the recording of environmental sound for broadcast – often natural, but always the sound that exceeded the scripted sound of the piece – was transaudient, simply available for hearing, signifying the real or adding realness to the core, structured work. In both cases, the sound itself, let alone the process of producing it, was not designed to be available in its own right for scrutiny – it was to pass into hearing.

The change in field recording from the 1960s on is that it became a means to bring sounds explicitly into audition. This followed the musicalization of the world led by musicians who focused on hearing and listening, such as John Cage and Pauline Oliveros, and the availability of more portable machinery for recording. As machinery became simpler, smaller and more capable of

Earlier version presented at *Tuning Speculation III*, Toronto, in 2015.

high-quality recording, fidelity became a medium in its own right, and the place for field recording as something autonomous, or even of superior value to other sounds, led to an aestheticization based on listening. This newly born attentive listener would be rewarded not just with the panoply of world sounds, but also with the spectacle of themselves listening. The listener would consciously attune to the world (as with the valorization of silence in Chapter 7 below), and the world would respond, through its self-elected transmitters, the field recorders. Digital technology enabled both 'quick and dirty' capture and also extremely detailed 'catching' or recreation, of the world heard microphonically.[1] Below, I will also track a certain sub-current, which is the consciously aesthetic and at least partially self-reflexive production of field recording albums, to explore how the field becomes more complicated, revealing what was always already not there – i.e. the field itself, until summoned, until decohered into the statistical valences enabled by the digital restructure and destructure of analogue sound for analogue ears.

Sound artist Lawrence English offers a way out of the problem of overstating the realness of the products of field recording, and although he optimistically applies the idea across the broad sweep of field-recording-based sound art, the insight that listening is the key is very valuable. He argues that

> The idea of objective recording in the field, thankfully now problematised and rejected, still lingers though like a spectre haunting the ways many listeners consider recordings. It is as if, somehow, because of where they are recorded they are *true*. The issue for anyone who undertakes field recording as part of their practice is to recognise that agency and ultimately a kind of creative subjective listening is vital if the work is to transmit, as Szendy puts it, the *listener's listening*.
>
> (English, 'A Beginner's Guide to Field Recording')[2]

English is keen to stress that artists and documentarist recorders are communicating their listening – and whilst this is a significant shift from the idea of capturing the real of a place, it has only shifted the location of the presumption, for English's reflection on the sound art of field recording still leaves in place the notion that real listening has taken place, and can be really presented. This is a type of new realism, but one still caught in the idea that, if we can place the real correctly, the problem of the real (in this case, the real sounds being caught, transmitted and heard) dissipates, whereas I think we need to introduce more of the wrongness, the arbitrariness of live sound recording in unscripted, non-professionalized spaces, to approach the real as problem, as opposed to surmounting the issue of inaccuracy about what or where the real is.

When field recording translates into listening, into ways of amplifying nature, into using natural sound, even into writing that features sound, it suggests that listening, and listening well, will enable hearing, 'real hearing', and this will bring the world into focus, perhaps drawing the listener's attention to matters of global import, or to the always-local problem of living in altering sound environments.[3] Outside of the reality and fidelity that might be claimed for field recording, I am trying to hear how noise infiltrates and first broadens the 'field', and how, in so doing, it legitimizes the practice still further. The practice of field recording operates as a progressively stranger device for processing the world the more its assumptions or strategies are brought into close contact with critical thinking.

There are two closely connected modes of conceiving the intervention of field recording in the world: the first is about space and time and concerns the object of research, the rare species of moth caught to be preserved forever. The second mode, in close proximity to the first, is about the process of sound catching, which is the process not of acquiring but of fixing into place in a form that can be consumed. Pierre-Yves Macé writes of phonography as being a practice that is isomorphic to photography, i.e. the recorded material re-presents an instance of the real, 'inconceivable apart from its demonstrable realness [*caractère réel*], of the having-taken-place of its referent' (*Musique et document sonore*, 52). Further, this re-presentation creates or structures the very belief it is trying to inculcate. Phonography is not the actual object brought to the here and now from then and there, a then and there that was the here and now of its moment of capture. Rather it is the idea of being a real that is presented to us as a thing that was present but now no longer is, just as Barthes claimed in his writings on photography. This idea of the captured real permeates the further use of field recording as marker of the real – an idea prefigured in Schafer's notion of the 'soundmark' that crystallizes the sonic presence of a given location, and questioned by François J. Bonnet as misunderstanding the possibility of either using history to understand sound, or vice versa, given the fleetingness of sound.[4] Finally, in this model of encapsulating the sonic real, musicians and sound artists play on the distinction between the musical and non-musical (or extra-musical), bringing this deconstructing relation inside of music, or art production. Macé emphasizes that music itself is always already the exclusion of what it is not, and this absence has been a permanent non-presence within all music as 'the element which is both integrated and not, brought within the space of the work, but as *other*' (*Musique et document sonore*, 21, emphasis in original). The advent of field recording as an established practice, such that it carries its own signifying codes (it is the carrying of those codes) merely serves to bring this inherent, if retrospectively found, connection to light.

If the first mode is one of the status of the object, the second is about technologies of object framing. Jonathan Sterne points out the mutual influences of anthropology and nascent recording technologies. As far as field recording is concerned, all early recording can be thought of as being an anthropological field recording – a way of capturing a real that could then be replayed in another time and place, thus fixing the fleeting interminable of sound into something suitable for study and appraisal – and beyond this, capture as control.[5] Ultimately, all recording carries something of this code within it, even if the growth of multitracking, editing and studio techniques introduces different elements into the ontology of sound. The material technologies of early recording of stories, folk song, speeches, carry discursive technologies symbiotically – the belief in preservation conducted from the perspective of an informed outsider drives the use of recording, and its dissemination under the banner of authenticity. All of this is admirably teased out by Sterne, and also by certain ethnomusicologists such as Steven Feld, but in addition to these knowledge/power dynamics is the deeper structure of access to the real through a combination of enhanced and mediated listening and the sense that framing a real event or situation will allow the real to re-present itself as it truly is, for the wonderment and instruction of potential audiences.

So, field recording captures an element of a pre-existing soundscape, the sounds it displays are a sampling of a wider population, but the sounds not only stand in for a wider ecosystem, they can be regarded as an entity that exists exactly as it is now to be heard via cylinder, MP3, tape or vinyl. Both models combine to set up the field recording as privileged transport of the real, a real which can be regarded as being brought to life or, just as tantalizingly, a marker of the real as that which is excluded from the representation in recording. Ultimately, the real is actually and actively extruded from the recording, such that it becomes the real that the recording says it is and, in so doing, becomes absent, just as any real thing does when either caught in its becoming or simply ignored/unknown even as 'the' unknown. The recording of something real, of matter made material (Macé, *Musique et document sonore*, 23–24) intervenes not as something external, but as something that creates a pattern relation between what it offers as real, some sort of concrete outside and the processes involved in the accessing of the sound that transports those relations.

The field itself then becomes problematic, as opposed to being the real that will either be captured or rendered for posterity. The field is no longer merely the place that welcomes, or seeks to repel, or is dispossessed by the recorder (a hybrid of human and machine, incorporating discursive prostheses that have led them to that activity and place). The field is not there beforehand because the world does not exist in a para-Heideggerian state of 'being-there-to-be-listened to'. Even imagining the world as field is the same as referring to the outside as the 'smoking area' in jurisdictions that ban smoking of cigarettes or vaping indoors. But – the intent to record in some way prepares the field for its ascension into fieldness such that it can be heard by humans not-present-within-the-sound-being-heard-but-at-home-instead. Only once recording has occurred does the field attain some sort of presence – a presence that has been distanced in the process of bringing into being. Tascam deconstruction, portably.

The field is not just the place recording takes place in, or structures in audible form. A field is also a space of possibility, a set of possible states for matter or particles to move into, within, across, through, etc. And so the audible field is one of potential – whether presented in full or highly edited, even mixed, form, the field recording presents this potential, and that the potential was brought to one place (the ultimate recording as presented). Whilst some do mix, use, alter, recombine, their field recordings, the field recording itself is often left intact, or presented as something other than a field recording if 'tampered with' – as if the field, once its potential and its presence have been deferred, absented, in order to be heard, to be subject to listening, needs to be maintained. As if the field will vanish if not kept complete, or perhaps the changes will travel backward in time to undo the field that the recording brought into being. Field recording might sit within an aesthetic piece, but its mobility is kept under control.[6]

If there is no field, that does not mean there is no world, only that for it to be field, it needs to have fallen into the realm of attention (not necessarily human – a local population of one animal could define it, a machine could, weather or geography might), such that it can be recorded. This conveys a surprising amount of power to the recorder, and no amount of self-effacement can undo the choice to transport sounds to other listeners. But the recorder is not the dominant figure that the early and quasi-imperial past of recording would suggest. Instead, they are brought into being as they bring the field into presence. Up until that point, there are plenty of actual things in existence (person, place, animals, factory, sandwiches, minidisc, fluffy microphone cover, waterproof clothing), all of which establish the conditions for the recorder to exist – but as the button is pressed (physically or otherwise) and recording begins – the field comes into being, and so does the recorder. At the end of the process, we have a recording, even though neither field nor recorder had any measurable existence beforehand.

The idea of the soundscape has always carried a suggestion of self-reflective awareness, a parallel to the move to ethnography, away from anthropology, but the self-reflection persists in maintaining the idea of there being a reality that exists 'out there' in the world and that issues of capture are only epistemological. Hence the persistence of an idea of purification, of progressive and self-critical advance to finally and correctly bring sounds from an elsewhere to a different place, while keeping the sound authentic, flash-frozen. No amount of self-reflection seems able to save the field recording from the logic of capture.

The fidelity of recording is far from being the only way in which soundscapes are an improving discipline, liable to induce better listening and then more democratic and ecologically minded social living. When R. Murray Schafer and his teams went hunting for the true sound portraits of specified places, whether Vancouver or the trip to Europe that became 1977's pioneering set of documents *Five Village Soundscapes*, Schafer's idea was that any human habitation would produce an individual soundworld that reflected its socius, and also its relative connectedness to the natural surroundings of the village.[7] The whole objective project to define locational soundscapes is shot through with judgements about what is good and bad sound. Bad sound is generally anything contemporary, but, more specifically, it is sound that blocks out other sonic events, so it is not what it is as such, but how it functions for listeners that counts (*Five Village Soundscapes*, 31). Of course, a further problem is that Schafer makes the second-level judgement on behalf of the inhabitants as to just how much interference traffic makes. The worst thing is when the unfortunate locals are so alienated from their soundworld, they no longer notice how disruptive it is (62). Much more could be said about the issues of acoustic ecology, but the point of interest for me is about how Schafer views the problem. That is, that the soundscape is in fact not all of the elements that truly occur, but a truth that is buried, instead of laden, with extraneous sounds in its inner unfolding (the presence of traffic hinders the soundscape, as opposed to being seen as an overloud instrument, let's say). Bonnet critiques Schafer for the moralistic presumption about specific sounds but also oscillating between an alarmism deploring the sonorous nuisances of modernity and a will to safeguard sounds on the verge of extinction, Schafer's approach is clearly under the influence of the syndrome of paradise lost, a phantasmatic space that is ultimately nothing less than a panacoustic empire.

(Bonnet, *The Order of Sounds*, 181)

Not all soundscapers are as picky as Schafer and the acoustic ecology imperialists, or if they are, it is on different grounds – traffic is boring, running water even more so and wind merely an indicator of slack recording practice. From Alvin Lucier (*I Am Sitting in a Room* [1969]) we get the possibility of a space as made of the noise of its existing when recorded in relation to another intervention, from others the happy accidents of sound recording are precisely what supply the real. Two works struck me here, and they have become deeply connected, even if the rush to attribute emotional content to them has diminished the extent to which their form drives any possible content, and these pieces are Stephen Vitiello's *Sounds Building in the Fading Light*, recorded on the ninety-first floor of the World Trade Center in 1999, released in 2001, of the sounds of the building reacting to its environment, and William Basinski's *Disintegration Loops* from 2002. Both have acquired a particular status connected to the destruction of the World Trade Center, the first in direct memorial mode (but released beforehand), the second in connection with Basinki's story about playing the loops while observing the fall of the towers from across town. So the content for both has become the space of melancholy, an absence to be filled with a reaction to that absence. Because there is no way back from that baggage once attributed, I won't dwell on it, but what is interesting for me is how the process of recording became the material. Vitiello's record is a document not of any real, but of the attempt to sonically uncover a real, very much like the practice of finding spirit voices on tape (known as Electronic Voice Phenomenon). Only in this instance, instead of sounding of ethereal beings, it is the sounding of the world that is discovered. The *Disintegration Loops* are likewise a formal practice of melancholy before their overdetermining (by Basinki himself), with the album being the sound of tapes of earlier recordings decaying as they played, the chemical surfaces peeling away under the friction of the tape heads, which go from being a mode of transport of the living tape to acting as pall-bearing delivery system to the morgue of the final CD. The soundscape here recounts the passage of an effectively two-dimensional space encountering the edge of its universe being scraped by the supplementary dimension.

This scraping of soundworld and device to bring the soundworld into being as listenable object is made excessive, direct and 'literal', in Koji Asano's noise soundscape *Quoted Landscape* from 1995. In this full-length CD, a microphone directly brushes objects it seeks to record, and so its entire soundworld is of the relation device/object. The space sound occurs in for human ears is rejected for an ever-reducing, reductive, limiting sound. The sound of a microphone scrubbing over surfaces makes this piece a rejection of the idea of capturing an aural hyperreality in favour of a low materialist trudge. In so doing, something like a universal sound is produced – the sound of sameness, of sonic equality, except where lumps occur in the sound-space-time. This work is artefact all the way down, and knows it. If what we were looking for was a triumphal statement of 'how to do field recording while questioning it', maybe this is it, but I'm not very interested in that. Far better is the idea of ever-increasing proximity to the object as sound emitter such that the capture of it does not just kill it like a gassed moth, shot dodo or tasty turtle (like the forty consumed on the HMS *Beagle*'s return with Darwin and his specimens). It does far more and far less – it sets up an entanglement of object and object, such that no reality can persist as it is brought into the realm of existing. And yet, all that production of nothing out of touching into nothing is not simply nihilistic, instead it produces stuff as residue: the something that is the sign of the nothing that is the real having (not) happened. And where this all happens is in the shortening of the distance between real world and recording such that both are acknowledged (or brought into being just as the addition of Lucier's voice in a room, then subtracted, leaves the room, as residue). And where all this happens, I think, is in the endless approaching of a true soundworld that includes its observer.

Others have taken different routes in their quest to solve the mystery of the real in audio form, and ostensibly offer more critical paths or guidance into the wilderness of the sonic pleroma. Francisco López takes a very broad view of what a soundscape can or should have, arguing that 'there is no purposeful *a priori* distinction of foreground/background' ('Environmental sound matter', 1, from *La Selva* [1998]). He has no problem with selectivity, editing, mixing or montage, and he claims both that the process of recording is an inevitable mould for the listening or 'processing' of place, *and* that 'recordings cannot replace the "real" experience' (2), *and* that people have told him how realistic his doctored recordings are, and that he is 'unrealistic' (4), *and*, most interestingly, that partial hearing is the natural norm (5). López tries to cover every possible critical angle, purifying his own mission, and every statement relates back to an admittedly complex idea of authenticity that both leaves the real intact as a thing pre-existing (really) in order to be recorded in the best way possible so as to come close but definitively, essentially, fail, thereby maintaining the sense of a real from which sound emerges, while being ultimately unattainable. But, in fact, López's attempt to cover every path, signal every avenue, does tell us something useful about displacing the realness that can underpin the moralistic value attributed to one-dimensional (literally one track) captures of time, place and culture or nature. López's real is revealed as absent in recording, yet hyper-really present, as a trace in the recording is a negative theology of field recording, where God has withdrawn.

The work that López produces alongside these notes is subtitled 'Sound environments from a Neotropical rain forest', but there are other attempts to recognize the complete embeddedness of the sonic bounty hunter. Steven Feld's paranoiac-critical shields around his recording of 'pygmy music in Papua New Guinea' is one such, Heike Vester's *Marine Mammals and Fish of Lofoten and Vesterålen* (2005), Andrea Polli's *Sonic Antarctica* (2009) and Hein Schoer's *Two Weeks in Alert Bay* (2010) are three further examples (all released by German label Gruenrekorder), each time more and more revealing of a self-reflection that seeks to hear itself creeping ever closer and talking to camera. Feld's *Voices of the Rainforest* is the corrective to the dominant sound gatherer and subaltern object people, and incorporates many aspects of life in Papua New Guinea, including natural sound, music, voices, and 'evokes 24 hours in the life of Bosavi in one continuous hour' ('From Schizophonia to Schismogenesis', 279).[8] That he has basically shoved the Kaluli people back into being part of 'Nature' does not seem to concern him.

In the Arctic listened to by Vester and her recording machinery, the community she seeks to make present to hearing is that of various sea mammals. This is a passive field, ready to be sampled, re-presented and used as a combination of aestheticized nature and naturally informed aesthetics. The high-definition hydrophonic sounds sourced, edited into tracks with high-description titles such as 'Acrobatic Atlantic White-Striped Dolphins' or 'Calling Pilot Whales', make *Marine Mammals and Fish of Lofoten and Vesterålen* part of a tradition of conveying the musicality of nature that informed mid-twentieth-century vinyl LPs of birdsong, and since the 1970 album, *Songs of the Humpback Whale* (recordings by Roger Payne, Katharine Payne, Frank Watlington), human wonder at the communicative capacity of cetaceans.[9] The titles lead the listener to understand not only the realness of the source, and the source itself, but also to understand that if a track has a particular length, then that is because the sound was interesting and well captured for precisely that amount of time. Other than the structuring of the album into discrete tracks and a certain level of editing/ selecting composition, this is supposed to be an album from the animal world, and for that reason it cannot fully convey an awareness of what it means to find, construct, define and hone the field of 'what was already there'. The simple finding (through labour, experience and technical know-how) undermines its own claim to realism, as the apparatus is hidden and less satisfying sections presumably edited out.

In the Antarctic, the hierarchy between human and non-human is less apparent, as is the space between recorder and recordees. An international community, ethnologically belonging to a shared scientific research elite, is heard interacting with its surroundings. In Polli's *Sonic Antarctic*, environmental sounds, wildlife, machinery, vehicles, voices and changing ambience convey a richness of enmeshed experience of the Antarctic. Far from being uninhabited, this continent has its own population, albeit without citizens, its own legal framework, outside of standard international models of sovereignty and a significant chunk of the Earth's biomass, even if it is not especially rich in biotic diversity.

Polli's structured recordings include the extraneous sounds of microphones, weather, with centred (interviewed) voices and more incidental comments from machine operators, and this adds up to a dense integration of human and environment, it would seem, and has the virtue of diminishing the Romantic 'last frontier' imaginary that deadens thinking about polar regions. Events but not drama, mundanity, normality developed through the recording, convey the human interest in the Antarctic, and incorporate it into the wider world. This technocratic environment, analysed in depth by Jessica O'Reilly, is presented as a complex and exemplary zone, through carefully selected sonic phenomena, including those more glitchy, awkward, noisy sounds.[10] The natural and technological sounds add to the normality, the world-as-untreated empirical being. These act as background, as *grounding* – such that the field being recorded, being collected, becomes not just the field made in the process of measuring, but the reason a field is generated in the first place. If this seems abstract, it is less so if we consider the voices of many of the interviewed meteorologists who all feed into an unmistakable message of global climate danger. Their activity (sonically presented in the electronic sounds of machinery, of transit, of the process of measurement translating into sound) provides a reason for the scientist presence on the Antarctic and the field recorder's presence. The resulting sounds of *Sonic Antarctica* are designed as empirical advocacy – Polli has a message, that humanity needs to act, needs to hear the science of rapid climate change. The sonically documentary nature of her project is designed not to show this as merely a point of view but as the actual fact of working in the Antarctic, and the shared culture based on discovery, data and dissemination of both of those.

Polli's Antarctic record recalls Sterne's warning about the early sonic anthropologists and sound collectors, but the community she has recorded is one that is highly technologically aware, not identified ethnically (all other continents have bases in Antarctica) and is not being caught by a representative of putatively imperial/Orientalist policy with more power. Instead, as a technologically based artist, Polli is able to move freely among people whose identity is predicated on the value of recording and dissemination. She is not as 'embedded' as Schoer tries to be, but it is clear from her aural integratedness that she is not other to a presumed other that needs documenting. Such anthropology as there is in *Sonic Antarctica* is based on elective community ideas about the value of practices, an incidental bonus, revealing a shared belief in the truth and superiority of their facts and data. There is no pretence at trying to record a pristine Antarctic, which would perhaps be the first move of an ecologically aware artistic project. Instead, Polli sets out to present the interaction of humans with the environment, and to keep the sounds of the place active in either background or foreground. The recorder is not omniscient, but physically present as part of that human presence. There is no pure nature, nor is there a pure human sensory communing with the location.

Hein Schoer's *The Sound Museum: Box of Treasures* (2014), with its lengthy curatorial text and images added to the 2010 release *Two Weeks in Alert Bay*, also gives hope that a good, honest, respectful and true portrait can emerge from a lengthy engagement that can be distilled for aesthetic and ponderously ethical listening.[11] The whole is reframed as a 'journey' to and through Canada's Alert Bay, a village on Cormorant Island, to the north of Vancouver Island, with track 1 the sound of the arriving boat, presumably Schoer-laden (echoing the helicopter intro of *Sonic Antarctica*), then the rest of the CD moves from conversations, storytelling, sounds of the location, whether the village or further beyond. The local First Peoples of the Kwakwaka'wkaw provide testimony and history, while Schoer also tries to get an illustrative range of sonically transmissible customs into his recording (also in the form of the accompanying materials in the second 2014 expanded edition). Schoer himself reads a mythical tale in 'How Raven

Stole the Sun'. Once more, the final setting or montage illustrates the web of interactions in a place as well as the recorder's perception, knowledge and aural mastery.

All of these examples look for a true listening that hints at a real event or place that is specifically absent (but otherwise present at some other time), and they do so through a conscious use of what would be regarded as artefacts, the ironic name given to errors in coding that produce unexpected sonic moments, particularly while editing.

In these 'sonic ethnographies' or 'ethnophonographies', those artefacts are not exclusively digital (Sterne refers to early recordings of Native American song by ethnographers as 'artifacts' [*The Audible Past*, 319]), but do arise presumably as a result of a transversal digitality – that is, through an interaction of ostensibly analogue and digital in the processing of air disturbance. The choice to keep these moments in is an act of digital selection, of closing the cut between analogue and digital and allowing the creation of a purposeful artefact that microcosmically works the same way as the recording as a whole. A way to retool the hermetic. In Schoer's montage piece, 'Two Weeks in Alert Bay – One Day in the Life of Raven', it becomes tricky to decipher which sounds are more or less artefactual, as bird sounds, water sounds, sounds of water displaced by a vessel all play against each other in the opening part, announcing the compositional strategy that is based on the extra-musical sound as present sound, evidence of presence through recording. Elements fade in and out evocatively and crisply (raising the prospect of the ultra-clear sound as the most artefactual of all – although the closing track consists of mostly incidental and digitally construed sounds). People walk, work, sing, move around the landscape, in a richly thickened yet flattened variant of Glenn Gould's hyper-embedded and layered *The Idea of North* radio essay from 1967. The fullness of life in Alert Bay is transmitted via the presence of incidental sound, as the listener is led around an indicative audio-locational survey, showing both Schoer's presence and the locatedness of the local people, like sonic exhibits.

Once the artefact has been accepted as part of the real and part of the recording, and not as an error in the transcription of the world (even then it is in the world as transcription, resulting from the interaction of different processes or forces), then the artefact becomes a possible paradigm for the field as a whole, or at least a glimpse into a new kind of field. This field is no longer simply the place in which recording happens. The referent in the referentiality of the sound captured is revealed as it is brought into being. The moment field recording enters the field, it structures the field as recursive product of its own activity. If there was a real there, safe from categorization as referent, it is displaced by a new relational pattern that emanates from the recording, or even the decision to record. English refers to field recording as a type of hyperreal experience:

> The most affecting recordings offer a focus that lays beyond the everyday listening we experience. They reveal a depth or presence that transforms the moment of recording into something hyperreal, to borrow Baudrillard's term, that can be meaningfully engaged with by other listeners at a future times [sic] and in different places.
>
> ('A Beginner's Guide to Field Recording')

I think, however, that he means this hyperreality to constitute a heightened sense of the real, as opposed to Baudrillard's notion of a realness that no longer has any relation to old models of reality. In this context, Chris Watson's *Weather Report* (2003) is instructive: this ultra-high definition recording could be seen to represent a strong belief in English's view that something important of the real can be conveyed, even if it has not been directly experienced or captured with 100 per cent accuracy. But perhaps the logic of the field as something created through recording, and recording through the field, helps us rethink these three beautiful recordings of weather in wildly different locations (Masai Mara, Kenya, Scottish highland glen and Icelandic glacier) as field constructions, purely real to the point of making the question of realness unimportant and redundant.

This is not to make the field a simple product of the recording, rather the field expands (as a phase-space of possibilities) to encompass what was called the field (the place of recording), its presence as sound within the recording, its absence as real, also within the recording, its absence as place to the displaced listener (who is both far from the actual place and made aware of this in the listening to the place that is other to his or her other place of listening). These different types of real, different types of place, form a new field of processes and wave-like interactions. The reason we can talk of this expanded field is not just the introjection of a deconstructive model, or nihilist realism, but is due to a recognition of the strange effect that producing the real in sound has, such that it sets off in different, unpredictable directions once activated. The sonic artefact is the structure of field recording as expanded relational field, a way of thinking the contingent and multiple instantiations of the real as occasional, fleeting and withheld, even as offered. The artefact can also be conceived of as the observer, as produced by what seems to be his or her own action of observing, or more accurately, the observer as artefactually located (not in the use of extraneous technology, but as a part of a set of connections that we call technology), artefactually subject.

It is López once more who indicates the contingent nature of captured sonic place, in his 2018 three-hour piece made available on USB (*Sonic Fields Vlieland*). This piece is an excessive version of an audioguide, a retooling of Janet Cardiff's soundwalks, but without additional narration. The listener is ideally supposed to return to the place of location, but whether they do or not, they are advised to use headphones or good speakers. Computer speakers cannot even generate the basic artefact of the sounds that demand to be heard, and López not only plays with place, he looks to create a sonically supplementary space of higher fidelity through curational recording.

Does all of that leave the process of recording as the only non-artefactual thing, even if not autonomously real? Well, no, because it becomes nothing but the arrangement of connections, locations and movements in audiospatial, audiotemporal hypersound (the place where sound is only a potential of all possible events, all possible sound, all possible recording activity, all possible listening).

3

The Empty Channel: Noise Music and the Pathos of Information

'If there were only one possible message there would be no information, no transmission system would be required' (Shannon, 'Communication Theory', 173).[1]

There is, then, a diminishing return in perfection, even in the quest for the best transmission of a signal, and for pioneering information theory writer Claude Shannon. Once there is more potential, there is entropy, and once there is message there is noise, or noise as risk of noise. Shannon's ideas are, despite attempts to think it otherwise, profoundly historical and contextual. But those ideas (often as transmitted by Warren Weaver) become richer, more noisy and more productive, once removed from the possibility of generating truthful models about all information transmission, and can be heard suggesting in their accidents a way of understanding the reason why noise music continues.

On the one hand, variants of harsh noise 'music' offer a practice-based deconstruction of simplistic ideas of coding, and open up an aesthetic path into a radicalized version of Benjamin Bratton's 'stack'. On the other, communication of or through music finds itself transformed in ways much more radical than those offered by hopeful (even if antagonistic, critical or subversive) musicians. This chapter traverses ideas of code, noise and entropy to complicate the idea of information, putting the emphasis on parallel circuits that undermine the idea of a channel as a route to functionality. Harsh noise, particularly in the form of the harsh noise wall, is a way of processing not code, but systems of coding, in ways that refuse decryption.

Earlier version presented at VAMH, Hamburg, 2017, and a subsequent rendering appeared in Nathanja van Dijk, Kerstin Ergenzinger, Christian Kassung and Sebastian Schwesinger (eds), *Navigating Noise* (Köln: Walther König, 2017), 244–66.

But perhaps we need to start by going deeper than the signal making its heroic way down a telephone line, and rethink noise's embedding in electromagnetism at a more primordial level. Maybe noise is basically about electricity – as source, product, consumer, producer – and emerging into perception as a result of its technological mobilization. As noted in Chapter 1, Douglas Kahn has written of noise's intimate connection to electricity, from amplification (in *Noise Water Meat*) to the non-human generation of noises on Earth and beyond (*Earth Sound Earth Signal*).[2] Noise slips out of our control, evading sense, escaping closure, and it is tempting to imagine it as prior to human existence. Hillel Schwarz talks at length, in *Making Noise*, of noise as a core component of origin stories, such as the noise of the Big Bang, still and always present as the cosmic background radiation, and capable of being received across the space it defines, even on planets.[3] This particular beginning helps us understand noise as residue, as something that can only be picked up later, in differed/deferred fashion, and that effectively only comes into being upon its being perceived/received. There is something more interesting, too, which is that while this sound might seem entropic, in fact it is the sign of the order that forms in its wake, and it too will be subject to entropy when the universe reaches a point of expansion such that energy is no longer transmitted far enough to have any effect. There will be only noise and absence-of-noise at the moment where each sub-atomic particle sits isolated in its own nest, equally far from anything else and equally silent. This 'heat death' is the ultimate implication of Boltzmann's broader conception of entropy, as 'energy will always go from a less to a more probable form' ('The Second Law of Thermodynamics', 20), which is equilibrium, separation and low-information, and 'all attempts at saving the universe from this thermal death have been unsuccessful' (19).[4]

The year 1913 sends us echoes of a perhaps familiar origin of noise, a way of encoding it as something cultural, as the Futurist Luigi Russolo produced his manifesto, *The Art of Noises*, that proclaimed that noise would be the basis of the future of all music, then of all art. He offers us two more ways of thinking about noise, which more or less contradict each other. He says that nature is full of noise, and that noise is life. At the same time, he proclaims his present and future to be the time of noise, because of the sounds of industry. On this second modelling, noise is an expression of the modern, even of the modern human condition. Anti-modernists might ruefully concur, and this bears later fruit in the hands of R. Murray Schafer, as he moulds the reactionary idea of acoustic ecology. But Russolo embraces the idea that noise propels us, structures us and destructures everything, through the motion of the universe, like Lucretius or Heraclitus, or nineteenth-century physicists James Clerk Maxwell and Boltzmann, who began to understand entropy as the statistically natural state of all being. It is from the industrial discovery of noise that nature re-acquires the noisiness it always had. And this results in the notion that music must expand, while our ideas of harmony, order and silence need dismissing. This of course is a path not followed by Futurism as it fell swooning into the arms of fascism, in Italy at least.

So maybe industry on a mass scale, in the ideal form of the capitalist factory, is the birth of noise, long before there is what we now blithely, yet restrictively, understand as coding. Certainly, a good case can be made for the increase of noise emanating from industry in the narrow sense of 'volume of sound'. The same is true in the increase in ordinances against noise, and the idea that noise is something subject to legal control. Alain Corbin, in *Village Bells*, talks about bells in the French countryside that became noisy (were deemed noisy) after the Revolution of 1789, and were melted down. Bells later re-emerge as tools of municipal control.[5] So, noise is heard as something to do with social activity and machine use, but perhaps pre-dates industrialized society as we understand it. Maybe the urban environment can itself be seen as a noise generator, with the mass of citizens, slaves, traders, soldiers in ancient cities already creating a noise network/trace/filament across Africa and Asia. The urban is not the only closed environment as European slave ships demonstrated as they rendered total bodily exploitation commercial. Noise in all these cases, and to different effect, can be a result of the unexpected, as well as the product of massification. Corbin's key point about the transitions within hearing is that the low-density rural world that most people lived in until the eighteenth century (in fact, 'most' people have only lived in cities in the twenty-first century) and that is largely devoid of noise, is quiet because life follows predictable, measured cycles, with hierarchies never shifting ground. Noise would occur in the form only of huge disruptions such as war, invasion, plague or enslavement and transport. Within that constraint of habitual non-noise, there would still be privileged moments of socially encoded noise, such as the village festival scene shown in Pieter Bruegel the Elder's *Fight Between Carnival and Lent* (1559) that is used for the cover of Attali's 1977 book *Noise*. The festival as an idea covered all major social events where the people featured directly, and includes witch trials, mass exorcisms and executions. These moments of ritual, as paradigms of sanctioned transgression, represent the excess of actual sonic noise and the metaphorical risk of other threats to social harmony.

What unites the above ideas is that noise is, or is the result of, some sort of concentration or condensation, whether continual or momentary. It is also something that organized, rational humanity seeks to either domesticate, punish or ignore. Which raises the question of whether noise can be an objective thing, whether it can be placed within a closed system or language, even in the interest of an apparently radical potential. I would say that it cannot, and any attempt to say otherwise is universalizing a concept or phenomeneon that varies according to the situation of the person identifying 'the' noise. Subjectively, what we all call noise varies; historically, it varies; historically or subjectively, it can flicker into and out of existence. Across cultures, what is noisy – what is disruptive, excessive or wrong – varies dramatically. Furthermore, noise is not even subjective, but it does traverse a subject to come into being. So the subject is not an external judge but part of a process of machinery based on cultural experience, location, social identity, income and so on. These *understandings* of noise illustrate that we can only ever imagine noise in multiple encodings.

Noise is always given an origin, a location, a home from where it can radiate, but Jacques Derrida has argued that the idea of the origin (or source, or place of ultimate truth) is itself something like an ideological construct, a metaphysical presumption, and that, in fact, all we have are origins that we must have made at some later point and then placed back into time so that they could provide us with the idea of what the origin was. Noise is a perfect rendition or paradigm of this paradoxical attribution, with a common tendency to look on noise as an origin, or something that can be identified with an original moment or point. Far better to take Derrida's philosophy as a warning about the use of origins as ways of defining essences, and instead conceive of noise as being very much like Derrida's idea of *différance*, as something like an operator, or process, than a thing. For example, noise might be other to music, but the more interesting 'noise' lies in the way in which 'noise' and 'music' relate or seem to be having their relation undone, by, say, a new piece of experimental music (i.e. the unfamiliar is not the location of noise, but the vehicle for the possibility of thinking noise, thinking music).

'Noise' is a position on the noise being encountered rather than present in 'the' noisy thing that has made its way into audition, no doubt unwelcome, uninvited, unexpected. Un. Noise is how we find it defined – a position based not on individual selection or delectation but one arrived at from multiple paths, pasts and factors – a statistically derived attribution at any one moment. In that context (an ever-changing, ever-to-be-not-yet-context) what continues to be of interest is the prospect for something called noise music. Without noise music, a soundchild of the 1980s and 1990s, the idea of noise, the idea of finding a use for the idea of noise, would likely not have occurred, for all of Cage's earfiddling. This 'music' pushed borders of genres, equipment, tones, notes, sounds into tangled messes of abstract noise collages, or exploded more monolithic practices through inappropriate and excessive performance of norms. But 'noise music' – because it is a category that you point to, talk about, share, buy, sell, discuss, value – would seem to not be noise anymore. Just like Dada's anti-art, noise loses when it wins. At this point, writers on noise usually like to find examples of 'good' noise that do not fall into any traps and manage to salvage the 'true meaning' of noise. Not here, not yet, maybe never.

Instead, let's focus on the coding of noise, how 'coding' intercepts noise at various levels, and how the failing to encode fully restores the value of coding as noise. All the examples of definition I have mentioned feature in the coding and decoding of noise as a concept, and of specific musics or musical works and performances. The question of how we understand those things is a sort of coding in the widest sense, as is the social reading and subcultural use of it as an affirmative marker. I think that those types of coding will help tell us something about the process of coding and decoding in a narrow sense and how those can only be subject to permanent recoding once thought about from a 'noisy' perspective.

[Current]

Electric hums, static: enabling conditions for electrifying music and the creating of teleaudition: for Kahn, they are resources from the restless elements on the sound-friendly planet of Earth, noise transformed into carriers of sound, and, not much later, images. But the history, or industry, of the production, transmission, storing, buying and selling of music has set its sights on a noise-free ideal sound. As each new technological leap made earlier generations sound noisy, inadequate and properly devalued, the dream seemed ever closer. Nietzsche, in *The Will to Power* (and elsewhere), said that truth exists only as a construct, a sort of wish-fulfilment, and is not out there, waiting to be discovered or attained.[6] So similarly, audiovisual devices just cannot stop getting better. Apparently. From hi-fi through the 1980s format wars in digital's first era as mass commodity to today's blu-ray (today's Betamax?), through 'lossless' audio and the endless precision-loading of remastered albums, perfection remains elusive. According to Jonathan Sterne, the widely held belief in a drive to perfection is just that, a belief, and that even in the context of the interest of consumer electronics companies to upgrade continually and resell marginally superior products, what we lived through in the end of the twentieth century and in this, is the progressive simplification of media for music delivery – with MP3 the paradigm, the apotheosis, the standard bearer (*MP3: The Meaning of a Format*).[7] Sterne also identifies a possibly unexpected source for this lowering of fidelity, and that is the reduction of sound quality in telephony, in order to maximize how many communications could travel along the same amount of cable. So, for Sterne, the heightened noise of the 'lossy' MP3 format is ultimately a product of post-war electrical engineering for communications (*MP3*, 7).

Sterne is looking in the right place – Shannon in the late 1940s, with help from Weaver, is the one who identifies the role of noise in any system or circuit. In Shannon's schema, noise is always there, lurking at the periphery of the communication circuit (or, more accurately, line), waiting to insert its input mid-message, mid-transmission or mid-pulse. The system exists despite the noise, and its functioning is to be constantly worked on to reduce the effect of any noise insertion. Weaver attempts to universalize Shannon's system into a model for all communication, and so provides us with a new origin: the origin is the sender, establishing a connection with the receiver, and noise comes into being, like the snake in the Christians' garden of Eden, to disturb that complete connection. Where Weaver took the model, many recent writers have followed, as there is something timely about Shannon's *Mathematical Theory of Communication*, coming as it did as part of the development of digital binary modelling that would increasingly define most music delivery, as well as sound and visions of all sorts, and not long before John Cage's first presentation of *4'33"* in 1952, Pierre Schaeffer's development of the idea of *musique concrète* in theory and practice, the introduction of both 33 and 45 rpm records, establishing new meta-genres – the single and the album and the fierce technological competition of the Cold War.

Shannon and Weaver's redefinition of communication as a sort of container that could be passed from one place to another helps create the sense of noise as a technical fault, a technical hitch, an extraneous interruption. Sterne notes the convergence of the technical move to improve communications technologies and the development of new terrains of experimental music as part of a dualistic 'domestication of noise' (Sterne, *MP3*, 94–95), and that both specifically include noise, only to dispose of its noisiness. For Cage, the noises of the world were now to be compositional resources for anyone in the world; for Shannon and Weaver, noise was a peculiarly integral part of the circuit, its incorporation dreaded yet always prepared for: noise as anticipation of noise. Weaver writes of the more or less organic generation of noise in any system, whether as by-product, or as lurking external force:

> In the process of being transmitted, it is unfortunately characteristic that certain things are added to the signal which were not intended by the information source. These unwanted additions may be distortions of sound (in telephony, for example) or static (in radio), or distortions in shape or shading of picture (television), or errors in transmission (telegraphy or facsimile), etc. all of these changes in the transmitted signal are called *noise*.
>
> (Weaver, 'Recent Contributions to the Mathematical Theory of Communication', 4–5)[8]

All of these phenomena occur in the delivery of electrified or improvised music. Reliability was 'rerouted' in several stages through the twentieth century, not least through the purposeful use of feedback – a very different, overloading type of feedback, unlike the reinforcing strength of systemic feedback, but still a willed use of noise, an overcoming, or even domestication. Detuning, breaking, turning up too loud, playing wrongly – all these mirror Weaver's warnings about other communications noise, and form a continuum of noise use in the circuit of avant-garde music or sound-making. In short-circuiting the means of music-making, noisemakers also subverted musical expectations of the communication of music in comprehensible, reasonably predictable form. As experimental music introduced elements of noise across a range of practices, the readiness of the receiver becomes paramount – in fact, if the sound producer is looking for noise to infiltrate the circuit and be heard as such, the listener needs to be switched on yet specifically not ready for the rerouting of musical forms. The listener is not only a decoding device, but has to occupy the position of transmitter – i.e. they have to be ready to re-encode the noise they encounter as music and effectively play it back to themselves as a recast message.

Although this process is fraught with the danger of becoming a faulty, 'noisy' receiver, as R. Haven Wiley notes in his explorations of animal communications in and through noise (*Noise Matters: The Evolution of Communication*),[9] the set of required actions and responses sets up a new pleasure circuit, and a new potential for noise. Decoding as a creative act involves the listener as producer, as hoped for by Cage with his many ways of musicalizing the world in the listening (Cage was looking for a non-noisy, receptive listener). Pre-existing knowledge, of the performance of known works, or of the functioning of tonal systems, scales and keys, the list of behaviours to be produced by audiences in different generic settings – this is supposed to be addressed, made audible once noise enters the system of a specific concert. Where once these audiences imagined themselves to be made through training and personal listening skill, they can now be made much more efficiently through data analytics, for example via the streaming service Spotify. Within that realm, listeners become fully encoded listening entities, a noise to be honed into meaning, accessibility and investment.

Noise does not arise from simply thwarting expectation through the novelty of creative actions, instead it consciously undermines the status of music, even the status of the performance in front of you, as machines, or even the whole concert, are opened to multifaceted failure, in a subversive use of what Shannon identifies as a 'secrecy system [which] can be considered to be a communication system in which the noise is the arbitrariness introduced by the encoding process' ('General Treatment of the Problem of Coding', 179).[10] This meta-coding is the machinery of noise music production, a known language to the fan, an initiation for the novice, a barrier to the sceptic. The production of extreme noise in the place of music can induce a panicked scrambling for the de-encryption machine. As Weaver notes, with dread, 'if you overcrowd the capacity of the audience you force a general and inescapable error and confusion' ('Recent Contributions', 27). Of course, it does not take long for listeners to adjust, to reset and move from one listening system to another, or they could of course leave, but it seems difficult for noise to not be reintegrated, leaving us with the still challenging, but less noisy sense of music in an expanded field.[11] This field is not just the use of new practices, the shedding of older skills, the physical assault of ultraloud music or enforced interactivity of a physical nature. It is also the spread of music into sound, and more curiously into the state of intermedia. Sound-making interacts with its own outside (and the inside of its inside, i.e. the machinery for its own production), its breakdown, and the audience becomes a medium in that construction.

Is noise a construct of the analogue world? It seems that the rise of auto-destructive sound-making goes hand in hand with the development of highly versatile and accessible digital music-making devices, programmed even to simulate problems such as glitching or the clicks and cracks of cosy old vinyl. All of the overdriving, distorting, damaging, retooling that we find in noise music comes first from analogue techniques and diagnostic machines, and from a time where analogue was developing hi-fi and advancing TV and video technology – Nam June Paik was misdirecting TV and audio devices from the mid-1960s. Japanese noise musicians often revert to the multiple possibilities of distortion that arise from analogue electrics and electronics, and make a point of the importance of the technological reversion, a para-humanism of autonomous machines in place of emerging soft digital humanity.

The digital seems to be a safe haven, where whatever tricks you would like to do can be reproduced and maintained at room temperature in CD/DAT/ soundfile formats, a realization of Shannon and Weaver's 'noiseless channel' (Weaver, 'Recent Contributions', 17). The smoothness and high functionality of the digital came under attack in noise music from the beginning, whilst using the actual capacities of digital sound-making to undermine the expectations of the recently constructed digital-listeners. Even earlier, electronic and computer sound devices were loved for their capacity to generate unexpected oscillatory sound excursions, and tape and computer held each other in a residue-generating bearhug. In short, an empty dialectic unites noise-making and new technology, where each empties and lowers the other, instead of virtuously spiralling upward in mutual overcoming.

Weaver has more to tell us about the noise he wishes to overcome. Firstly, he sought to clarify that entropy is not the same as noise – entropy is a feature of the message, the transmission – a sign of the level of possibilities to be contained ('information is a source of entropy', 'Recent Contributions', 17). Noise, though, is an addition, leading to 'the received message contain[ing] certain distortions, certain errors, certain extraneous material'. Uncertainty increases, 'but if the uncertainty is increased, the information is increased, and this sounds as if noise were beneficial!' (all ibid., 19). Noise becomes part of information received, and is part of an excessive transmission, so needs 'subtract[ing]'. One way in which listeners do this is to understand noise as message, to recode the entropic and supplemental information as the message. The avant-garde listener's qualification as listener is coded via this skill, perhaps in line with Wiley's observation of bird-listeners' 'adaptive gullibility' (*Noise Matters*, 167) where many birds operate on trade-offs between the benefits of making more listening errors with regard to other bird sounds and the risks of missing out on opportunity (e.g. mating) through over-caution in listening. In an exact obverse mirror process to that of Shannon, Weaver and also Norbert Wiener, the delivery/transmission/message becomes irrelevant – the circuit vanishes to be replaced by another, through which new content exchanges via the malleable receiver with their flexible, fast-coding listening. In fact, recent technologies have created a computational Leviathan, a stack-like convolute of circuits that intertwine, knot, layer and subtend each other, as Bratton notes

> The Stack, as examined here, comprises six interdependent layers: *Earth, Cloud, City, Address, Interface, User*. Each is considered on its own terms and as a dependent layer within a larger architecture. ... Each layer is understood as a unique technology capable of generating its own kinds of integral accidents, which perhaps counterintuitively, may ultimately bind that larger architecture into a more stable order.
>
> (*The Stack*, 11)[12]

The definition of entropy is somewhat contradictory in cybernetics – on the one hand it is clearly stated as part of the sea of possibilities that information could pick a point within, whilst on the other it is the direction of dissolution. Like the quantum particle, both seem hard not only to measure but to define. For Cécile Malaspina, in *An Epistemology of Noise*, communications theory and physics share a view of what entropy is.[13] However, it would largely seem that Shannon and Weaver's model is more simple than Boltzmann's radicalization of the universe as statistically empty and entropic, with the collapse of local order a mere sideshow. To summarize, Shannon and Weaver picture entropy as the threatening disorder of *fullness*, that can be harnessed into signal – in fact, information itself is greater, with more entropy, as long as we do not misunderstand 'information' to be 'meaning'. Information and entropy can both be sources (Weaver, 'Recent Contributions', 17). Weaver even closes his introduction to Shannon's text in *The Mathematical Theory of Communication* with the cryptic idea that 'entropy not only speaks the language of arithmetic; it also speaks the language of language' (28). Boltzmann sees entropy as the emptiness that is the statistical reality of the universe, with dissipation so normal we cannot even understand how unusual our isolated reality of order is.[14] Entropy, in his modelling, has nothing much to do with stuff, but is about absence and its intrusion. In no sense, other than the very local, could we misconstrue information modelling of entropy as input, source, stuff, with Boltzmann's empty and ever-emptying universe. Notwithstanding this opposition, the local process of entropy, where things lose definition, is where the two models meet – with noise one part of one of four subsets of entropy (Weaver,

'Recent Contributions', 21). Shannon ostensibly builds his model for controlling the intrusion of noise on Boltzmann's local, dispersive thermodynamics. In Boltzmann, we could imagine that noise is the ripple of stuff, of meaning, coming into being amid near-total entropy, which is the more probable form, such that life (on Earth) or negative entropy exists only as a result of evolutionarily selective entropy in the dispersion of the Sun's rays (Boltzmann, 'Second Law of Thermodynamics', 24). Suffice to say, it is very hard to map noise and music onto these conflicting, *différantial* and almost mathematically differential models. Entropy proves to be source, backdrop, intrusion, input, information, absence, lack of information, movement *and* absence of same.

So, in noise music, the surface of it is superficially entropic (in the commonsense view), massing information in a formless cloud (something like overload in Shannon and Weaver), and perhaps noise music offers a very good way of understanding both noise and entropy as complex and indeterminate processes as opposed to being things. For all its apparent disorder, noise in music is arguably just a more complex system than the telephony model of noise promoted by Shannon and Weaver. Noise music's use of many devices, such as overdriven analogue synths, or no-input circuits, purposely generating non-linear sound structures in a variegated, wobbling or lurching whole – and if we were to stick with Shannon and Weaver, we will accept the integration of all noise into the stack, as it will end up carrying other codings, other signals. Routinely entropic music systems or sound works can also be noise, but the noise occurs in the dissipation of sense: 'a steady degradation of energy until all tensions that might still perform work and all visible motions in the universe would have to cease' (Boltzmann, 'The Second Law of Thermodynamics', 19).[15] And in this model, noise is not outside the stack but the premonition of its collapse. The listener may have to accept a highly paradoxical way into this form of entropy, in the solidity of harsh noise wall, where there is no space for information to communicate internally, so the listener is shunted back out into other codings (genre, connoisseurship, idiocy, existential gloom), but in the absence of event (Boltzmann) as opposed to too much eventfulness (Shannon/Weaver). Noise music goes far further than Shannon and Weaver. Apparent entropy in their model masks Boltzmannian entropy that is more like noise, and, in so doing, noise music acts as Shannon and Weaver imagined their telephone lines doing, using noise as a way of establishing a different circuit. Only in this case, the meaning is not within but in the resolution of noise into a medium or genre, or, better still, a listening possibility or affordance.

Noise at its emptiest, or strongest as an emptying device, is a proper mobilization of entropy, not just in the sound produced but in the removal of concentration, seriousness or solidity of the listener's sense-making. At the extreme, such as Satie's *Vexations* (from 1893), with its 840 repetitions of an atonal piano sequence, noise as music (and as the nothing that shuttles between noise and music) acts as a condensation of time, transformed into the planing away of concentration and/ or attention. Just such a possibility is present in white noise, or 'white thermal noise' as Shannon and Weaver call it. This multiple bandwidth/frequency noise is still a set range of sounds, and corralled by Weaver into a controlled, factorable phenomenon. In music, or in noise, white noise would seem to be the ultimate expression of noise and entropy together, combining the two definitions in one solid mass of resistance. But we should also be aware that white noise, or noise of other colours, has been used for decades as a diagnostic device, a way of policing the accuracy of sinewaves, currents and, in general, signal delivery. It has also been widely used as a soothing device for humans, the multiple frequencies luring in attention only to slow it into restful inertia. In both cases, white noise acts a sort of barrier, both seemingly infinitely mobile and static. Only the passage of a needle through the furrow of a record's surface or the obstinate movement of a CD player/digital device's clock shows us that normal time is still elapsing.

[The Miscellaneous]

This still leaves us with Weaver's 'etc'. On four occasions in his introduction to Shannon's theory he slips this most unlikely word in:

'the selected message may consist of written or spoken words, or of pictures, music, etc.'

('Recent Contributions', 7)

'these unwanted additions may be distortions of sound (in telephony, for example) or static (in radio), or distortions in shape or shading of picture (television), or errors in transmission (telegraphy or facsimile), etc. All of these changes in the transmitted signal are called *noise*'

(7–8, emphasis in original)

'If the signal being transmitted is *continuous* (as in oral speech or music) rather than being formed of *discrete* symbols (as in written speech, telegraphy, etc.), how does this fact affect the problem?'

(8, emphasis in original)

lastly, a list of things that could make up a message: '(letters, words, musical notes, spots of a certain size, etc.)'

(12)

You will note the inclusion of music – it is a regular indicator of the universal application of the idea of communication in Shannon, as Weaver reads it. But what is the 'etc.'? This strange surplus diminishes the clarity of explanation, so what does it do? It could be there to future-proof; it could be there as a way of Weaver acknowledging the limits of his own knowledge; it could be there to indicate that content is irrelevant; or flexible; or open; or universal. But its apparent laziness suggests something much deeper – and that is the presence of noise exactly within the entropy of overall message potentials. Its peculiarity is not only in its openness, but in its display of the openness of the system – an awareness that noise is, if not exactly integral, then something more than extraneous. The presence of the 'etc.' is Weaver's attempt to bring the noise in, to contain it within the safer entropy of message potentials.

Noise is a threat to the transfer of encoded material, it eats away at the encoded thing in transit, but never seems to affect the source – this is always a pure, intentional moment of sending (countered by Wiley's hyperbolization of noise in communication circuits as applying to all phases and elements of communication [*Noise Matters*, 136]). The sending brings sender and receiver into being, and they gather into existence as the message travels. The presence of the formless potential of 'etc.' tries to bring noise inside as 'known unknown', and does illustrate that the 'whatever' of noise can be brought into the signal. But noise as the external input that *adds* itself as content and form still threatens the existence and nature of the terminals in communication – both encoding and decoding would reveal themselves as without foundation if noise can infiltrate the message fully. Noise music, as a music based on breakdown, excessive pushing of machine and music, tries to do this – to unmake the connection between music and the understanding of music, in a way that further eats away at meaning and understanding. Is this intended? If it isn't, why is it happening in place of music, where music should be? The place of noise in the cybernetic circuit is less and less clear: yes, it is inside and out, yes, it helps define the other parts negatively (the bits which are not noise, but are in some way correct and in the right place).

Sterne says that noise travels along the circuit, even if still conceived as extraneous, parasitic, and that MP3 is the culmination of the exploitation of noise, in order to transmit more: 'rather than fighting noise, one could simply distribute noise in such a way that it would be inaudible in the presence of a signal' (*MP3*, 110). This happens through 'perceptual coding' (*MP3*, 2), which, in short, is a technique developed in the 1990s to exploit the noise in listening: i.e. not all of the sound of a high-fidelity music product is actually necessary, and some of the redundancy (or 'quality') could be removed with no loss of perceptual signal, thus increasing bandwidth on cables, and vastly reducing the amount of bits of data that could usefully represent an audio track. But even this model presumes we know what noise is at any point, whereas noise is broader or perhaps fuller than a technical specification. In addition, the universalizing drive of the cybernetic model needs adjusting. For one thing, the technical circuit of sound delivery is doubled by a perceptual circuit. These circuits then flow into wider social and listening contexts and structures, receiving feedback and further noise from them. Digitalized culture expands the two-dimensional conception of the circuit into a complex structure of interlocked, transactional and nodal channels.

Once again, the advent of a positively construed noise music will also introduce the possibility of noise moving location, and new circuits will have to be grown that allow noise to move not just as message ('here's some noise', transmitted and received knowingly, at say, a concert) but also as reconfiguring device. Experimental music has spawned, or fractured into, a myriad microgenres, and each variant slides into a slot where its coordinates, or its relative position, is known. The now-defunct Paris record shop Bimbo Tower offered an alarming plethora of genres, extending to a dedicated 7-inch section for Australian and New Zealand noise. It had divided sound art into multiple variants, noise into subgenres, localities, labels, constellations; generations of performers found themselves touching fronds with newer hybrids ... such definition shows the twin impulse of the noise receiver: on the one hand to keep it noise, highlight its uniqueness, its contingency, and on the other hand to bring it into the realm of message, of containment. The rage to code noise knew no bounds in the shop, but they could never keep up. The 'etc.' was always there, spilling over, finding, filling and exceeding the ecology building of the shop's human inhabitants.

Japanese noise in Bimbo Tower had got so big, it was allocated not only its own section, but its own domain, with individual artists who produce dozens if not hundreds of releases provided with their own niche. The thing called Japanese noise represented a multiple flowering of an excessive retranscription not just of noise but of genre.[16] Within that growth, the height was the 1990s, and creeping through the entire landscape was and still is the anti-monument that is Masami Akita's Merzbow with the 300 or so releases under that name. In so many ways the epitome of noise music, his peak moment as something new for East and West alike was the mid-1990s – and yet it seems impossible to fully say this music is no longer noise.

The sprawl, I think, is what keeps Merzbow noise, just as it does for later artists such as China's Torturing Nurse. Even as listeners grapple with the sound mass, the endless churn of plastic and nanoscale file objects, they know they cannot conquer. Merzbow's insistence on the material is a continued resistance to the supposed dematerialization of music, a maintenance of the object as itself a noisy thing. But the CD releases offer the highest possible level of noise in terms of volume and a sense of the multiple layers that feed a Merzbow piece. Albums such as *Hybrid Noisebloom* from 1997 still surprise with their onslaught. And, Merzbow's *music* might no longer feel like noise for those hoarding their symbolic listening capital as they look for new listening to master, but until Merzbow (as hypostasis of Japanese noise) reaches a mass public (one that never seems to arrive), it still has scope to suggest noise as other to music. It still seems like an expression of the formless, a bringing to form that never coalesces, just as hi-fi can never reach its false ideal, or just as noise can never reach its apparent ideal.

Practically speaking, even if we allow Masami Akita his own genre, this stuff that he makes has a clearly defined place to live inside the ecosystem of avant-garde sound-making. It has a place in a history, however discontinuous, of noise. It's easy enough to find, and you can now listen to loads of it in degraded audio. Paradoxically, or not, Merzbow's distortions are at their best when allowed a reproductive format that can hold all the detail, that can make the message transmit. To the CD player, a Merzbow release is probably no more detailed than a 1970s prog album, maybe less so, despite what it sounds like to human ears. This is not quite the case when producing or recording tracks, when the editing and mastering is a constant battle with software, or when the record-pressing plant does not know which sound is supposed to be there, and whether a master is a correct rendering of material for pressing onto vinyl. This occurred for me when releasing 'La Puissance de l'erreur' by Vomir (in 2011), when the GZ Media vinyl press said on numerous occasions that their machines could not identify the track of harsh noise wall as a 'proper' track, nor, if the mass of noise was the track, could it tell how to decide when the track should begin or end. But for the machine player, even when conceptually wrong, it is all information. Even in the live setting, anything other than complete machine failure is mostly information, or at least transmission.

The CD itself represented a way of playing with the digital, and much has been made, over time, of the potential of the glitch to revolutionize music, as it was produced from the failure of already-produced sound. As time went on, writers such as Caleb Kelly and Greg Hainge looked a bit closer, and developed the idea that, far from challenging the digital, completed glitch projects rely on the apparent perfectedness of the format.[17] Normally, a glitch comes from the laser misreading a CD, which can be the result of mispressing, dirt or disc rot (a surprisingly common fate for early CDs and many cheap CDRs). Artists like Christian Marclay and Yasunao Tone used this effect to make sound art works from the late 1980s on, others such as John Oswald and Disc redirected pop energy into fractal ecstatics. Many decided to record glitches, or produce them digitally – creating a sense of a format under attack, but actually mostly creating a disturbance for the listener through extended play. While the sound indicated 'stuck' or 'damaged' to a human, the laser continued reading – the glitch had been brought back into the circuit, and achieved its aesthetic effect through the combination of a sense of failing or noise while precisely depending on the reliability of playing and reproduction that digital formats offered. Glitch musicians therefore move the glitching from noise to information content, altering the habits of the listener and how they not only hear coding but how they are obliged to decode the music heard as properly coded.

It is no accident that these examples all derive from the 1990s, and despite the continued sprawl of both Japanese noise or music in the style of that noise, and also of glitching, we might wonder where noise is now. We might also wonder does it extend beyond the production of things as standard as records, CDs, soundfiles, concerts, installations, broadcasts ... this brings us back to a certain living-on, the sur-viving not just of noise, but also the paradigms laid out in the 1940s and early 1950s which established the places of messages and noise in seemingly definitive yet in fact utterly time- and context-bound ways. Beyond the optimist universalizing of the cyberneticists lies a way of maintaining their thought of noise as that which waits to intrude and which awaits controlling. Maybe there is some definitive way to keep noise going if we think that noise is in some ways always there. If that 'there' is not exactly 'here', if it is not inside or outside, if it is both behind, aside and ahead of us. Maybe it is like Timothy Morton's hyperobjects – something we can glimpse but that exceeds human comprehension whilst having a profound effect on the world. If instead of noise being an 'is', perhaps noise is a 'not' (like Blanchot's *pas*): not-this, not-that, not-quite, not-here, while all the time proliferating as if it were true, as if it were a thing, with a place, a being, a sense, that would be nearly something. Or at some point, not now, it would be. Maybe.

Maybe we can hear the last noise as it emerges only to fail.

A few years ago, harsh noise wall tried to counter the pervasive colonization of the term noise by a host of post rock, quirky performance, improv and electronic activities. This time, noise would be not only full, it would be an emptying, an ending, a constant ending. Harsh noise wall, or HNW, is both the final tragic throw of the noise dice, and also the undoing of the portent of noise, as it congeals into absurdity. Its solid masses of throbbing noise, rich yet nauseating, comforting yet oppressive, its chunks of full spectrum anomie, are a resistance not just to meaning and music but to noise itself. Since the advent of harsh noise as music in the 1980s and 1990s, the debate between those wanting to make something that is still noise (i.e. a new avant-garde) centres around whether music should be layered with the noise or not. The circuit of music is totally reversed in this world, as noise becomes message that many would-be novelties in music wish to communicate. Avant-garde music continues, as does avant-gardism in many terrains, despite the cod-tragic destiny some attributed to art thirty years ago or so, condemning it to reference-rummaging, crate-sifting.

Maybe the ubiquity of available sound consigns noise to a terminal periphery, leading the way into the entropy of everything everywhere all at once. Maybe formats can be subverted, manipulated, turned to good (sharing as redemption). MP3 as noise? Return of cassettes as noise? Material culturists would like us to focus on consumption, on machines, on software. New materialists and agential realists offer para-empiricist takes on what is really going on in ways that assess the mechanics of industry, technology as well as subcultures, listener groups, connoisseur publics. Noise behaviour, or noise generation, is not where we expect. It is certainly not in the stockpiling of soundfiles, neither is it in the giving away of same. Instead, it seems to be in the refusal to let music escape the commodity – only it has now become contentless content, as dreamed of by Shannon, Weaver and Wiener's cybernetic models, to the point where we can talk of 'content providers' as means of delivering a 'medium', and by medium what is meant is purchasable hardware, network connections and patented software. Today's (human) wetware has never been more capitalist about music, and the reterritorialization of listening into its devices matches not only corporate dreams, and the activities of consumer, but is increasingly validated by the machine focus (material culture) of cultural studies of music or indeed of sound in society. We need to not forget that there are listeners enmeshed in the stack, inhabitants of a purported all-availability of sounds and that these listeners are made in circuits that exceed the machinic.

However, do they escape the algorithmic? What would the dream of escape entail? I have mentioned the material resistance offered by artists suspicious of the process of dematerialization. But this material resistance can come across as an elite strategy, and even limited editions and rare concerts need publicizing. But where the internet facilitated noise musicians to reach a threshold via a global audience, high-speed broadband has meant that presence in the form of concert-playing, for example, is secondary, or only takes place as part of an extremely low cost, not-for-profit boutique festival. Far beyond the functioning of code to make, listen to or distribute sound, it has enabled a full proximity that brings everything near, as long as it does not need paying for. There is no more space in which to mediate (as Baudrillard predicted back in the 1970s) and, as Hito Steyerl argues, 'the all-out Internet condition is not an interface but an environment … Networked space is itself a medium … that contains, sublates and archives all previous forms of media' ('Too Much World: Is the Internet Dead?').[18]

Softly predictive codings, known as algorithms, track and shape the listeners of today. Any material resistance, even the nihilistic thickness of harsh noise wall, happens elsewhere than everywhere. Streaming services, with Spotify as the brand leader, have redefined not just the function of coding, not just what gets coded, but the overall shape of the stack that has music at its centre. Maria Eriksson and a group of co-writers have carried out an extensive and multimodal study of Spotify's practices, form and mission. It becomes apparent that the company's mission is not the simple exploitation of musicians and listeners to make money, as this is only part of a broader mission of which music is an incidental part. But in terms of music, they note that

> [t]hrough their entanglements with algorithms, global music metadata arrangements, and automized web-scrapers, streamed music files get wrapped up in the whirlpools of data traffic that surround digital streams.
>
> (Eriksson et al, *Spotify Teardown*, 78)[19]

They then go on to map out an empirical reading of the multi-coding machine that is Spotify, where music is 'redefin[ed] as a data-driven communicative form – with audio files and metadata being aggregated through various external intermediaries, and with user-generated data being extracted from listening habits' (80). Music, including experimental, or even noise music, has experienced multiple codings, whether in terms of message, (un)desirability, genrification [*sic*], commercialization, commodification (including in symbolic connoisseur capital), formatting, and now all of these come together in the 'ease' of streaming. The listener, of course, is the most coded part of all. Noise music has no way out of this, but at least it has understood from the start the risks of dematerialization, as all small scenes or micro-avant-gardes have witnessed the complete asset-stripping of even the small amounts of commercial value that the globalizing internet had initially provided.

Noise has nothing to offer, no salvation. Streaming can be played with, critiqued, and data-collecting misled, but it is all interesting, all data. Noise is not the intention to be noise, but will often be accidental by-products of refusals, rejections or unwitting resistance (the absence on Spotify of silent tracks that were initially part of CD albums, for example). Noise cannot disappear, nor can nihilism (philosophy, not attitude) be adequately monetized, in cash or signifying value, but maybe it can think of itself as an isolated pocket of stopping capacity, like literal electrical resistance. Like this resistance, it enables even as it withholds or slows, and this is the expected fate, always, of noise, to not be noise, or never come to be. But that is better than annihilation in the soft integral reality of streaming utopias. Flatness, emptiness, lack of development, too much development, too much sound, not enough sound. There is almost something there, 'even emancipatory programs of disenchantment' (Bratton, *The Stack*, 72).

Eon Cores: Noise Prospecting in
A Personal Sonic Geology

Noise is a beginning, noise is an ending. Or so many have said. For lovers of the origin, the *arch*-ists, we have the Big Bang, and we have cosmic background radiation. Hillel Schwarz tried to put this end to end in his *Making Noise: From Babel to the Big Bang and Beyond*, which, as the title suggests, imputes to noise an epistemological and constructionist character. We have the sound that somehow subsisted before meaning and yet could be defined as noise, and we have the world of sound that surrounds us, which many imagine is full of noises. For those that embrace the end, the *teleo*-rs, noise sounds like the clanging chime of doom, the third knock, the final trump. But of course the first will be last, and if we do hear the sound of this universe coming into being in the form of background radiation, then this will also be the last sound. In fact, if it is noise, or sound, it is not the sound *of* anything. It is the sound that remains as excess, as residue. Residue is noise – the unwanted, unexpected, formless, uncontained.

But residue accumulates, acquires form. In the case of noise, this form has occurred in the modes of practice and process. In other words, something a lot like noise appears in solid recognizable form, while the truer, deeper noise is what moves between forms, sometimes enigmatically. Noise can be there at the beginning, or it can occur later, or stand as some sort of endpoint, but it seems that noise has appeared and will continue to appear. Film-maker/curators Philippe Decrauzat and Mathieu Copeland have probed for noise as all of these things: going back to original and influential sources, then letting noise occur, creating a space for it and finally making noise into material to be used. The 'personal sonic geology' presented in the exhibition *A Personal Sonic Geology* (Le Plateau, Paris, 2015) is the localization of noise in a set of new processes that cross between media, and find a strange destiny in a series of films that took sound as their source, extracting noise as material and transmuting it into a new noise in the final forms – artists they included in their geology include

F.M. Einheit, Gustav Metzger, Ellen Fullman, Lydia Lunch and Alan Licht, along with others, other locations, words, places, events, music and images.[1] The final forms were not closed – films (audio and images) doubled on each side of films (material), interacting with each other, recombining in a permanent evolution into which the viewer/auditor would be drawn. In so doing, this exhibition opens up the prospect of noise as geology, genealogy and as strata that drift and re-layer one another over time.

Noise is continuous, some opine: you cannot close your ears (even Deleuze and Guattari fall for this one),[2] there is no such thing as silence, everywhere sound awaits as a figure of the unexpected that, nonetheless, can be marshalled for ethical good through listening, sound-making, environment shaping. Noise is everywhere, they say. Noise is so good it is the material for all else, with Michel Serres asserting that 'white noise [*bruit de fond*] the heart [*fond*] of being … white noise is the base – "white space", as it were' (*The Parasite*, 52), thereby both ingratiating himself with the unknown, and identifying what it is, what it is not and where it comes from.[3] Others say that noise is nowhere, unattainable. Noise is not only discontinuous, it is the paradigm of discontinuity, the way we can recognize or sense fissure, rupture. Noise would be a dissonance that opens up a break in time – something like a beginning and end in one. This is primarily how it has featured in music production and criticism – a term applied to whatever music is the most extreme at any one time. It was in 1977 that Attali saw noise unfolding over time as a sign of the future (and unfolding in this book as a sign in its own right, a sign to remember the endless disappearance of noise and its rejection): at any one time, the new sounds noisy, and is hard to process. Over time, though, the noise becomes meaningful, understood, categorizable. Over time, Attali's Nietzschean breach in historicity and ontology has been sealed over through complacency (he too has written out the properly nihilistic parts of the original).[4] In an even deeper flattening of the prospect of noise, Alex Ross has identified the tasteful incorporation of what was previously foolishly seen as noise, by the world of classical music. Not only does Ross's *The Rest is Noise* salvage a genre, emphasizing one micro-avant-garde over all others, it also presumes that noise is defined only once it has made progress happen, as opposed to when it is noise.[5] Unlike Attali, who identifies a process (that disrupts linear time) within a variety of types (an open set in fact) of music and musical practice, Ross identifies a process of Hegelian overcoming where all that is relevant has been seen to feed into the monolith of music as advancing culture. For Ross, it is easy to tap in to this resource, but what if it is ever-changing, always slightly out of reach? Because once you know noise, the noise is gone, it is just a different type of music. Once you know noise, in hindsight, it became not a harbinger of change but a premonition of sameness.

To undertake geology is to explore geology. The latter is the structures and processes of planets, the former is the study of them. And noise has always been caught up in ideas, representations and theories of noise. To make this activity *personal* is not just an act of autobiography, but also a way of recognizing that noise flows through people, perceptions, constructions of subjectivity, and to do this consciously means to flow through artworks. So what better means than an open-ended, multi-artist, multi-temporal action culminating in multiple form(s)? Geology here, like Nietzsche's idea of genealogy (or Foucault's archaeology), is the way in which Decrauzat and Copeland can perform an acoustology, making their mobilizations of sound, of sound and bodies, of sound and vision, into an explicitly subjective set of operations. Copeland has previously ventured into artistic versions of noise activity with his exhibitions *A Retrospective of Closed Exhibitions* (2016) and, as curatorial collaborator, *Voids* (2009) – neither of which included anything other than emptiness in various forms, or an emptying of the presence of art. In *A Personal Sonic Geology*, the curators do not empty art but instead empty the idea of historical procession, in favour of a complex temporality of influence (also addressed below in Chapter 14).

There are so many things to say about noise, it's such an enticingly rich and vacuous signifier. This should not surprise us, because noise meant gossip and whispered storytelling first, just as *bruit* did when it was not referring to gentle natural sounds, which was for centuries its primary meaning. Somehow we got misled that noise and nausea were forever tied together (one example of this is Pascal Quignard's doleful fantasia *La Haine de la musique*), rather than a loose connection among many possible entanglings.[6] Noise is a negativity, I have said, and people are uncertain about this, because they say they *like* noise. So, to be clear: *firstly*, it means that noise cannot exist independently – it exists only in comparison to other things, such as meaning, or music, or normativity; noise is always enmeshed in what it rejects or in what seeks to reject it, or define it as 'the rejected'. *Secondly*, negativity has to include the sense of noise being thought of as 'the thing that is bad', the negative thing we (some **we** that represents **us** all, and with the power to define for the **we** that is **us** all) sought to exclude. For me, these two 'negative' thoughts are the core of noise, and everything else is in permanent motion, constant change, with a new model for every entanglement. I do mean entanglement, in the sense of quantum physics, as seen through the agential lens of Karen Barad, as two moments emerge and even as they separate, the apparatus of reactive listening keeps both senses in play. Even decohering will not prevent the parallel twin existence of the entangled.

The set of works that constitute this *Personal Sonic Geology* exhibition play through and on this negativity. Artists are put in relation to one another, all of them are brought out into the sphere of Decrauzat and Copeland, firstly in their own right, then as material. But they were always destined to become *material*, as their works were commissioned in the knowledge that they would inhabit twin temporalities: one in the performance or recording of the artists' work, the other their presence in the films of the two curator-artists. This non-simple temporality is one example of relational 'negativity' at work here. Another is through the sonic disruption of the works, which works as disruption because it goes against expectations of 'correct', polite, 'appropriate' gallery sound. The sonic geology plays on this and exaggerates it further in the final film phase, where it is the works themselves that act on one another in creative dissonance. This exhibition illustrates that the demands on 'correct' curating do not need following, and can be played, turned back by artist and curator alike, in a reinstallation of noise between artworks and times as well as vibrational sympathy.

Noise is not positive, it is disrupting, unsettling, affective and maybe too close. Or it is not noise. When 'noise' is used positively, it is only a commodity, a capitalization. It can bring 'positive' outcomes, particularly in terms of protest, or subverting social categorization as other, but this gain should not be misunderstood as noise itself, which is not only more likely to feature as a 'negative' but, more importantly, it lies in the play of positive and negative and their continually changing valences. Noise is that marker, or even the movement, of the negative, not the 'negative term'. Another way of seeing it could be through Fred Moten's 'cut', where black performance can undo and remake (in one move, the cut) hierarchical claims about cultural production and reset what is going to count.[7] And the geology at play here does not settle, it never can, as it mutates alchemically in the variegate forms Decrauzat and Copeland pull it out of, into, around. A rolling magma. This is where the history of noise appears in a *Personal Sonic Geology*: across fissures, across time and space, from individual works that are often literally, actually, aggressively noisy in some way, to their remodelling. This happens as and in the noise of an intermedia practice that unfolds over the many months that accrete into the not-final film exhibition.[8] The unasked question the exhibition did answer was how to use music as source, practice, material and recharged conclusion, all in one place, and they returned to many who had modelled this helical relation, expanding and extending it on so that it became excess.

The idea of noise, in all its paradoxicality, has always been connected to its practice. Historically, this happens with Futurism and Dada, both noisy in their own ways. Luigi Russolo, of the former camp, not only made orchestras of boxes designed to make precisely the kind of sounds that music deemed beyond its purview, but also established early ideas of just what noise is and why it is important. He did this in the 1910s, just before the outbreak of the noise to end all noises.[9] In so doing, he felt the need to argue that noise was natural, and should be used in art because of that. At the same time, he said that noise was a product of human culture, and so should be used in art. Finally, noise was the sound of the future, and therefore was ripe for use. At this emergent point, in the early twentieth century, noise was coming to be seen as a radicalizing device. As noise was something within a nature, and a culture and an industry all deemed too rowdy to be directly present in art, it could work as a marker of disturbance: take your pick from modern composers such as Hector Berlioz, Richard Wagner, Igor Stravinski, Arnold Schoenberg or the inventor-composers of the seventeenth century.

As a way of geologizing and auscultating these resonances, and taking those sounds as a heuristic device, *Personal Sonic Geology* helps remind us that at the same time as Russolo discovered and brought noise out to play, Alfred Wegener was proposing his theory of continental drift based on shifting tectonic plates.[10] He was held in even more derision than Russolo for this foolish idea that is now established fact.

Is there a lineage of noise as invention and ultimate marker of greatness through canonization in the heroic progression of great white Western composers? Even the exciting riots that accompanied premieres of major works (such as that of Stravinski's *Rite of Spring* performed by the Ballets Russes in Paris, 1913) are just part of the soft progression toward sonic colonization, a small flurry of aristocratic resistance to (bourgeois) gentrification.[11] It is at the periphery of that tradition that we see the attempt to gather or harvest the more disruptive moments and bundle them into a parallel canon of *improving* dissonance. Classical music connoisseurs may have helped play a part in rejecting some sounds as noise, so they could be positively dissonant, but when the 'wrong' sounds came inside, what changed? The sequence of 'noises' that has resulted does not bring us as far as the equivalent breach that was Dada: is Erik Satie noise? Are Henry Cowell, Charles Ives, Edgard Varèse, Pierre Schaeffer,

Pauline Oliveros, Eliane Radigue, François Bayle, Karlheinz Stockhausen …? Maybe, probably, even. But then what about improvising jazz musicians? Genre-troubling jazz composers? Rock, punk? Music's Dada moment did not happen until the mid-1970s, and when it did, it crossed jazz, progressive rock, funk, punk and industrial. But it was industrial music that redrew the line. Let's note at this point that the same criticisms could be made of experimental music outside of the classical genre as of that within it, but those other genres, other micro-avant-gardes, have had to define new places, as opposed to finding acceptance within a well-funded 'conservatoire of noises'.

The Dada-esque moment of genre-busting, convention-pulping activity was best found in and around what was quickly identified as industrial music (in the late 1970s). Of course, there is something really specific, rather than absolutely open-ended and novel at its core, and even the name is a misnomer (as it is based on the name of Throbbing Gristle's record label). But something happened in that moment, something very noisy, as performance, visuals, sound and discourse were mobilized not to praise industry, as Russolo may have hoped, but to accuse the oppressiveness and politicized misery of the post-industrial, media-controlled, consensually fascist society that industrial musicians saw around them. This moment is at the heart of Decrauzat and Copeland's work in *Personal Sonic Geology* – both personally for them as artists and curators but also as a precise rendering of what it means for any personal geology to happen in a society that wants no individuality, no critique, no art that does not follow approved models (and even when it does, it wants them packaged, commodified).

Industrial music covered a very broad spread of sound, just as 'noise music' would, slightly later on, this transition from one to the other marking another way of traversing and/or reinvesting the 1980s (industrial moved into other modes, hybridizing with other electronic musics as the 1980s and 1990s progressed). It was the gateway genre to junk noise clattering, the playing of metal, concrete, concrete mixers, found sounds. Lots of broken things. Lots of the wrong things. Even more bad playing of those things. Noise here is less about creativity, and more a summoning of a strange sort of fatigued creativity, the rejection of a failed crypto-capitalism of avant-gardism that builds into a canon. And although not present in this/that sonic geology, we could imagine a sonic geology of uncovering, of excavation and re-placing of genres, practices that also represent a source to later artists, and a source that can be turned (changed in how it is perceived, how its relations work) in how it is returned to by the later artists.

But is noise necessarily anything to do with music? Maybe it should be made to sound more like science? Certainly, we have the quackery of neuroscience, and will-to-scientize aesthetics, along with the willingness of funding agencies to promote either art or writing that crosses (i.e. mentions) technology and art in one eructation. Geology is not at all like this: what it looks for is hidden within solidity – some of which is dark enough to end up in extractable noise. Like prospectors, Decrauzat and Copeland scope, probe, align, organize and dip into the reservoir of the well. Between the solid rock are the channels and pockets – and these are exactly, alchemically, hermetically, magically the same (structurally, logically, aesthetically) as the sonic works here, and also the same as the clearly solid yet fractured history of noise.

Recent flavours of discussion have moved away from thinking of sound and noise as things we need to imagine in relation to music (as Brian Kane's 'Musicophobia' article attests). That may well be true, but the thought of sound and noise did not spring from any other place than the reflection on music or art, other than when it was thought of as a nosological issue or an engineering problem. The history of thinking about sound, in the West, takes place in the context of music, or its parallel in meaning. This may be connected (it has been) to the history of recording, or it may be that the history of recording has 'blinded' us to sound beyond that and what we need is sonic archaeology: a sonogeology to reveal the material, a geology that concludes in flowing audiovisual form.

Everywhere that noise is there to be heard, be it in music, ideas, art, social dissensus or in the many sonic vibrations of the universe that only humans were arrogant enough to think silent, everywhere, there is potential for betterment, for learning. And all of that is caught up in the normativity of early adopting, i.e. of firstness. *A Personal Sonic Geology* gives us a method, a process and a set of things that massively disrupt a logic or validation of 'firstness' in favour of a complex temporality where now and then combine, where parallel nows intertwine, sonically, in the space of the exhibition. It is no small thing: this exhibition (and book, including further essays reflecting on and into the processes of geologizing, such as an early variant of this chapter) is a geology that has reorganized spacetime along noise lines.

The avant-gardes that have littered Western cultural history since the mid-nineteenth century have ossified into piles of the culture they sought to break down. The twentieth- and twenty-first-century attacks on culture, from Dada to industrial to the soft suffocating of art in relational aesthetics tried to do more than develop, change or improve. They sought to eliminate, to create but also destroy. Turning Mikhail Bakunin on his head, these blasts of noisiness that defined (post- or de-) industrial music, made creativity destructive – and made a show of it, made a show of themselves, from Duchamp's coal sacks, through the epic puerilities of Fluxus, the refusals and self-defeats of Gustav Metzger, and the flows of COUM Transmissions. These were ultimately accepted, they found a safe space in which to be part of history, but they can all actually be kept alive, as opposed to cryogenically lined up in the stately march of art history, within a geologized noise that keeps the noise in play, through a new audiospatialization. In so doing, we also see established a transferable paradigm of audiotemporality that does not insist on the present or consumption of a completed, processed past.

Metzger was not only influential in directly inspiring rock and industrial musicians, his auto-destructive actions excoriated the drive to produce and create that offers a legitimating crust to extractive capitalism. Art, if it was to be anything, needed to not be, to not labour the world by its presence, but instead exist only to fall apart, decay, collapse, and be actively futile. Metzger's permanently irruptive destructions are essential to Copeland, who has acted as curator and editor of Metzger's collected writings.[12] The processes mobilized by Metzger are therefore essential to any geological approach to sound and noise – an alternative to building, and also to creating value through revealing/extracting. Auto-destruction is more ecological in spirit and material reality than the massive efforts to make, distribute and preserve (or indeed see or hear) cultural artefacts.

Maybe noise can be something outside of hearing, that way we could shut noise off once and for all, unsound, un-noise, ur-silence. Only the sighs of relief of the tunefully eared to interrupt the *bruit* of the gentle breeze, unpeculiarly wafting its normative sociability. Maybe noise can be … Maybe it can be, even if it is not 'it' and it cannot 'be'. Once you can point a finger at it, either in warning or in insouciant knowing, it is not, and it is not *there*. But what if the pointing can never settle? What if Decrauzat and Copeland have used their *divining* of the strata of noise to constantly undermine the ready tendency to categorize, to fix, to understand? What if they have changed the object nature of all the works that flow into theirs (and back out again, and into each other)?

But noise is also tiring, a tiredness that knows only the bounds of an ever-decreasing zone where possibility even matters. Once noise music became a thing and ruled the ears of the avant-garde globalized hierophancy, everyone heard what they wanted when they heard the word 'noise', but for good noise to turn bad (i.e. be good) it is necessary that there be interstitial noise, a noise that undermines the solidity of the parts of the whole. Noise is not the opposite of meaning, music etc., in an inherent way, but the opposite as a result of noise in the relation between in/out, noise/music and other binaries based on power differentials.

The geology is also a seismology, tracking routes and locations of noise amid all the sound, or even the silence, of solidity. The solidity is one of power, of habit and custom, and this is what can be reassessed, felt differently, used differently, once we have the means to undermine and measure a desirable undermining as it happens. *A Personal Sonic Geology* does this through its own fracturing method, unleashing new combinations, counter-flows, explosions, stridulence (like crickets' legs, sounds brush against each other, producing frictional sonicality). More than finding, Decrauzat and Copeland manufacture their own sources in a radically material exploration of what lies beneath. And this material *sounds*, so sound transforms from being fleeting experience to a new solidity, whilst at the same time losing its internal solidity to merge, blend and hybridize with all the other sounds. This builds a complex and shifting structure of sounds, sights and embodied sensations for the auditor/viewer's encounter with the realized geology.

All this noise, this worlding, has been a way of changing the way people hear (and here, in combination with other sense-impressions). And so 'noise' is something both more and less than the people who 'make noise'. Noise is not the sounds those people have made, it is the effect of what they have done at given times, and how we hear it changes over time, over the course of history, but noise as process, as the almost-present of something threatening because unknown, cannot be stilled. Those processes continue before, around, beneath and across us, and in mutual flux in the continually relocating, re- and de-subjectivizing geology.

Maybe noise needs to still noise – the last noise shall be the emptying of all noise, and this is exactly what those who can genuinely be identified as having something to do with noise have done: they have sought to end all expression, not to overcome, but to empty. The emptying goes on. The exhaustion in seismic acoustological geology is one of potential, not of closure or closing in – a way out of the newly solidifying genre, perhaps, a restatement of noise as mutability. Not noises in mutation but as metamorphosis, geomorphosis, making the ground shift every time. And so here noise cannot be fixed, absolutely not (there's the return of the negative again).

Noise is not there to be signalled from afar, but as a non-presence that rumbles within the transmitted personal sonispheres that have been cracked open to flow. Sound is a survival construct, a limited perspective, a biologically terranormative experience. Noise is only the history of how humans have come to understand it or reject it as not-understood. Noises/sounds give way to noise, which is both more and less than the individual component or the particular moments, the particulate forms – just as the personal sonic geology works as a noise channel by tunnelling through noisy practices, moments and objects. This is geology as a willed, auto-cross-contaminating disorder.

Part Two

Unsettled

Noise is not just, or even, a formal question. It hinges on relation, on context. Noise in or as music is no different, and whilst often ahead of normative 'mainstream' society in its approaches as a 'community', it is not immune from social ideas, social critique and imbrication in broader problems. In this section, I look at how this is the case for noise in music, moving beyond simplistic and anecdotal accounts of audience configuration or debates about political views that may or may not have been held by specific artists, to bring back the question of how form and content relate, in order to look at how race and gender are mobilized within or across a range of experimental musics.

The first chapter in this section extends out from Fred Moten's ideas about disruptive form as a response to socialized racial hierarchies, and also to think not about 'race in noise', but about blackness across noise as a particular instantiation of the question of race. In order to devise a model of 'collision musics' for blackness in proximity to, in, against, over, noise music (often starting out from genres under-represented as 'black music', such as metal), the chapter moves away from recanonizing to emphasize the noise of form and content in particular settings and artistic choices. The following chapter addresses the 'place' allocated to women in avant-garde music production, and, having established some 'placings' in a way that is 'noise-ful', it moves on look at contemporary examples. It might be tempting to establish a counter-canon of female artists, but as with any countering, the point is to provide a different structure, and in this chapter I set out a different way of thinking about women's presence at the margins of noise in many genres. To do so, I revert to the experimental art of the 1960s and 1970s as an example of an area of practice that was both still very much responding to gender hierarchy and presumption and free from a long prehistory that had been recoded male all the way down. The second half of this chapter brings the focus more closely on Pharmakon and Puce Mary, not just as representatives, but as operators of a willed marginality, played with through the latticing of distorted voice and harsh electronics.

The closing chapter in this section listens, unwillingly, to silence, and to the ways in which silence has become valuable, such that listening is a moral (liberal) value. To get to this I do consider some canonical moments in sound-making, but the focus is on recent books (and to a lesser extent films) that use silence as a tool for survival, betterment or happiness. This chapter closes with the idea of quietness as interference, and disrupted silence as closer to the expressed wishes of the silence-seekers whilst leaving their liberal universalism behind.

Is There Black Noise?

Is there black noise? Is there black noise music, is there black noise in the place of music? Is blackness part of noise, against it, lost in, underneath or away from it? Is black too noisy? Where, amid this set of questions, is the question of race in noise, noise music and noise as music?

In one way, noise has thought itself beyond questions of race, culture, ethnicity, gender, sexuality and nation. That is not to say that these have not featured, or featured as that which is excluded, but noise when it occurs in the place of music (which is what I take 'noise' to be) has many presumptions that have taken it out of the contextual. For good reason, much experimental art has sought to move beyond the biographical, the essential, the determining, in search of creative freedom. Experimental music, whether defined through noise or not, has been no different, and to some extent has imagined a *global* hierarchy in the progress of what counts at any one moment as avant-garde. New music that has taken place in experimental genres other than Western classical modes has not excluded non-Western musics or performers, but it would be legitimate to see exactly how *present* those musicians, musics, cultures are, and whether or not the various types of noise music that have been at the forefront of experimental music in recent decades have actually been as open as they imagine/conceive themselves to be. What if the openness is actually a whitening of noise sound, part of what Lloyd Whitesell identifies as canonical late modern art's refusal and erasure of race in its wish to approach emptiness.[1] This idea will resurface later on, and also to some extent be problematized. For now, let's think about race in what counts as 'noise music'.

To the visitor to a DIY gig in a small venue in North America or Europe, noise music's audience is very white – no more male than most rock audiences – and likely less heteronormative. This could lead to speculation that something about the 'music' is based on, at best, a rejection of the significance of race in the lives and creative prospects of many, in favour of an unconscious peer group bias.

Maybe metal gigs would look the same in 'the West', but the experience of noise and/or metal is not restricted to ex-colonizing white majority countries. At the core of noise music is the explosion of experimental and excessive variants of Japanese noise in the 1980s, 1990s and early 2000s. Before we start to activate the worry that what is Japanese noise is to some extent a mishearing on the part of non-Japanese audiences, or that it is appropriated, we need to reflect that noise music as processed through Japan is an already-hybrid form, full of cultural references to music from outside of Japanese culture. Like most music, there is no authentic ownership of noise. Musicians claimed the right to steal and distort from whatever sources they found (progressive rock, free jazz, electronic music, metal, for some examples) and were in constant dialogue with non-Japanese audiences and musicians. Furthermore, the spread of the hybrid genre that is noise coincided with the globalization of music consumption via the World Wide Web, and so influences quickly crossed cultures, musicians became known in 'the West' and formed the backbone of future developments of noise music (in the strictest, record shop style, genre coding definition). Musicians from around the world have worked in noise music, played with noise musicians around the world – it could be that noise is the properly alter-global music that roots music advocates seek for their silo.

So what is the issue about race and noise music – music, let's not forget, that is all about mixing, distortion, outsiderness, freedom, twisted technology and performance expectations? To some extent, I'm even asking myself, why entertain the question? Why go backwards and racialize sound? Even if it would of course be 'racializing', an intervention based not on essentialism but in recognition of lived race differences in many cultures, and with very specific historical constructions and facts based around slavery, when considering the West, at least. I do think that questions of the whiteness of noise are interesting, and set against the backdrop of increasing racialization of hierarchy/hierarchization of race, that to hope that noise is beyond such questions is potentially ideal, but certainly not sufficient. Presumption of such a situation is inadequate, but, nonetheless, in considering race in noise, I want also to problematize what it is we are thinking about if we worry about the whiteness of noise, what complexities of noise and music and their interaction would we be ignoring? Which 'we' are 'we' even talking about? I am also aware that society as a whole is not really concerned with, or by, the activities and attitudes of micro-generic scenes, compared to the attention to these issues in say rock music, EDM or hip hop and genres that come after them.

The recent expansion of critical race-based critiques of cultural phenomena has led to a rethinking of exclusion, occlusion and the turning away from complex interactions between publics and performers in the context of societies striated and triaged on the basis of pseudo-biology. But often 'race' is a synonym for 'black'. Jennifer Lynn Stoever's *Sonic Color Line* unproblematically does this.[2] There is one very good reason for why writers might do this, and that is to represent the particular and enforcedly exceptional position of a group of people transported from Africa as slaves by the colonial West in massive numbers, and then oppressed and denied equality ever since. This makes the position of the descendants of those people, in the societies that profited from their exploitation, a unique and precarious one. And this is not based on people's physical characteristics but on cultural attributions that may have altered but still 'inform' a militaristic low-grade civil war conducted by the American state on one group of its citizens (the basis for Body Count's 2017 album *Bloodlust*, of which more later), and the recent terrorizing of one group of British subjects who came to the UK from the West Indies in the late 1940s and through the 1950s, with the threat of deportation, after a life paying taxes, and often working for the very State that hoped to hit its targets better by going after people so loyal to Britain they never got a passport to go anywhere else, or let their passports lapse. So let's recognize the particularity of the colonial exploitation of one racially identified group, brought out of Africa into death, slavery, exploitation and then inequality, imprisonment and segregation, and not think of 'race' in the context of noise, in ways that homogenize non-whiteness, but think about blackness and noise, and the massively noisy music produced by black America through the twentieth century and into the twenty-first century.

It is tempting to establish a counter-canon of the most significant experimental moments in African American culture – and, paradoxically, some of the music of black America has been too successful to still be defined as noise in any meaningful way. So, on the one hand, we have all the jazz pioneers feeding into the free jazz and fire music exemplified by John Coltrane, Alice Coltrane, Ornette Coleman, Archie Shepp, Zeena Parkins, Pharaoh Sanders and Albert Ayler … and the proximate Afro-futurism of Sun Ra, funk, dub, early hip hop, whilst on the other hand, imagine Missy Elliott or Kanye West had never been massively successful – they would be regarded as major avant-garde figures (the same could be said of Björk and no doubt others). In other words, the main story is not about appropriation (as in rock 'n' roll stealing rhythm and blues) but about a massively experimental experience that is yet outside of the canons of sanctioned avant-gardes, even many noisy ones. Fred Moten has pinpointed ways in which this creativity can be theorized without essentializing, without being determinist in history either, and his thought, especially as seen in *In the Break* and *Black and Blur*, is central to the question.[3]

Those questions raised above, at the beginning of the chapter, were not rhetorical. They are a sequence allowing a recalibration of the various ways of conceiving blackness in musical, and in noisy, terms. They structure a way in to the thought of modes of transposition of cultural experience that does not insist on people's being limited to that history (as Adorno does when considering jazz).[4] Ultimately, they conclude in a consideration of recent cross-genre music from Death Grips, Moor Mother, Flying Lotus, Zeal and Ardor and Body Count.

Tricia Rose, writing in 1994, argues that 'rap music is a confusing and noisy element of contemporary American popular culture that continues to draw a great deal of attention to itself'.[5] The 'confusion' relates to the content of lyrics, video and imagery which combine liberatory writing with misogynistic elements. More recently, Jennifer Lynn Stoever has written in depth and detail of a 'sonic colour line' that places black Americans on the outside of the line which crosses between aesthetics, policing and ways of perceiving action and activity around predominantly Black musics. This colour line 'codifies sounds linked to racialized bodies – such as music and the ambient sounds of everyday living – as "noise", sound's loud and unruly "Other"' (Stoever, *The Sonic Color Line*, 12).

Beyond the music of hip hop, rap provides a voice to an otherwise unheard sector of American society, and also acts a lightning rod for fears of violence among what Moten calls 'the sociopaths who call themselves the mainstream'.[6] From the late 1980s on, this otherness has been 'assumed', taken on and turned back on this mainstream. Rap and hip hop had long since spread beyond black America, in a cultural diasporic re-engineering, a black secret reverse global technology, and it continues to maintain this sense of danger, of combining radical social critique along with accusations of encouraging violence, drug-dealing and so on. It was not, and is not, just the members of this notional margin that potentially understood rap lyrics this way, but results from a persistent characterization of black community as a proximate menace:

> The social construction of rap and rap-related violence is fundamentally linked to the social discourse on Black containment and fears of a Black planet. In this light, arena security forces [at hip hop concerts in particular] are the metaphorical foot-soldiers in the war to contain African Americans' public presence and public pleasure.
>
> (Rose, '"Fear of a Black Planet"', 279)[7]

Rose continues, identifying the massing, communal noise of Black music fandom, 'because Black youth are constructed as a permanent threat to social order, large public gatherings of them are viewed as dangerous events' ('"Fear of a Black Planet"', 283). She further warns, in an argument that has lost none of its pertinence, that 'the return of the ghetto as a central black popular narrative has also fulfilled national fantasies about the violence and danger that purportedly consume the poorest and most economically fragile communities of color' (*Black Noise*, 11), such that the very assumption of stereotyping, prejudice and (defensive) anti-police sentiment plays into the hands and fantasies of the legal, entertainment and media institutions.

Ultimately, rap is identified as threatening in its content, form (loud and repetitive beats, possibly played in cars with open windows, recreating the Jamaican soundsystem as a mobile, nomadic and drifting vehicle and signifier of the presence of a community – urban black youth, especially male, especially in groups). Twenty-five years after the appearance of Rose's book, how is this still the case – how is rap still so potent as crystallizer of both community ideas and (other) community fears? It can only be because the fear is only partially about the content that created so much panic (notably with the arrival of gangsta rap in the late 1980s), and predominantly because the situation for most black people in America (also other countries where hip hop is a massively successful form such as France) has not changed. In fact, maybe 'fears', that code word for unreasoned, essentialist dread, selectively stoked by crypto-racist appeals to nations' earlier greatness, are greater than they were. The financial success of several rap, hip hop, trap or grime musicians cannot disguise the discourse presented by local authorities, by local police, by venue owners or licence granters, of the threat that a live event is deemed to pose.

For Rose, then, rap is noise in its message, in its structure, in its source, but above all, in being the representational core of minority America, and the sociopath mainstream defines rap and hip hop as a threat.[8] As I have argued before, noise is not a thing, not a clearly definable autonomous thing. Instead it is bound up in judgement (hence noise is never just a creative source of potential), especially of the majority, whether this is via political, juridical or cultural authority. The judgement imposed over and over on rap, more than on other censored musics such as metal, is that it is a danger unless and until it proves otherwise – which is the case for how US police (and other police forces) presume danger when 'dealing' with black people to a far greater extent than when dealing with whites – and act with incommensurate and lethal violence as a result (up to 1 in 1,000 black men are being killed by police in the USA as a whole, over double the rate of that of whites).[9] In some ways, Rose's idea of 'black noise' is very much in line with the ideas of Attali, in *Noise*, where noise is defined and redefined in conflict with moral and legal powers.[10] In other words, the location of noise is not so much in the music, but in the set of activities and images that surround it, and judgements, presumptions and decisions made about it. This is a 'black noise' that attempts to push at the barrier around the world of secure, poverty-tolerant middle classes, offering self-definition to the localities from which rappers emerge. It is a 'black noise' that is shoved forcefully away, except once it has crossed a wealth line that ensures transition from invisibility to colour blindness. When Public Enemy offered to 'bring the noise', they referred to their music, but also their lyrics, militaristic image, assertions of community resilience that echoed the Black Panther movement of twenty years earlier, and, ultimately, their power to act as noise in crossing from margin to mainstream.

While gangsta rap had begun before the arrival of Public Enemy on the scene, it was they that took on the lyrical force of pioneers such as Schooly D and moved on from simple repetitive backgrounds to develop a torrent of sound to drive the lyrical and conceptual conceits. Public Enemy stand as a paradigm of technology diverted to radical political ends, similarly to industrial music in Europe. Hip hop had always been about such retooling, whether in the practice of (vinyl) scratching and using turntables as musical devices, or in the loop itself, heard even in the breakthrough rap hit 'Rapper's Delight' by The Sugarhill Gang, fifteen minutes' music all derived from a small portion of Chic's then recent hit 'Good Times'. The radicalization of minimalist repetition, in actual repetition of found sound, echoes earlier Black American minimalist work such as that of Miles Davis, and subverts the permanent change of composers such as Steve Reich. These deviations in music machine functionality are what Julian Jonker explores as black secret technology (after A Guy Called Gerald's early drum 'n' bass album *Black Secret Technology* from 1995),

> taking white technology apart and not putting it back together properly. Black secret technology is finding the secret life of hi-fi equipment like the Technics SL-1200 [turntable]. Black secret technology is discovering the mis-uses of the Roland TB-303, a machine originally intended to help rock guitarists practice over synthesized basslines.
>
> (Jonker, 'Black Secret Technology', 6)[11]

Nothing could be more appropriate to noise music than this deviation of equipment, just as jungle threw together dub technologies and new software allowing time stretching to get ultra-fast percussion tracks.

The loop is a core part of the noise proper to the actual sounds of Black American late modern music – a rejection of meditative simplification as well as of instrumental virtuosity.[12] In the early 1980s hands of Afrika Bambaataa, it represents a co-option of Kraftwerk and European experimental electronic music. This co-option would go on to have a new life in Detroit techno, but Afrika Bambaataa and Soul Sonic Force used the sample as backdrop, as part of a music whose layers were not instruments working together in any established genre convention, but were instead genres of music. Public Enemy take looping practice, via the core presence of a DJ inside the band, and develop a soundworld that can incorporate the soundworld beyond the music, an extra-diegetical sound that is brought within, troubling the distinction of what counts as musical sound and what as not-music, as sound, or, in the context of music, noise. The repetitive rhythms based on samples become part of a musical approach based on a politically performative statement of power emerging out of chaos, new communities arising out of disorder that was the product of accumulated unequal power relations.

Public Enemy, and Chuck D in particular, certainly intended for their project to contain a strong message, but also that it would be formally radical, taking off from the subtle and sparse use of non-musical sound in 'The Message' by Grandmaster Flash and the Famous Five (released 1982). The harsh and disruptive structure of individual songs on *Fear of a Black Planet* (1990) is extended into the jagged flow of the album as a whole. This does not prevent Public Enemy from making 'rap music [that] is also Black American TV, a public and highly accessible place where black meanings and perspectives – even as they are manipulated by corporate concerns – can be shared and validated among black people' (Rose, *Black Noise*, 17). Rose's point is that all rap carries valid messages and interaction, even if the then-recent centrality of Public Enemy, Ice-T and NWA carried a new and potent mix of ideas into the public domain (once MTV, media market-monopolist of that era, allowed hip hop videos onto its platform). Public Enemy also established that groups did not have to be domesticated by the major labels, although ironically, this would thereby prove the viability of even 'anti-social' rap to those very corporations.

Hip hop and rap would continue to be privileged targets for concerned citizens and cultural censors (UK authorities' fears over grime concerts, for example, have not gone away with the genre's second coming and higher media profile), but its move into commercial and critical success demonstrates perfectly its Attalian characteristic as noise phenomenon. Consideration of its sonic aspect reveals that Public Enemy matched this negative definition from outside with a negativity that is the true developmental part of avant-garde production: in other words, their music was complex and also noisy in its complexity. But apart from this clear and still-present noise in cutting-edge hip hop in all eras, more subtle and/or formal modes of blackness are in play in avant-garde music production and listening – either as absent or as absence-identifying re-noisings.

If blackness is a 'mainstream' signifier of social danger due to the content, social origins and intrusive sound of hip hop, as massively testified over the last four decades, is it also excluded from avant-garde mainstream practices, audiences and the like? The leading global experimental music publication *The Wire* would certainly suggest there is no exclusion – having started out as a jazz-based publication in 1982, it has perhaps always been aware of the issues of cross-pollination and trans-audience reach of musics, whilst acknowledging the need to make these explicit. But more broadly, it is not clear that we (the globally connected fanbase for various avant-garde musics 'we') have truly escaped from what George Lewis identified as a structural segregation of experimental musics in the 1960s, with 'the' avant-garde still seen as essentially classically-based, with black musicians hived off through 'the implicit racing as white of the notion of "avant-garde" itself' (*A Power Stronger than Itself*, 33).[13] Above all, 'whatever separation was developing was accentuated by the fact that black and white avant-garde musicians tended to perform in separate spaces, often with vast asymmetries in infrastructure' (36). So, segregation was genre-based, location-based and, more insidiously, furthered by (white/would-be-universalist) moves to empty art of content, origin and context. Free jazz, as politicized form,

> was being formed in a historical period in which so much art and music made by white artists, particularly Abstract Expressionism, was framed as progressive due to its non-representational quality. In that light, the insistence by blacks that music has to be 'saying something' becomes part of a long history of resistance to the silencing of the black voice.
>
> (Lewis, *A Power Stronger Than Itself*, 41)

Nobody needs to actively silence black performers for there to be structural racial issues in play. Even the presence of black performers, inserted into an asymmetrical structure of colour-blind presumptions, would not remove this entirely. The prospect of non-narrative, even more or less empty art would suggest newness, openness, looking to the future, equality. But Lewis suggests otherwise, and Lloyd Whitesell goes further in his 2001 article on whiteness and avant-garde music, with a focus on minimalism.

Whitesell begins by dealing with the appropriation made by Western composers of non-Western musicians, but, he goes on to argue, this 'borrowing' is quickly hidden, removed from the foreground, maybe we could even say it is 'backgrounded'. From here, he explores a range of avant-garde moves to empty their artform of content and context ('White Noise', 171–78). In so doing, two moves occur which heighten the (unstated) whiteness of avant-gardism when predicated on removal: firstly, the absenting of content and context presumes this can be done equally by everyone, and its desirability in sanctioned avant-garde progression would exclude artists identifying as black; secondly, the emptying reveals a quest for purifying that is about neglect of, or looking away from, history. All roads end up in whiteness. Arvo Pärt is singled out for making 'symbolically white' music ('White Noise', 178), which is 'expressive of a white racial value in its striving toward an ideal of purity' (179). John Cage's silent pieces, such as *4'33"* 'enact[s] a rhetorical structure analogous to that assumed by the white subject. In its vanishing viewpoint, it echoes a white perspective' (184).

The claims made about whiteness are polemical and sometimes extravagant, not least because Yoko Ono is presented as white and Western (173) and Zen itself is shown to be able to withstand the racial appropriations made by Cage and many other 1960s US artists. Empty art, attacks on the contentuality of music, visuals, performance, concepts or objects could be seen as whiteness through its refusals, if not its inherent quality. But what about the empty works that used black? If Robert Rauschenberg's white paintings are uncritical conflations of art and surroundings (184), and not a critical gesture, then what about Ad Reinhardt's 'ultimate paintings', which consist of only black painting, albeit composed in nine squares? If Kasimir Malevitch's white was a problem, was his use of black ok? It would be just as easy to say that avant-gardes' use of blackness was the problem, making black material contexts into surface coloration. But behind the partly justified claims about individual artists lies a very strong critique where the removal of content actually reveals that the context that allows the lack of content is itself a white space, not literally the white cube, but a space of colour blindness that posits a universal experience of emptiness, erasing, covering and, for the audience, viewing and hearing.

Beyond the prospect of a shared universal opening where everyone's experience of silent musical works can be, if not the same, then equally rich and unhindered, lies the materiality of different levels of access to the emptied work, to the work where there is no content or context. This is not due to anyone's inherent physical characteristics, nor is it *determined* by social constructions such as race. But institutions (including genre expectations, venues, audiences) act as Foucaldian *dispositifs* or vectors of creative power, and they do this not only as they include, but also as they exclude without knowing, performing excluded exclusions. Or, to say it differently, there are exclusions that are latent, denied, unstated, probably unintended but whose effects are as solid as if they were. To return to Whitesell, the argument is that claimed universality is also problematic, and then to create a universality based on the aesthetics of an experience of the empty work adds a layer of denial even as other cultural layers of control are genuinely stripped away in such work.

> At a comprehensive level of ideology, certain cultural values will be taken for granted to a point where they are all but invisible and so fall outside the arena of contention. The racial character of whiteness is just such an unmarked field of values.
>
> ('White Noise', 183)

This unmarked field is there to be heard in minimalism, post-minimalism, conceptual and post-conceptual art. On the question of whiteness and listening, Marie Thompson has posed the idea of 'white aurality', following Nikki Sullivan's notion of 'white optics'.[14] Thompson continues the thread identified by Whitesell, tracking a way into ambient music and sound art that pits itself directly against the notion that all humans can have the same sound experience whether they are field recording or being (part of) an audience. Thompson identifies

> The role of white aurality in constituting a sonic materiality that can be cleanly distinguished as preceding sociality, discourse, meaning and power, and its role in consequently defining the virtues of 'modest' sound art. As with whiteness more generally, the presence of white aurality is marked by its absence.
>
> ('Whiteness and the Ontological Turn in Sound Studies', 274)[15]

None of these ideas prevent anyone from making whatever sounds they currently wish to, nor do they reinforce pre-determination of audiences or performers. Instead, the revealing of the whitening of sound in the quest for a future sound that is the true and timeless sound (including how 'we' hear, or, hear music in neurological para-science) is an alerting mechanism that tells us how genres of music have helped stabilize gender, sex, race, ethnic, national and linguistic differences. Even eclecticism helps stabilize those divisions, but recognition of a 'racialized' avant-gardist [divide] is itself a new noise (i.e. still capable of disruption) in the sonologic of thinking about sound.

In 2004, Danger Mouse (aka Brian Joseph Burton) produced and released *The Grey Album*, which combined the a capella version of Jay-Z's *The Black Album*

(2003) with samples from the Beatles's 1968 album *The Beatles* (aka 'The White Album'). As this was at the height of now prehistoric battles and concerns about copyright, despite the a capella version of *The Black Album* existing precisely to be re-used, and the approval of the Beatles, it did not receive an official release. So its greyness pre-empts the model of grey open access publication, public but not official. The 'grey' of the album refers to the mixing of albums, and the collision of two styles that are clearly identified with white or black musicians, genre expectations and, to a lesser extent, audiences. The grey is not a loss but a heightening, a kind of resolution that nonetheless maintains tension. But how much does it play out issues of race in music? *The Beatles* is referred to as 'The White Album' because its cover is entirely white, with the band name also in white, embossed. Jay-Z's cover features him limned in pale light against a dark background, face shaded by his cap. The singer is present where the band absents itself – adding to the sense of the white cover as purifying, or perhaps as ultimate statement, while Jay-Z is about materializing, presencing, perhaps.

But the black/white of the albums 'titles' is more interesting – the white of *The Beatles* is pop artist Richard Hamilton's perverse undoing of the burgeoning trade in concept covers, not least that of fellow pop artist Peter Blake, responsible for the cover of 1967's Beatles's release *Sgt. Pepper's Lonely Hearts Club Band*. The 'white album' was not only a self-contained statement about content and its removal, it also displaced the location of content into material history, as the copies would be subject to change over time, and the very 'purity' of the cover would lead to its discoloration. Hence artist Rutherford Chang's interest in amassing multiple copies of *The Beatles*.[16] As a title, *The Black Album* had also been used by Prince for his unreleased 1987 record, and earlier still, by Non (aka Boyd Rice) in 1977, for a release of proto-harsh noise. All this to say that the intersections marked out by 'greying' are richer than the simple stirring of two colours might suggest.

Danger Mouse did not just play the records on top of one another, but instead re-recorded the music for *The Black Album* using *The Beatles* to replace the largely already sampled backing for Jay-Z's release (it is worth noting too that 'Revolution #9' on *The Beatles* is already a sound collage). The collision of two albums, styles, artists, under the guise of flags of colour is in itself an act of noisiness, though the methodology to me ends up in making a different *Black Album* rather than removing the specificity of both records equally. While this could be one statement about unconscious or universalist-based blindness to whiteness being a move in a racial production and consumption of music, it is still not clear that anything more is going on in that vein until we reach '99 Problems' which uses samples of 'Helter Skelter'. Jay-Z's original track used sampled guitars again, so it is as if Danger Mouse smooths differences even as he introduces them – or makes the change more uncanny by bringing it closer to what was present in the track at first. For racist mass murderer Charles Manson, 'Helter Skelter' suggested the dawning of a race war that would see whites triumph. Killing wealthy white people in a bid (presumably) to suggest black people were responsible for the killings was going to be the ignition of the prophecy that only Manson could hear. The use of Beatles song 'Piggies' on 'Change Clothes' also connects us back to the word 'Pigs' daubed in blood at the murder site ordered by Manson, in Cielo Drive, Los Angeles in August 1969. Manson was obsessed with *The Beatles* as a whole, and as a marker of the racial tension being stoked as a backlash to civil rights the album has acquired an unwanted signifying status. The distorted samples of already distorted overdriven guitar from 'Helter Skelter' add another layer to the racial discrimination that is the backbone of the lyrics in '99 Problems', and, once more, the greying is a thickening, a noising of layers.

When the layers of sound, any sound, cover the full spectrum of frequencies, then what we have, acousto-scientifically, is white noise. No clear signal is detectable, and the meaning of any particular note or tone is lost in an overall fuzz. The phenomenon of white noise is deemed white as this is the (absence of) colour that combinations of light spectra make. It is often presumed that 'white noise' is the goal of harsh noise music, and if this genre, method or practice is somehow more white than not, then the randomness of the nomenclature of 'white' for full-spectrum sound takes on a different hue. In fact, even before that, we should consider that sound has no colour – even for most synaesthetes, what we are talking about is a perceptual response to something that does not reflect or refract light into 'colours'. Indeed, very full noise sounds, where individual notes can be hard to discern, can be identified as brown, or red noise – and these more closely approximate the multilayering of electronic sound that is harsh noise wall. So, while white noise is not any way actually 'white', we are entitled to think on what it means to use the identifier 'white' for it; and if the audiences or makers are mostly white in racial origin, then this heightens the legitimacy of the question.

As I mentioned at the outset, in terms of practitioners, if not always the audiences, of different types of noise (as opposed to thinking all noise is a variation of FX pedal-based sub-punk noise), it is not possible to think of noise music being white, unless we predetermine what counts as noise, and it seems counter-productive in some ways to raise the question of race again in this instance. But the hope of a full-spectrum noise community cannot rest on an unquestioned belief that the term 'white noise' is neutral, without consequence. This is not to say anything about the performers of noise music, or any experimental form we (I) might like to identify as structurally noisy, or their motivations, or indeed to call what they do white noise. But the whiteness of noise lies at the horizon of all noise potential. This means that a predominantly (historically, canonically) white avant-garde has taken the positions of emptiness *and* fullness. Or, more noisily, *and not or* fullness, where the fullness of noise can only fail to complete itself: human noise will never actually be anything like complete noise, it will always fail due to a noisiness within the noise that is generated by the act, even imagined, of listening, hearing and making.

With emptiness, whiteness structures a complete neutrality, regardless of the motives of the artist, which in fact excludes that which can either be neutral and vanish, or declare itself, and fail to reach the zenith of disappearance. With fullness, completion in white noise suggests that all difference can be wiped out in the anti-harmony of white noise. This is in some ways reflected in the use of white noise in aids for sleeping, particularly for small children (and whereas it is almost never used in noise music, it is available to be added as a 'colour' in music production and production software). But the aspiration to a completed loss of meaning in fullness is there in all noise (from jazz to Japanese noise, from fuzz-based jams to jungle to wall noise and noise to come), and this unstated ground is white noise – more liberal democracy than radical politics, it advocates a totality where individual voices can all express themselves, and contribute to the one universal buzz of phatic humanity.

So is there black noise? Yes, and this will only help the argument that the use of 'white' for completely full-spectrum sound is not neutral, just as the use of masculine pronoun in many languages ('ils' in French) stands in for any mixed gender group, as if it were neutral. Black noise is empty, mostly absence of sound, punctuated by occasional stabs of sound or, as US telecommunications standards have it, black noise 'has a frequency spectrum of predominantly zero power level over all frequencies except for a few narrow bands or spikes'.[17] Where white noise is structure, however indeterminate, black noise is ground, within which sounds emerge, such that the blackness of black noise is both black ground and black in the non-black and black mix of sound that emerges from the (sonically) absent (yet present in absence, as Moten has it) background. So, these entirely neutral uses of metaphorical colour have led us to white = full, black = empty, other than disruption ... It would be an easy step to simply mirror Rose's sense of black noise as socially excluded, socially pre-emptively identified as danger, as something sonic, and then to say black music is in some way inherently noisy, in the context of colonial history and the ensuing non-neutrality of race in avant-garde art and music production. And that works, but if we wish to narrow the idea of black noise to blackness as noise in noise production itself, then we have a model for disruptive and nihilistically grounded genre-breaking in the acoustic term 'black noise'. If we take this back to Danger Mouse's *Grey Album*, we can read white noise back in, in the fullness of granular synthesis in the sampling, mixing and layering, black noise in the appearance of a new construction (*Grey Album*) in the space where there is no sound: between two existing 'completed' recordings that close themselves off from the world. And if this album is one example, we could imagine mapping a new zone of black noise, an infra-dimension of diasporic music, often hard to place within avant-gardes, yet precisely for that reason, operating as noisy avant-gardes.

For Moten, blackness is the outside of the outside of the avant-garde (*In the Break*, 32), always in motion, circling in, through and out, and capturing some part of the core of the black historic experience of the Middle Passage (perhaps more akin to the excluded Hegelian middle in terms of its recognition in Western official avant-gardism) at the same time as being almost an *essential* avant-garde. We will hear

> the universalization or socialization of the surplus, the generative force of a venerable phonic propulsion, the ontological and historical priority of resistance to power and objection to subjection, the old-new thing, the freedom drive that animates black performances.
>
> (*ibid.*, 12)

With its core of avant-gardism, a pushing back, a pushing forward epitomized in the work of Cecil Taylor, 'black performance has always been the ongoing improvisation of a kind of lyricism of the surplus – invagination, rupture, collision, augmentation' (26). These actions are to be heard in music that drifts free of genre, that radically replays the fusions of 1960s and 1970s musics, so that the moment of fusion is suspended. Outside of the academic variants of so-called New Music (attenuated Western classical musics), experimental music reception is unbothered by genre, so for something to be noise in a way that drives black performance as it sounds in Moten's thinking, what we need is some sort of cross-generic and unsettled music. For me, Flying Lotus, the project of

Steven Ellison, is one such music. Like artistic intermedia, Flying Lotus creates a post-genre space in between many musics, most audibly hip hop, drum 'n' bass, jazzes of free and fusion directions, sampling, trip hop, progressive rock as remediated into the jazzes that to a large extent drove it, and parallels math (rock) complexities of Braxtons old and young.

Flying Lotus creates massively complex soundworlds that do not settle internally, let alone generically. Recognitions come and go as different styles overlay one another, or succeed one another at rapid intervals. At a very basic level, it all happens very fast. A further 'invagination' is that of digital and analogue, a distinction which in one way is profoundly uninteresting to contemporary musicians, but which Ellison purposely revisits (for example, in reverting to acoustic drumming in more or less drum 'n' bass patterns on *You're Dead* [2014]) to highlight an inherently deconstructive relation between the modes. In other words, the digital in sound requires the analogue; digital forms pick up forms initially driven by analogue technology and vice versa as Flying Lotus quotes musics unconcernedly from 1970s and 2000s in an internal Afrotemporalism. Digital methods heighten acoustic set-ups, digital sampling reiterates analogue nostalgia in crackles, voices from a netherdigitality. *You're Dead* ramps up the broken, cut beats of *Cosmogramma* (2010), the jittering turned from a flicker experience into a generative mode – that is, instead of disruption being a cut, the disruptiveness of *You're Dead* is after the cut, a set of processes that pulse with potential and do eventually set up a utopian choral ending in 'Your Potential/The Beyond', seguing into 'The Protest', which proclaims 'we will live on forever', with small sonic slices sutured out of the lines as they repeat and the cosmic jazz introduction gives way to a skitter of competing beats before settling into a muted sampled beat that tails away. All of which indicates that the performance of utopian sound acknowledges the danger it navigates, the need to make statements against, in order to exist autonomously as creative producers. Such worldviews are not limited to black musicians but are part of the world-capture specific to modes of music identified as Afrodiasporic, as experimental yet not regarded as mainstream avant-gardist (initially at least).

From the point of view of noise, of black noise, perhaps a privilege needs to be designated for something like collision music, a mode which not only breaks free of genre without stabilizing into a new one, or replicating an old one, but that can maintain competing discourses at the same time, again taking Moten's idea of blackness not as absence but presence playing out across absences, some enforced and hierarchical, some integral to all social existing. Such a collision music would be where that Afro-diasporic resistance to the very conditions of possibility of the African diaspora often manifests itself as a kind of internal strife – between musician and instruments, between (and within) locales and their corresponding styles and between confinement and fugitivity in the constitution of political aesthetics.

(Moten, *Black and Blur*, 87)

Flying Lotus acts as an outcrop, or a new silting of always already mostly Afro-diasporic and Afrofuturist/Afrotemporal genres, and their example leads out into music that reappropriates whiter genres in order to produce a further radicality of black collision music. From Death Grips to Body Count, this infiltration not only cements the unsettlement of black avant-garde music, it also returns us to the basic phonic positioning that Moten sought to capture 'in the break'.

Death Grips are readily described as combining hip hop with punk, or with metal. Alternatively, they can be heard and read as experimental hip hop. While there are many more-or-less rapped sections across their overall output since 2011, hip hop really is only one element of their sound, caught up with several types of metal – from doom to death, to where metal crosses over with hardcore (punk), and also electronica of many paces and rhythmical expectations – from breakbeats, glitches and stuttered micro-edits, through samples and on into steadier pulsing rhythms. Where Flying Lotus might be as far-reaching in their genre crossing, Death Grips offer an even more disruptive sound, and with MC Ride's extreme approach and extreme variation in his vocal sound Death Grips are a proposition based 'against', as well as on, sound. The aggression owes a debt to the many outlaw musics that have been gradually subsumed into normality and these are then bent into continuously morphing shapes with harsh sonics combining with lyrical or conceptual harshness. The very mutability of Death Grips' sound at any one moment does lead to a weird sort of flattening over the entirety of their releases – like the cut-up and fold-in novels of William Burroughs, the aural consumer of Death Grips seeks refuge in defining or imagining all that unpredictable and properly mashed-up sound as somehow consistent.

Like many of the musicians in this chapter, Death Grips are far from unknown, and, as an avant-garde proposition, have received much wider attention that much of what gets defined as 'noise'. Their approach to the business of being musicians is purposely awkward and disruptive – bringing out albums online for free while signed to a major record label, suspect cover art (see *No Love Deep Web* [2012] in particular, which may or may not be an homage to Whitehouse's *Erector* [1981]), breaking up, bringing out work more or less secretly … But this element is not that 'noisy'. Instead, the biggest artists play continually with listener-purchaser demands and desires, with bootleggers/pirates/gift-givers and chart-compilers, in increasingly sad ways to subvert the market to make a living/massive profit/publicity. But Death Grips are not obliged to subvert their own profit-making, so reflecting on their music should acknowledge their self-conscious locatedness in an economy that wavers and wobbles between freeness and entrepreneurial manipulation.

Death Grips give us a collision genre that combines and throws together (throws against) multiple genres to finally emerge as a para-industrial sound – an industrial sound from another universe, and up-to-date, with its sampling, aggression, interest in control and its breakdown or limits, and a belief in violence, of a literal noise as establishing a type of noise that works on the audience as irritant. Lyrics and vocals are supplied by MC Ride (Stefan Burnett), and, as the black 'element' of Death Grips, he is able to supply what Moten terms an 'irruption of phonic substance' (*In The Break*, 14). MC Ride is the most visible member of the group, as its 'frontman', but in taking word, in physicalizing voice as aggressive resistance, Ride/Burnett embodies the 'convergence of blackness and the irreducible sound of necessarily visual performance at the scene of objection' (ibid., 1).

With this (hard)core representation leading its sound, Death Grips mobilize an atemporal blackness as that which plays with essences attributed to blackness and to mixing. The relentless auto-disruption of the sound (including of the vocals) makes Death Grips a resistant yet often opaque standard-bearer, even for Moten's complex ideas – and this is precisely the interest – that difficulty in *assimilating* Death Grips, in neutralizing it. MC Ride's voice operates in the same way as the collision-genre of the band's sound – it never seeks to settle, to allow a consuming ear to master the sound, and instead it crosses between many registers, sounds, styles and levels of processing. Nobody could imagine that MC Ride exhibits the raw expression of feeling, idea or reaction. And where there is no 'raw', there is also no essence, no inherent expression. Death Grips precisely master this unlikely way into an avant-garde radicality whose 'nature' is to refuse, undermine, attack essence.

The more significant part of the radical noise of Death Grips lies in the sound, and the collision of sounds, styles, modes, categories, genres, analogue and digital (whereas with Body Count it will be precisely the content that is of noise interest). In 2015, Death Grips released *The Powers That B*, which brought together two online releases, *Niggas on the Moon* and *Jenny Death*. While there is not much that is more overtly political on these discs, the title of part one is hardly neutral, and neither is the opening track on part two, which is 'I Break

Mirrors with My Face in the United States'. References to blackness surface on part one, but so do many things, and if anything, far from being more interested in blackness, it continues Death Grips's interest in polysexuality, freedom, controls social and personal, multiple cultural references and an insistence on physicality, or embodiment that is not so much about strength or presence but sensation and the play of surface and depth. *Niggas on the Moon* may not get albedo into the content of the lyrics of the album, but it does reflect back on Gil Scott-Heron's sardonic 'Whitey on the Moon', from *Small Talk at 125th and Lenox* (1970) which rails at the absurdity of black poverty in a country that can spend billions (even in 1970s money) on manned flights to the moon. It also offers an Afrofuturist or black secret technology history of exploration, or even the idea of either utopian dreams or dystopian exile – circling us back to the slave trade to the Americas. Where that part of *Powers that B* refers to blackness, it is as part of a wider contemporary culture, sometimes American, sometimes more amorphous ('Black Quarterback', lines about the free capacity or not of 'my people' in 'Say Hey Kid', or the likely references to Barack Obama's complicity in 'Powers that B'). This is a culture that is not divided as such, but fragmented, centred on power and potential abuse. But around that is sexual and personal freedom (including the freedom to be abject), as the individual, encapsulated in the narrating/shouting/garbled voice, acts out living in a semi-existentialist assertion of value in the face of valuelessness and wilful, oppressive devaluing.

All that destructive economy is there in 'I Break Mirrors with My Face in the United States', the propulsive rhythm of which recalls for me Tricky's quasi-metal 1995 take on Public Enemy's 'Black Steel in the Hour of Chaos' (1989), for part two of *Powers that B*, which is *Jenny Death*, is a very metal album, but which veers from one style to another, and maintains a sampling, electronic and discordantly industrial mode in so doing. The repeated title line is a metonymy for Death Grips's aggressive approach to cultural production and political culture; it is about refusing the racism of how blackness is 'seen' (and not seen) as the dangerous reflection that needs to be kept behind glass; it is a signal of how the mirror of racism can be cracked through using it from the 'wrong' side; it is about one-way surveillance cells transposed into an entire culture and, finally, it is about the assertive assumption, the taking on, of the role of reflection, of being secondary, in order to become not just primary, but to break up any such hierarchical system. In philosophical terms, it is Moten on Hegel … a supposedly progressive dialectic up-ended, architecture noted and displaced, chipped, where reflection becomes mirroring dissonance.

MC Ride's vocals are perpetually scrambled through filters, fast speech, purposely compressed lines, agrammaticality, odd song structures (less so on *Jenny Death*). From the opening 'Up My Sleeve', *Niggas on the Moon* establishes vocals as ground, surface and disruption. The album is based on chopped short samples of Björk's voice, and MC Ride alternates between analogue (unprocessed) and digital (treated, distorted, sampled, used as beats, in parallel to rhythms or even against them). The complex movement of vocal lines across layers of the tracks (i.e. in relation to other parts of music or musical samples) leaves the album afloat, a rejection of solid ground, in favour of a juddering sensory directness. This music is not so much made of tones, but of pulses, clips, clipped sound, digitally detuning tones, a voice that cannot stabilize but instead leads listeners into a dislocated engagement where in is no longer inside, secure, being led along a line of meaning, but out, out 'the activation of an exteriority that is out from the outside' (Moten, *Black and Blur*, 33). In other words, as each part of the music and vocals is unstable, subject to change, yet driven with an outsider's violent resistance, the presence of complexity, contingency and uncertainty in Death Grips is a performance of blackness that eschews all possibility of authenticity, even of the hybrid collisions and Afrofuturities opened up by Flying Lotus.

In a parallel micro-avant-garde to Death Grips is Moor Mother (Camae Ayewa), also part of Black Quantum Futurism with Rasheeda Phillips. Moor Mother offers 'chillstep' (a Zen blade style genre descriptor where the drum 'n' bass part of dubstep is smoothed out …) as one of their bandcamp descriptors, but *Fetish Bones* (2016) is more of a mono-breakcore experience, with sequences of unchanging single drum electronic percussion, voice transformed in pitch, grain (through short reverb, among other FX, filters and simply being caught within multiple layers). These layers offer sounds progressing at different speeds, caught at different levels of 'fidelity', ranging from lo to somewhere around mid, but also lower than most lo. Content matches vocal delivery, as variations on anger and strength give way to loss (as the tracks are short, there is no realization or triumph, even if there is considerable power). Colonial history, history of slavery, current race-based brutality and danger filter through all the sounds and the collision aesthetic. The urgency of the political is formally matched in the rapid attack and decay in each track – more so than an uninterrupted stream, which could build tense engagement, the stop/start of the thirteen mostly brief tracks of *Fetish Bones* propose a series of lurches into pre-existing worlds that the listener is cut into, breaking the space the listener has in which to listen, in a very subtle escalation/de-escalation process. Even more than the resistant Death Grips, Moor Mother has broken into the avant-garde 'mainstream', with work (in summer 2019) at London's Institute of Contemporary Art (previously drilled into by SPK, bled on by COUM Transmissions), curating spots, completed a work with the London Contemporary Orchestra on slavery and colonialism (touring UK in late 2019), but Moor Mother retains a jarring and dissectional approach to sound, voice, pacing and lyrical themes. Their voice detunes, de- and re-genders and plays at the edges of identification (as well as changing 'spatially' where it is within the other sonic layers) such that it can comment on and dwell in border conditions, where there is threat but also creative force, and noise in the resistance to the imposed force, its dispersion and reconfiguration as a process of re-cutting where the border condition can be.

To introduce a non-hybrid form of contemporary black performance (i.e. where blackness is at stake in content and use/subversion of form), I see a continuum from the above artists that stretches into Ice-T's metal band Body Count, active for over nearly three decades, infamous at the start for the song 'Cop Killer' (1992), and still addressing power, hate, community, defence, racism and abuse of the law, and that then leads us to the hybrid Zeal and Ardor who directly and consistently address the legacy of slavery in the unequal position to which African-Americans are consigned in the US.[18] Body Count's 2017 album *Bloodlust* features numerous references to the power inequities in contemporary America, and its highlight as noise (because there is nothing inherently noisy about either metal in 2017 nor a metal band with black performers) is its take on 'Black Lives Matter', which targets the misguided or wilful counter-statement that 'All Lives Matter'. It does this through the reverse-counter that 'No Lives Matter'. This apparent nihilism is highly complex and purposeful, and seeks to undermine 'All Lives Matter' in order to boost both resistance and critical capacity in the argument against racism and the unconscious white privileged imagination where everyone is treated equally in democracy.

What started as the hashtag 'Black Lives Matter' in 2013 had become a much broader protest movement, with a strong focus on the apparent State acceptance of police killings of unarmed black men in 2014 and 2015. Many, in the course of 2016, thought it would be a good idea to 'broaden' what they saw as a simple slogan, and assert that all lives matter, while at the same time racist politicians had the nerve to call the Black Lives Matter movement racist. Ian Astbury of post-goth band The Cult did it (July 2016), and Corey Taylor (Slipknot, Stone Sour) attempted to explain how all lives matter was one idea but that black lives were under threat right now and the movement was about legitimate and necessary defence. What Taylor could not quite do was address the white privilege that his strong liberal position relied upon, which is that if we just fix this one thing, we can all live as one harmonious humanity because everything else is basically fine.[19]

The move to 'All Lives Matter' diminishes the real and present power and need for 'black lives matter', argues Ice-T in his spoken introduction to 'No Lives Matter'. The claim of 'All Lives Matter' is sanctimonious and meaningless, as it presumes that all lives are seen to matter equally, whereas, as the first verse makes clear, history has never believed black lives matter equally or, more importantly, in their own right. There is no need (and this is where Ice-T pushes out from Taylor's position) to bring in a comparator. If we do, continues the song, we will see that power ('they') cares for no one, and no lives in fact matter. This is not just a facile inversion of 'All Lives Matter' (i.e. all lives are oppressed, reduced, worthless), as Ice-T builds on this opening to say that whilst the poor, all poor, are marginalized, left out of the system except to be treated as aggressors, that black is coded poor ('black skin has always stood for poor'). So, when 'no lives matter', it is still black lives that are the 'privileged' target for State abuse and liberal neglect.

Body Count uses metal's distrust of authority to advocate a rigorous apathy, but underneath (within, out of outside) is the deeper helix that alternates between black/all/none, to show that the unity is indeed there but inflicted, not built through solidarity. The solidarity has to come from recognition that different groups are not treated the same, and in terms of social power, discipline, surveillance, control through drugs, murders by police, in America, that group that needs to matter most is expressed in 'black lives matter', and Ice-T's lyrics use a paradoxical nihilism to *strengthen* its critique of power.

Unlike the bulk of this chapter, I am looking to the words, and the deep structure for the noise in 'No Lives Matter', and this is to bring back Rose's sense of black noise as the excluded, and also to take a different path through Moten's ideas, because for him words (Amiri Baraka's in particular, but also Cecil Taylor's words and voicings) could also act as powerful breaking avant-garde tools. There is one more subtle way in which Body Count's track moves beyond an angry statement of metal intent. In the first refrain, the lyrics alternate between one split line, divided by a comma, such as 'They can't, split us up' and a line that talks up the unity of the oppressed. This comma is ostensibly about a racial divide, about the power of racism itself, but also it is the divide that stems from pitting 'Black

Lives Matter' against 'All Lives Matter' liberals. The comma separates 'them' from 'us', while the alternating lines act against both the words and the punctuating splits of the awkwardly broken lines.

If earlier, I picked out ways in which writers have thought about the blankness of the empty modernist work, or how the whiteness of white noise might be an issue, then it will be as necessary to note that despite the longstanding activity of black performers in metal bands, and the presence of metal around the world as a genre that represents the poor just as hip hop does, metal is seen as a white genre, and to use metal to explicitly, coherently and consistently take on race is actually a noisy mode of music-making. So what, then, of black metal? This movement started in the early 1980s, and is strongly connected to Norway and Sweden in the early 1990s. With its assertion of pagan traditions and rejection of most social or communal convention, this is not a promising ground for black noise. So what is the 'black' of black metal? It is the assertion of a turn away from the perceived good, particularly of white Christian moral control and hypocrisy. But it is not neutral to take black and make it a new value precisely because black is in some way bad … Recent years have seen other metal genres take up the term 'blackened' as a qualifier, to note a turn to harshness. But again, this blackening is not neutral … despite an actual right-wing tendency in black metal (Varg Vikernes of Burzum, NSBM) it is not inherently 'white' – there are black black metal performers, including in South Africa.[20] But Manuel Gagneux started his Zeal and Ardor project as a response to racist 'suggestions' on 4Chan about music genres that could or could not be fused, and it combines black, death and doom metal with spiritual blues songs, and politically and critically purposeful sound effects.[21] The first album, *Devil is Fine*, came out in 2016 and was followed by *Stranger Fruit* (2018).

Having taken on the challenge of merging two musically divergent genres and genre receptions, Gagneux builds a multilayered soundscape within which vocals and instrumental parts drift across one another, using a range of effects to distance and bring close the song part, or the musical component. The effect is of a cross-temporal as well as cross-generic collision genre, one that uses audiopatina to drive home the critical-historical purpose of Zeal and Ardor, lifting it out of the dangers of pastiche. The opening and title track of *Devil is Fine* consists of a deep-throated blues-ish song, and the clanking of chains. In the background, a fast-riffed but muted guitar track builds and falls away. The 'devil', as heard with the chains, is both the slaver and the devil that offers a better bargain, as mythically struck by Robert Johnson, a way of dealing with danger in order to escape current oppression. The way out is music, not through a music that turns its face from oppression, but musics that instead face into a historic and deeply physical marking in order to exceed, to be out from the outside.

The musical track of 'Devil is Fine', like about half of the tracks on the album, is properly black metal – alternating between riffs with no space between them, filling audio space, and twin guitar note playing; blast beat drums and growled vocals. Gagneux alternates between part-spoken, part-sung blues and more metal stylings (especially screams, throat-based growls), and the genre clash is managed as a kind of mutual grafting, as different elements emerge in the course of the short songs. 'Come on Down' starts with a blues song part that is almost too clichéd, suggesting that the metal is only decoration, and that actually what we have here is an attempt at a turbo-charged authenticity instead of an experimental working-through. But given the arbitrary base of the choice of collision Gagneux has made with Zeal and Ardor, one of its main achievements is to elude the demand for authenticity that often accompanies music that aspires to social commentary. The blues parts are always subsumed, even if they hold court over background sounds for substantial parts of the songs, and in 'Come on Down', the changeover is at its most effective. The song part, describing the transition from the devil being in the fields to 'the' house burning down is presented as if through an archaic recording (not just referencing the long history of racial oppression but also the history of blues anthropologizing by collectors such as Alan Lomax), and this yields to fast guitar, drum and howled vocals. 'In Ashes' has 'burn the young boy burn him good' intoned as its opening line, and the metal musical backing gradually builds, driving the anger of the song.

Zeal and Ardor's second album continues in the very direct lyrical line established on *Devil is Fine*, with its title, *Stranger Fruit*, an extension of Billie Holiday's performance of 'Strange Fruit' (first performed by her in 1939, written by Abel Meeropol, about the mob murders of mostly black people in the US, often through hanging, and so common as to be normalized through documentation on postcards). From start to finish, *Stranger Fruit* does not let go of this theme, ending in 'Built on Ashes' on the same topic. The relentless focus is in itself a metaphor (barely) for the continued oppression and sanctioned mistreatment of Afro-American people in America. Rightly or wrongly (bearing in mind Moten's warning not to make the American setting the dominant or even exclusive expression of Afro-diasporic experience), the treatment of minority populations in the US has supplied many chilling examples of persistent and murderous racism in that place, but its significance as generator of imagery is that the US is to some extent built on the history of slavery (as well as the dispossession of people that already lived in America before it was called that), and so its journey through slavery, into emancipation, segregation, supposed equality and evident lack of same, carries a broader story about an exploitation so immense that it cannot be wished away under an 'All Lives Matter' liberal blanket. Zeal and Ardor carry this fight for a recognition that is not granted but *created* through resistant culture, re- and de-appropriation, lyrical and musical intensity, and a grounded, if paradoxical, avant-garde noise.

Zeal and Ardor have become more successful than many musicians addressed in this book, and this will ultimately mean a diminution of the noise in that sound – but it will always already have set itself up as a counter-argument, a music that uses 'negativity', i.e. relational connections between two things that seem opposed, or that seem to be opposites. In fact, it dwells in negativity – which is not to be miserable, defeatist, or rejected – but to create work that lives in a between-zone, a collision-genre whose very existence is critical, transgressive as opposed to easily subversive with a too-clear message. The clarity of Zeal and Ardor's song content is not the same as it having an easy message – there is much more here than 'racism is bad' or 'racism is in the world, watch out'. This is its noise, its refusal to simplify (like Flying Lotus, like Death Grips) with its refusal to let lyrics dominate (like those projects, like Body Count), and its quest for a musical form that can do the work of critique as much as words can.

There is an interesting contradiction in Zeal and Ardor's embrace of black metal (though their music is far from constrained to this particular variant of metal). Black metal, at least in the 1990s in Northern Europe, was interested in restoring pagan origins to music, to culture, and even though it was using guitar music that ultimately went back to the blues, it sought to find new/old origins in the forests of Old Europa. We could just criticize the racist potential in that, but far better to listen properly to Zeal and Ardor as a way of rethinking 'origins'. Instead of an authentic expression of some true soul of his, Gagneux consciously, even cynically, took two forms (at least) of music and threw them together. That the results are powerful tells us about authenticity as a result of formal expression as opposed to expecting natural expression to emerge in an organic way: in so doing, black metal is revealed as not specific to (or authentic for) any one culture, as not being a specific cultural expression. Or – better still, if it is in some way an authentic way back to non-authentic origins it shows that the 'paganism' of what would claim to be 'true' black metal is something that can have very different content – to the extent of being about a historical, cultural and physical oppression. This, and the diasporic cultures that emerge from it, constitute a new type of cultural belonging, much more effective than the vacuous belief in true origins that could ever be found.

Whilst I have tried to explore or even establish a continuum of black musics that are not black merely by virtue of the inherent characteristics of the performers, not of the genres, I have looked to locations in cross-genre, hybrid 'collision musics' where blackness, or racial exclusion, is made into form and content of the work. This is not an upward continuum, but the prospect of an always-present noise of blackness that can emerge through different forms, many of which will be hybrid, unexpected and immediately critical in ways that are avant-garde, even when the music might not be so designated. What we do have is an extended array – a range across which the idea of noise can be clearly seen and heard as that which is outside, moving in through being an 'out of the outside', in ways that are not merely illustrative of an eclectic reception that does not 'see or hear colour', as in the way free jazz is consumed, in some ways post-racially.

Noise is not absent colour.

After Generation: Pharmakon, Puce Mary and the Spatialized, Gendered Avant-Garde

I

It is a commonplace that the avant-garde unfolds over time, one movement or practice cresting and falling back as another surges on, replete with the discoveries of the preceding roll. Whilst avant-garde art wants to be radical, to embody radicality in the unseen, unheard, unfelt and unexpected, it constantly drops away, and instead of a wave, an old avant-garde is the silt over which new art surges and flows. But is noise like that? Does noise learn? We can certainly fabricate a story that seems, at first, or sadly, at last, to be a succession of privileged moments. But these moments do not add up – and whilst noise fails, and enters the realm of listening (appreciation, understanding, gentrification), this does not mean that there is a single monochordal path on which noise treads, or on which we tread. Noise begets its own loss, inspiring hope for more noise, and an endless disappointment. Some imagine noise differently, but without this unheard, even unwanted element, talk of noise is actually meaningless, not interestingly paradoxically meaningless, just devoid of relevance. Noise is about destruction, a sequence of breaks, perhaps, but a sequence that does not hold except in the pathetic imaginary of the jaded fan who maps a path of increasing extremity or noisiness.

This putatively melancholy effect is not, however, either psychological or subjective. In fact, it is subjective, but only in the Kantian sense of requiring a subject on which to work, not in the not-even-pathetic sense of 'it's noise to me'. Noise is social, cultural, historical and profoundly contextual. It is obviously relational (connected and opposite to many things), a negativity in the sense devised by Hegel to explain the world as a set of oppositions that mutate over time but never merge. For these reasons, noise cannot only be envisaged as temporal, even as it occurs as a facet of time (just as music is the passing of time as structured in time – Hegel pre-hearing Cage). Noise is spatial – at a 'quite literal' level it actually occurs in space before (arguably) it takes on metaphorical form, as a transmitting medium is shaped and reshaped, in turn moulding responding modulations via an organism's ear and brain. I would argue that this sound effect is nothing (yet) to do with noise. Noise is what we think/how we feel/the way we are feeling about those vibratory transformations, and without a pre-existing sense of what could or could not be noise (as opposed to sound or meaning), it would not be *heard* or *felt* as noise, even if it was physically dangerous and damaging. Admittedly, some of this pre-existing could have happened on an evolutionary basis, as the unshocked and blasé were inexorably culled by the acceptance of noise as just some sound like any other. But spatial, yes, and spatially disruptive, even disruptional, as the acquired capacity to locate, and so make sense of one's environment through hearing sound is disturbed by the non-normal, non-normative intrusion of what could be called noise.

Noise needs to be conceived spatially as well as temporally, in broader terms than mere sound, mere ears. Spatially speaking, noise comes from outside, or is the indication that there is an outside, or, as Moten has it, an out from the outside. Noise is outside as the non-processed, non-structured. Noise is outside as that which is excluded, and exclusion happens not only on the basis of unpleasant sonics, or a conservative failure to hear new sounds as musical, but as a political failure to not make barriers. Experimental music, art, behaviours, interests are all placed at the margin – and to a large extent the margin is a desirable place to be – a conscious self-placement, or adoption/assumption of an instilled marginality (through illegality, undesirability, immorality). What artist would not want to find their place on the margin, the edge? Not everyone finds their way to the edge the same way – the temporal pile-up of avant-gardes has often adopted a very restrictive formula for who correctly dwells in the right kind of margin. As Martha Mockus writes of Pauline Oliveros, who in her later life was accepted into the correct marginality of being a composer 'like the rest',

> While she is often discussed in music histories of the twentieth century, she is positioned as the only woman working in experimental music. Furthermore, because most musicological narratives focus on the male-dominated field of composition, too many scholarly accounts of Oliveros's work perpetuate sexist and heterosexist assumptions, trivializing her commitment to feminism and her life as a lesbian.
>
> (Mockus, *Sounding Out*, 3)[1]

Apparently objective sequences of the great composers, improvisers, bucketscrapers and tech wizards have relied on the great normative of the Great

Man, and that from a very limited set of cultures, or carefully delineated into genres where perhaps whiteness was less obligatory. Women, as experimental sound-makers, have found it difficult to receive recognition, and still only make up a minority proportion of performers and audients. This is of course in line with much of contemporary social hierarchy, but it is arguably more of a failure of nerve than in some other sectors – as experimental music is a realm dedicated to valorizing the new, to changing existing ideas (apparently), and yet the place of women is small to negligible to absent.

This chapter is actually not about female visibility or presence, but about not being in the margin. Experimental music (particularly in the zone of composition) does not open the margin to all. This is not a chapter about women as experimental musicians. But in the context of not even being in the margin, what could the place be that opens up for noise performers such as Pharmakon and Puce Mary, both leading lights in contemporary noise, insofar as this is a genre; in the radio noise walls of cross-media artist Marja-Leena Sillanpää, or the anti-voice of long-established noise pioneer Junko Hiroshige? These are performers who all operate in types of the 'genre' of noise music (as seen in shops, or their online avatar-successors) that have habitually been identified as masculine, due to a combination of audience and performer demographics, and a sociological transposition of those largely true situations into the sounds.

Between sociology and aesthetics lies the kind of question asked by Tricia Rose of race as noise: is the presence of women musicians itself noisy? Are women deemed to be the wrong kind of noise when it comes to inhabiting the places (physical, metaphorical, virtual) where (non-musical) noise is likely to happen? Women musicians testify to a constant struggle to be heard – in terms of music, opinions, competence, knowledge or professionalism. From Oliveros, Wendy Carlos and Annea Lockwood to today's musicians, there is a dispiriting record of exclusion, discouragement or simple non-membership of scenes that build community dynamics in music. Noise music today is a much more open realm than many, in terms of income, sexuality, gender, race, access and political will of self-organizing musicians to think about and act on such questions. Even as noise music fails in its noisiness, it begins to act more as a punk arena, at one level, while the more celebrated musicians attempt to have careers.

Despite the failure of academic music to move past its prejudices, electronic music began to open up access to musical experimentation that at a formal level, or as medium, did not immediately impose a barrier of there being only familiar male faces and names as predecessors. There were few, if any. Far more than a notional parallel lineage of women musicians, I think we can see the possibility of non-male actors arriving in experimental music (or being recognized at least enough to persist, or to be recorded) as paralleling other new forms and media (or intermedia) in the 1960s – notably performance art and video art. Without the dead male hand of the Greats, these new media were more located in the present, in the person, in the political and in the accessible mode of production suited to actual new practices. In making a lineage or line of precursors for today's exponents of harsh noise, we should consider the input from those artists, with both the physicality of performance art and the media techniques and self-reflection of video art essential to industrial and noise genres and subgenres.

Performance art moved on from the rethinking of dance embodied in the mid-twentieth century by Simone Forti and Yvonne Rainer, just as it realized the logic within Yves Klein's conceptual events, including the problematic *Anthropometries* series where women daubed themselves in blue (International Klein Blue, or IKB), as an orchestra played his *Symphonie monoton* (see Chapter 7 below), and he conducted proceedings. Even at its most problematic, this work brought out what would be a common problematic for female performers in art and music – in addition to one's identity as an individual, or as realizer of art idea and practice, to what extent did the female body need to be made to appear? Performance art revealed the bodies of many young and/or new artists, male and female, but essential in this crossover form was the work of Yoko Ono. In her *Cut Piece* (1964), she held a kneeling position in front of an audience that she invited to come forward and cut her clothes with the knife placed in front of her. In surviving documentation from a 1965 version in the US, viewers can see Ono adjusting to the new breaches of her 'personal space' and boundaries, as her clothes are gradually cut away. The piece is not only about borders, it is about inhabiting those borders and illustrating their persistent fragility and contingency. More than vicarious, the piece aims to hold viewers in an increasingly empathic and worried yet attentive moment. *Cut Piece* offers many possible and conflicting readings – is this stripping away the fripperies of consumer individualism and the interest in appearances, or is it precisely an enactment of what is worst about women's position as objects to be stripped at will? Ono's piece is not about oppression or the status of being a victim. In fact, it is not about representation, as it is not even in the realm of representation – this is a removal of representation, replaced by the presence of a person as locus of art-making. That is the political aspect – the placing of self as art-maker into the art – and then we can open up what the actions, or the action of submitting, mean. Pauline Oliveros, as a pioneering electronic composer, advocate of listening as music-making and rigorous feminist group collaborator, found that being included involved not being included as a woman but as a neutral being. Her complex position can be found when she wrote to Kate Millett. In this long letter (of 16 April 1973), she argues that defining a 'woman's music' is problematic and has been used to keep women in their place, on the outside, albeit not within the sanctioned outside that is the avant-garde. Some male-dominated genres could be 'occupied' by non-male people, but what she is interested in, above all, is the presence of women making music, 'exploring sound with other women without regard for established forms' (Oliveros, in Mockus, *Sounding Out*, 47). This position is subtly different from making a 'woman's music' based on an inherent and unchanging gender or sex nature, and opens a path to contemporary debates around inclusion, recognition of inclusion through, rather than despite, gender difference.

As a sculptor, later to become a leading feminist installation artist, Judy Chicago found the same exclusions, and noted that 'neutrality' was actually only available to the men.[2] The inclusion of gender as a material was seen by many as the only way to overcome, surpass or exceed the unstated (because 'neutral') strictures on artist-gender-neutrality. In work that traversed performance, film and video art, Carolee Schneemann opened up re-physicalized bodies to play in *Meat Joy* (1964) and women's bodies as exemplified in her own, in numerous works for a decade, not least *Interior Scroll*, where an unclothed, paint-covered Schneeman takes a rolled-up scroll from her vagina and reads text about male artists, film, painting, gender and bodies.[3] Martha Rosler addressed women's socially delegated roles in another knife-based work, *Semiotics of the Kitchen* (1975), video artist Dara Birnbaum played with social expectations of women's activities and emotional responses in and to popular culture, while Joan Jonas worked across media to shape newer (still critical) feminist identities.

The story of art in the 1960s and 1970s tends to be quite focused on the US, and it is worth noting the significance (to the prehistory of noise) of Gina Pane, VALIE EXPORT, Rebecca Horn and Marina Abramović. These artists, along with Chris Burden, Vito Acconci, the Austrian Actionists and much of what Fluxus did, laid the ground for an art that would use physicality as a mode of social critique. The form would often move from product to extreme personal locatedness. The genealogies could be endless, but the 1970s witnessed a new type of extremity, one that would track directly into COUM Transmissions and Throbbing Gristle, the Schimpfluch-Gruppe and 'industrial music', a generic naming most artists active in the late 1970s and early 1980s completely reject.

Into that mix came punk, and many have linked punk into noise, or fashioned punk as a type of noise, but the connection between performance art and noise, through the practices of 'industrial' and/or experimental non-professional music is one with a clear and vital chain of women as actors, and not the rare exceptions that were women in composition or free jazz.

In parallel to performance art and video, women composers were carving out a place alongside music, in the shape of sound art, sound work, field recording. Whilst female composers might languish as the token representative of a mass of excluded, devalued or absent women – with only 1.3 per cent of US repertoire played in US concert halls in 2016–17 being by women, sound art has had no such limit – the rules were different from the start, or, more accurately, less groundable in a neutrality that merely preserved hierarchy.[4] Pauline Oliveros wrote about the need to find a new music, in the letter to Kate Millett cited above:

> Does it become women's music when a Symphony orchestra has all female instrumentalists, a female conductor playing a score written by a female based on musical ideas out of a music tradition developed by men? I am concerned with the power of sound! and what it can do to the body and the mind. I am not sure at all that it is 'SAFE' to borrow forms which continue a sexist message such as rock, rhythm and blues, sonatas, symphonies, etc. Maybe we have to search around and find something else.
>
> (Oliveros in Martha Mockus, *Sounding Out*, 47)

The ideas in the second part of this quotation do not mean that the first part contains only practices that should be avoided – Oliveros devised and worked with many all-female ensembles, but what she did not do is maintain a hierarchical structure of composer/conductor as source of all creativity. In field recording and sound art, into the 1970s, Annea Lockwood, Hildegard Westerkamp, Christina Kubisch and Janet Cardiff established women's involvement in zones later identified as sound art. This other side of women as leading experimental musicians combines with that of the performative, such that women's 'noise music' takes up these two realms, and in measuring and balancing them in different proportion, those artists offer work that is transgressive as well as socially subversive. It should not be that women making actual noise music (insofar as such a thing as possible for anyone, or for very long, or for it to be heard as noise by all) is anything new. Yet the combination of a material/physical presence and harsh electronics seems only now to be a 'normal' experimental practice. Of course, many women performers have worked in experimental music and 'simply' or 'neutrally' not received as much acclaim or notoriety as their male counterparts (more on this shortly). Websites such as Audible Women, Feminatronic and Hernoise, as well as sites on women composers or female metal bands, have been working at rebalancing the historical record in order to correct the current and future moments, and often explicitly state that they are interested in artists who identify as female.[5] But as well as acknowledging marginalized contributions, raising the profile of the acknowledged yet not seminal, and promoting all who make noise (i.e. with a bias against supposed gender-neutrality), the forms noise has taken, through key figures, emerge not from individuals nor from lost musical histories. Like most experimental music, art has often provided the material precedents, and in this case it is worth dwelling on the space carved out by Marina Abramović.

Abramović has reached levels of fame that could not have been predicted when she started in the 1970s. This global figure of performance art was part of an embrace of extreme physicality with a strong focus on duration and ability to take pain. Her work in the 1970s in the *Rhythm* pieces often included an important sound element. *Rhythm 10* saw her take up a knife from a selection (ten in the first iteration in Glasgow, 1973), jab a knife as fast as possible between her fingers, then, having listened to an audio playback of the taped performance, replicate exactly the same movements. At this point, she listens again to the two recordings together, and the performance is over. Other pieces included suffocation, collapse through exhaustion, induced seizures, repeating 'Art Must be Beautiful, Artist Must be Beautiful' while brushing her hair with a constant intensity. *Rhythm 0* (1974) echoed the challenge set up by Yoko Ono. Seventy-two objects were arranged on a table as Abramović stood still and naked for six hours. The threat of violence was continual, as sharp objects were used on her body and at one point an apparently loaded gun held to her head. The title of the 'rhythm' pieces suggests not only the sound component but a musicality – or, better, what takes place in the place of musicality, as if it were music.

Although these rhythms engage (to a high degree) with the audience, a double and conflicting process is happening as the performance unfolds: firstly, the rhythm is imposed, and seems to be occurring as part of the alienation or isolation of the performer; secondly, though, the border between performer and audience member also falls away – very directly and to explicit levels in *Rhythm 0* as it does in Ono's *Cut Piece*, but the border crossing happens even in the other works. The audience is called on, even interpellated, to experience the duration physically themselves through their simple presence, no matter how engaged, threatened, affected, excited, bored they might be. Abramović's work conjures the prospect of transgression – rules disappearing, a body and person under threat, damaging themselves, passing out, cutting themselves, in the sanctioned ritual space allowed the performance artist. For this transgression to do anything beyond being content, reference or representation (as arguably her works have been since the mid-1990s) it needs to cross that space even while constrained by it – i.e. she cannot attack other people who come to the performance, but she can let them participate by enduring the spectacle that loses its imagistic quality in favour of the presence of a physical embodiment being brought into being. All these phases are needed for transgression to actually occur. And all these phases aligned in the work of COUM Transmissions.

As Abramović staged her physicalized time in numerous performances around Europe in the early 1970s, COUM Transmissions began a process of combining extreme body art with media critique and occultism. COUM was for the most part Cosey Fanni Tutti with Genesis P-Orridge, and a changeable list of others (some of whom, like Peter 'Sleazy' Christopherson, would join them in forming Throbbing Gristle). Tutti, Orridge and collaborators would writhe in a range of physical actions, ejecting and consuming fluids, setting up conceptual live installations with a purposely infantile feeling and approach, all based on a bedrock of simplistic sound and music and a mix of William S. Burroughs and assorted hermetic ideas that all sought to provoke awareness and consciousness of self and the world that mostly sought to restrain it. COUM's notorious moment was the *Prostitution* show at London's Institute of Contemporary Arts (ICA). Tutti had for some time been working as a 'glamour model' for pornographic magazines, building a portfolio of work that made real the nature of women's cultural role as available visible objects of sex, as opposed to active sexual beings. *Prostitution* was based on that portfolio and is exemplary of how COUM, then Throbbing Gristle, used sexuality as a way of levering open prurient attitudes of 1970s culture.

In consciously using pornography as a tool or vehicle, Tutti had already put herself forward as sexualized object, but had always already been turning that back on the image consumers. Now this turn was extended and twisted such that the images and performance actions could be consumed as a continuum of sex culture, and sex culture being in the open, with its power relations, exploitation, shabbiness as well as orgasmic fun, would change attitudes as if by visceral force. That was the project, in any case. For Tutti herself, all of this activity was not about feminism, but more 'aligned' with 1970s Gay Liberation (Tutti, *Art Sex Music*, 114) though later study would change her view partially to recognize that, while it may not have been feminist in intent, it was in practice and in actualization (ibid., 340).[6]

Part of the interest in Cosey Fanni Tutti is her influential work in both COUM and Throbbing Gristle as realizations of something that was disruptive of patriarchal control societies (I leave aside the personal relations within the groups), even if not overtly feminist. Today, we would certainly identify the work of proto-industrial culture as something like genderqueer, and also pro-sex, all processed through an understanding of interpersonal society based on what was then sadomasochism, now BDSM. But, sadly, the other part, for this chapter, is the sidelining of Tutti in the grand story of the march of avant-gardes. P-Orridge (later Genesis Breyer P-Orridge) dominates the story. By the time you read this, maybe someone closer to events will have changed Wikipedia, but as of September 2019, the entry for COUM Transmissions is, shall we say, singular, in its focus, and that focus is not Cosey Fanni Tutti. She addresses this on numerous occasions in her book. On one exemplary occasion, P-Orridge worked as part of the editorial team on a book about contemporary art that came out in 1977, 'Gen[esis P-Orridge] had an entry under his own name, with a half-page photograph of me and him and doing our 1976 COUM action in Milan. Neither COUM nor myself were listed in the book' (*Art Sex Music*, 164).

The great opening up of industrial music's take on cut-ups, performance art, extreme yet argued rejection of society-induced anomic normativity, never completed its mission for everyone. As variants of noise-based musics emerged from industrial (or from no wave and punk in the US), from elements of sound in art and from an almost inevitable raising of stakes, only Lydia Lunch, Kim Gordon, Diamanda Gálas, Anne Clark, Karen Finlay, Beate Bartel and Gudrun Gut had any sort of profile at the extremes of 1980s music production.[7] Of course, there are others, but as 'noise' became a genre, sexuality and complex, almost Foucauldian senses of power gave way to representations of victim-women, sexual objects once more, under the glossy cover of sexual freedom and positive deviation. To paraphrase a more recent cultural moment, 'not all industrial noise bands … ' went down this path, and some that did were doing it in fully critical mode. Tara Rodgers points to the 'sexist imagery that has characterized many electronic music albums' ('Introduction', *Pink Noises*, 6).[8] Rodgers is using the term electronic to define a broad cross-genre sweep of experimental music, but I'm presuming she means industrial and noise albums, as she goes on to note that 'the origin story of the Futurists infuses one's orientation toward electronic music with violent noise' ('Introduction', 10). This noise is not seen by Rodgers as good, and is contrasted unfavourably with theremin maestra Clara Rockmore. Whilst the legacy of Futurism in sound-making would actually seem to be more prevalent in hipster instrument-making and extracting sounds from unfamiliar objects, the point about a presumption of violence is a good one. The violence, though, is from the process of warring avant-gardes, that from Dada and Futurism onward set themselves up as rejections of earlier practices, and even of art or music as such. I would argue that there is nothing about this violence that is masculine, except in a very stereotypical or obvious way, but the representation of violence, often against women, in the genre, is something that mirrors existing gender inequality and patterns of gendered violence, and so in that sense carries nothing radical at all. This may have been less clear in the 1980s where artists still saw themselves as sweepers away of convention through transgression or subversion of norms, but is certainly clear today when misogynist violence is present in word, image, deed and mainstream politicians' actions, then there is nothing left for a would-be avant-gardist in the depiction of graphic and one-directional violence.

Not that any type of noise music has ever sought a role as a social worker or a respecter of social concerns. Not that there is not a place for an aesthetics based on violence, but what is it doing, why is it and why should anyone regard it as anything other than a hindrance? To raise just one counter-intuitive counter-example, Jessica Rylan recognizes that something more, even if still something to be barely tolerated, is going on in the music of Whitehouse (in *Pink Noises*, 154).[9] The supposed barrier of violence for women to afford themselves space in the genre is not about the presence of represented violence in itself, but its complicity with a gendered (and heterosexualized) system. Being at the margin of a system is essential for something like avant-garde production, for noise as infiltrating musical or social model. But being excluded from the margin, or having the margin withheld, is another problem.

In parallel to European and US scenes, Japan saw a growth in noise that brought together harsh electronics, free improvisation and repurposed and excessive rock and jazz strategies. Within the Japanese noise world, a combination of punk-style DIY approaches (as detailed by David Novak in *Japanoise*) and multiple contemporary international reference points contributed to a range of radical political perspectives barely present in the surrounding society.[10] Women musicians had a stronger presence in Japanese experimental music (since the 1980s) than one might expect. Long recognized as key participants in variants of noise music, musicians such as Junko Hiroshige (aka Junko) solo and in Hijokaidan, Yoshimi P-We in Boredoms and OOIOO, Chie Mukai, Sachiko M, all have substantial discographies and performance credits, while Melt-Banana and Boris also have female core members (Yasuko Onuki and Wata respectively) and Acid Mothers Temple has featured numerous female members over the last twenty years.

Junko has been highly active in recent years, having been an essential part of Hijokaidan's confrontational approach since they began in 1982. Her commitment to extreme vocalizing is constant, and over the years she has collaborated with numerous musicians and noise artists, such as Michel Henritzi, Mattin, Sutcliffe Jugend and Sachiko M. Junko's album with Mattin, *Pinknoise* (2004) is a perfect example of what is harsh about harsh noise – strong, almost screamed vocals continues throughout the thirty minutes, joined by mostly higher pitch electronics. The vocal is mostly used for sound, and cycles around a few sound patterns we could not really identify as motifs. As opposed to a glossolalic improvisation, Junko manages to convey a stasis, a constant pushing against, whilst refusing resolution.

The Sutcliffe Jugend collaboration is more surprising – Junko's aesthetic is more of a formal harshness where Kevin Tompkins and Paul Taylor, as Sutcliffe Jugend, combine power electronics sound with a consistently aggressive lyrical probing of abject human being. On *Sans Palatine Uvula* (2013), they instead frame, respond and on occasion manipulate Junko's voice track she sent as her contribution. In so doing, they heighten the already formal approach taken by Junko, without lessening the charge of the structured yet harsh screamed vocal. With Sachiko M, the noise of the collaboration is in the bringing together of Junko's (naturally as well as assisted) overdriven voice with Sachiko M's mostly analogue electronics, often played with extreme quietness. Here, on the one-track CD *Vasilisa The Beautiful* (2014) Sachiko M surrounds Junko's voice with layers and swathes of different sounds – from dragged tones, through howls to soaring notes and squeaking. All the while Junko persists, a vector for intensity – not just in terms of an intense expression, but also as a realization of Deleuze's idea of intensity establishing nodes of richly thick affects, as opposed to the linear experience of things happening or actions being completed.

The challenge for the listener who is processing works like those of Junko, is how much to move beyond accepting the individual without recognizing or seeking to influence the levels of presence of women in noise. Despite the long tradition of women making extreme, harsh, uncompromising or odd musics, it is only in recent times that attempts are made to move beyond stereotyping, even if sometimes meant positively (expressiveness, earthfulness, maybe today witchery) *and* get out of the simple universalism of imagining all artists to have the same opportunity.

II

A new generation of noise music makers (Rylan already notes in 2010 the growing number of women involved in the [US] noise scene), includes two very prominent female performers – Pharmakon (Margaret Chardiet) and Puce Mary (Frederikke Hoffmeier).[11] Both make harsh soundworlds that rehybridize micro-avant-garde styles and processes. Both stretch out from power electronics and harsh noise, and can be heard as inheritors of Japanese, US and European noise from the recent past. Although they have engaged in collaborations (a key feature for all noise musicians as it introduces unpredictability, improvisation that is not a circular assertion of identity or skill, as well as new sounds, new machines), they operate, as many female experimental rock and pop musicians do, as self-contained equivalent of bands. Electronics, digital tools and the establishment of music scenes in spite of the low financial 'value' of experimental music have all enabled the solo performer, and to some extent we can say it is as natural to see a solo performer of any gender as any other.

Pharmakon makes brooding and harsh electronic music with processed vocals. The overall strategies resemble most those of power electronics, and while there are noise elements in the music this is perhaps not 'literally' noise music. The noise happens in other ways (as it does in all 'noise music' – this is a genre, a multifaceted genre, but the noise of noise music or of any music lies in very specific strategies, moments, sounds, aesthetic choices), and some of this lies in the simple fact of the presence of Chardiet as a woman, making the sounds, using or presenting her voice in particular ways, and the expression of an aesthetic through internal dislocation as opposed to a unified one-directional application of strategies. *Abandon* (2013) opens with Chardiet's processed scream, voice preceding all, in line with expectations of any female presence as creative musician, but this voice never settles, is only occasionally 'normal' and moves (through processing, through pushing vocal capacity) to being outside of gender, but from a female starting point, as opposed to achieving neutrality. In fact, 'Milkweed/It Hangs Heavy' begins with a short gargled growl, ascending – so the voice of Pharmakon follows a path to the outside of directed vocal expression, and then settles into a scream altered by effects. As the voice arrives through many machines, it drifts apart from being a human expression. In 'Ache' the words are separated out equally, removing expressive connection even as meaningful units of speech are presented. Across the album, the voice often also sounds of microphone interjection – i.e. distortion from either being too close to it, or knocking it, and certainly by not enunciating clearly into a very expensive microphone in a studio designed to empty the human into a warm bath of bad faith human sound used by mainstream rock, and at its height in the 1970s (before the faltering first years of digital recording and releases) and twenty-first century compressed over-focus on vocals in mainstream recording practice. *Abandon* brings what is supposed to be inaudible (the means of capturing voice) into audition.

Chardiet's voice does hit forceful peaks of expressive growled words and non-linguistic sound, but for the most part (and even at that moment) it lies in the middle of the mix: this is not a singer rising out of the background to convey their message but an embodied voice that emerges (painfully and never fully) in a morass of sound. The electronic part does not change much, and, despite not having beats, it adopts the relentless emptying of techno to demonstrate inescapability. Occasional sampled sounds offer percussive effect and the album closes on one such crisp sound. The predominant musical sensation is of clogging, of urgent stillness. This is constructed through repetitive loops, samples and layering. Although there is never a sense of a pile of strata, density is made through the strategies mentioned above. Lastly, if there is a direction, it is downward – most of the tracks wobble and waver, either in electronics or in processed vocal, or both, but tones slip downward, the exact opposite of suspension. This slow but unrealized fall, is I imagine, the abandonment of *Abandon* – a lostness or fall, and also a flight and fight within gravity's pull, a constrained ecstasy, a melancholic and other-than-human excess.

The same anti-human aesthetic permeates *Contact* from 2017. This album is richer in variationism (the term used by Darwin and his predecessors to refer to speciation and change), as if Pharmakon is testing whether adaptation works or is desirable – and all variation is caught, not contained but vibrating within steady throbbing pieces that lurch into the dramatic ending of three massive electronic thumps. There is massive vocal variation, Chardiet testing, pushing, edging her voice into many directions, but always caught within as opposed to rising above. To rise above would be to make the historically masculinist error of the sublime, of destiny, of transcendence. Pharmakon stays in the mud (or among the mealworms of *Abandon*'s cover, or the greasy fingers of that of *Contact*), offering a way in to a low, material, physical yet unhuman soundscape. The presence of the voice seems to be reaching for distinctness only to be lost in the overall effect, in the purposeful tenderizing of the lyrics in excessive vocal performance and perverse phrasing. More forcefully than if there were no voice in those albums, there is a play of excesses around and often against the voice, or against the clarity of voice. This in no way undermines the strong presence that the voice attains, that the tracks and albums attain as complete pieces, but this presence is a distributed one, a positioning that de-positions, that thwarts easy consumption as either female or as the performance of a style that aspires to neutrality.

In performance, Pharmakon is rigorously embodied. She goes against the will to disappearance of many sound artists and electronic musicians (as noted by many of Rodgers's contributors in *Pink Noises*).[12] The same tense relation between processed electronics and electronically processed and physically overdriven voice subsists in the live setting. As with the recorded music, Pharmakon 'adopts' an approach that has been presumed to be inherently masculine – aggressively harsh sounds from mouth to microphone to effects, a physicality that owes as much to performance art as to rock performance, subverting the 'masculine' aesthetic exactly through performing it (we could imagine going in the other direction, as recent noise musicians have, in parodying the styles of noise as well as other genres).

Pharmakon combines the two poles of noise/electronic/harsh performance: on the one hand, a careful attention to launching samples, loading layers, altering sounds, tracking the progress of the musical part of the track as she considers the machinery in front of her; on the other, she moves out from behind the desk and forces her vocal into the rich sonics of a voice that is being pushed out of shape, away from solid expression. She moves into the crowd at various points in her sets, an often static crowd (as can be seen on numerous filmed concerts on YouTube), again emphasizing that what may be a standard move for hardcore (punk) musicians or other performers is not so for a woman performer. Even as she presents as forceful, propelled by voice as much as body, she touches audience members as she goes by, daring them to escalate, through this semblance of interaction. This is not the communality of the hardcore moshpit, but the intrusiveness of a foreign body lodged in the host public. At the same time, Pharmakon is separating herself from the voice we hear, as the microphone delivers the full volume at levels she has set, and the distortions she has programmed/planned. As she walks by, audience members pick up a pre-echo of proximate human sound, lungs and open mouth expelling shaped air into metal but also into those near ears, while at the same time the electronics deliver another, thicker voice above or behind the moving figure of Pharmakon. This division of voice, which relies on the two vocal moments being connected and different, is the closest Pharmakon comes to the pharmacy Derrida talks about when he writes about Plato in *Dissemination*, and so Pharmakon offers a way of illustrating not only the primacy of writing but how voice and something like speech, if not exactly speech, are not nothing in Derrida's system, particularly not when in performance, as opposed to delivering a supposedly truth-filled discourse.[13]

This is not a gratuitous insertion of Derrida's ideas, as his mode of thought can help rethink Pharmakon's 2015 album *Bestial Burden*, which can too easily be read as the expression of authentic catharsis based on Chardiet's own failing body. The album is the result of her illness, subsequent urgent operation and then recovery. Of course, it is not a result, but more of a surplus, a Bataillean ejection. Reviewers have picked up on Chardiet's explanation of the album as being about the sense of her body betraying her, and the fragility of illness, but also of being subject to the practices of surgical intervention. Listening to the album, especially in relation to other Pharmakon releases, tells a more subtle and interesting story about Pharmakon as machine interface.

Starting with the title, it would seem as if Pharmakon poses a Cartesian problem: a mind suffers through its body-vehicle, and wishes it could not be subject to those physical pains, dangers and sensations beyond rational thought. Fear of death and damage would then be the mind trying to protect itself against further system failure, and *Bestial Burden* a cathartic expression of overcoming the limitations of a feeble and secondary body. Or: Pharmakon is stating that the mind has no separation from the body and that is where the danger lies, and then the expression would be the affirmation of a unity that is not unified and simple, but at least partly holistic. Looking further, the 'burden' that is 'bestial' could be the body, but it could be a description of some other burden – the burden a beast carries through living, or indeed, having a mind that can reflect on troubled physical circumstances. While all of these are possible, the presentation of sounds on the album, aided by the saturated beauty of carefully arranged meat parts on the cover, tells of a weight and sensation that is neither fully physical nor mental, neither internal nor simply external, but rendered in the crossing of a border between inside a body and beyond.

But first, and unheard by many reviews of the album, is the simple sonic fact that contrary to the expectations established by the accompanying story, the title and the cover, four of the six tracks on this album are much more ordered, rhythmical, almost structured like songs, and only two approach the physicality of the abject de-bordering that apparently drives the whole project. One, 'Vacuum', opens the album, with looped and slightly ragged breathing.

After two rhythmical tracks, beats, electronics and vocals getting clearer over the course of the tracks, comes the second half of the album, opened by 'Primitive Struggle', the track that most conveys physicality as opposed to representing it, with coughing to the point of retching, over heartbeat style double pulsing beat. This is followed by two more usual Pharmakon tracks, dominated by sine wave oscillations, but also containing her voice at its clearest. 'Autoimmune' declares that 'I'm a stranger in this vessel', a revelation that has taken the aftermath of the sputum heaves of 'Primitive Struggle' to arrive.

The 'burden' of physicality is that it threatens the stability not of a pilot in a fleshy vehicle, but the combined and usually unitary body that can think as one of its attributes, and that controls its functions as one of many others. The late arrival of the sense of alienation from one's own body to me suggests that the 'I' of the track is other to both mental and physical actions of the Chardiet entity. Or, that Chardiet has been ejected from where she usually is, from both, and, for once, a human is as if other to its body. It is not just the fallibility and reaction of the wounded body that alienates but the time and constant effort of those reactions that eject the 'I' of 'Autoimmune' just the same as clinging drapes of spit that take effort to spit clear of lung and mouth – just as the propelling of Pharmakon's voice in live performance. This is a state of exception that in some occasions is chosen, but the true state of exception is one where 'I' is cast out, spectating, auditing, rattled about. The ill body touches the 'I' of 'Autoimmune' in the same way as Pharmakon pokes at the crowd in performance, taunting it to respond, and this clearly voiced rejection of the body's actions is that final response. Just as the title suggests, 'Autoimmune' is a complex set of feedback moments, in relation to the spluttering and liquid border crossing of 'Primitive Struggle'.

Going back to the overall concept and structure of *Bestial Burden*, the sequencing provides a scaffold for the more overt moments of voiced/sounded distress. They represent this struggle through heavy beats, sliding electronic sounds and vocals that are mostly close to impenetrable even with the lyrics available to read. This is because Pharmakon, as she does elsewhere, strips syntactical construction of meaning through rhythmically and harshly pushing out words as units, as opposed to allowing the cumulative effect of paced sentences to deliver content. So while we can see lyrics about being beyond, or not belonging, only some emerge – precisely indicating how Pharmakon is caught within the physical – and her anger, disappointment and realization of the limits of a body lead to a point where embodiment is not just the problem to be complained about. Embodiment is the complaint.

Puce Mary (Frederikke Hoffmeier) makes all the sounds we hear on her albums – sounds from electronics, samples, live sound-making and sampling from objects and voices that come to the ear only through sequences of sonic reconfigurations. As with Pharmakon's combination of voice and other materials, the voice is caught within the other sounds. This is a voice under pressure, but one that emerges from within layers, as opposed to pressing back against them from within. Hoffmeier's voice is treated electronically, rises and falls in and out of audition, in and out of meaning and through a fluctuating set of distorting effects. The pressure that this voice is under exemplifies a broader bodily pressure, where autonomous, defined subjectivity (as human, as female) is under something like threat, but perhaps more accurately under erasure, under the skin of identity.

Puce Mary's voice falls away as something identifiably, naturally personal. It becomes individual through its processing, its supplementary oscillations and the moments where, in language terms, it (purposely) fails. As an exercise in comparative retching, we have 'The Viewer' from *Persona* (2014), a more formal take on what carries a superficial resemblance to Pharmakon's 'Primitive Struggle'. In 'The Viewer', which uses the soundtrack for the short film *Gynocracy* by Tao Alexander Sabella Hansen, a female voice coughs and begins to retch (in the film this is while she has red paint daubed on her naked body by a serious-looking naked man). Far from the personal presencing of *Bestial Burden*, this track frames physical vocal sound as part of a broader narrative, holding it in auditory callipers, turning it this way and that, as it comes up out of the rumbling electronics, tape hiss and synth sounds. Highly composed, these retchings can be heard after *c.* 2.20 and again at 7.20 in the track, when they are accompanied by metal thumping. After this, the retcher is left to fade out and the music washes out around this fade. 'Impure Fantasy', later on *Persona*, also carries voices beyond language. Percussive sounds and gasps surround the spoken word part. The narrative would seem to be a violent sexual one, and this the soundtrack to it, but we can also hear the soundworld as one of merging and indistinction between object and vocal, a situation where person can become object, object can acquire character. But above all, they cross borders, as exhalations, as solidifications of affect from hybrid actions. The voiceover is also not straightforward, as Hoffmeier's voice is slightly downtuned to make it more gender neutral, and as a result less in line with traditional and largely current normative-binary humanity. In short, it is easy to hear this piece as a variant of industrial music's fascination for BDSM, and in a way it is, but it is also something much more sonically tangled, a deliteralization of representations of erotic submission in favour of a sonified exactness about surfaces and interiors being repositioned in a Moebius strip, or what Jean-François Lyotard identified as the 'libidinal band'.[14] Toward the end of 'Impure Fantasy' there is a moment of excess as undoing, where the slowly gasping voice is cut, giving a light glitch effect (at 6.29, and adding a second inhalation, almost within the previous one). This unexpected moment, whether accidental or purposeful, acts as noise to the message (even the hybridifying message effect) of the track. It is a final breaking-through of an illusion of depth, as the voice is revealed to be a horizontally moving set of wave forms to be edited on screen, and one in which that two-dimensional representation of audio data can alter the shape of wave forms carried in the air.

The emergent Puce Mary voice is one way in which Hoffmeier undermines the composed, narrative forms her tracks take. Almost all of the tracks on her albums have clear beginnings, middles and ends – which is one of the ways in which listeners get not only narrative but also atmospheric development. The layering builds and falls away, not always mirroring in top and tail, but mostly resolving in some way. Within this, her often liquefying voice (perhaps through a phase shifter) trembles even as it shouts, its edges uncertain, changing shape as each vocal moment merges with the preceding sound and laps into the new, thickening all the while – this is a favoured sound across *Persona* and also appears on 'Masks Are Aids' on *The Spiral* (2016) though in more solid and differentiated form – i.e. less thick, less wavering.

Puce Mary's sound is closer to industrial music than to the genres officially identified as noise, but noise is here, tangled within the composed soundscapes. *The Spiral* continues to contain elements of machine operating (hisses, audible microphone use, sporadic intrusions of object percussion) that dominated the debut album *Piss Flowers* (2010), heard in Chapter 16 below. The voice is part of the machinic soundscape, very evidently 'not itself' at almost any time. Even when Hoffmeier speaks, it is never aiming for the highest clarity, and the choice to pitch a voice 'wrongly' for its gender is of a pair with not highlighting the vocal as the major occupier of sonic space. This is what is done in music designed for formats such as MP3, where the 'bandwidth' is filled by ostensibly crisper sounds and more vocal than either in the past or in experimental music. Even power electronics can succumb to the dominant placement of vocals – although a 'music' made exclusively of massively overdriven effects-laden, possibly shouted or growled vocals could be considered an ironic take on the pop sound enjoyed through mobile media. Puce Mary's placement of the voice not only goes against its usual highlighting but also emphasizes the layeredness of the sound, again undermining the narrative developmental part of her soundscapes in favour of density.

Maybe this placement, by both Puce Mary and Pharmakon, of the voice in the midst of all other sounds, tells us about the usual placement of the female voice: even experimental vocal pioneers ranging from Nina Simone, through Joan La Barbara, Diamanda Galás and Laurie Anderson, to name but singers from one limited area of the world, had the voice as the most prominent of instruments once engaged. Hoffmeier and Chardiet take pains to physicalize something more unexpectedly 'noisy' – which is the voice as something that can emerge in situations that contain many givens, and this emerging can stay part of a formally democratic soundworld as opposed to vaulting over the sound to the meritocratic heights of symbolic power.

On *The Drought* (2018), it is not just the female/human voice that emerges, but the sounds of wings flapping, or of a trapped animal – at length on opening track 'Dissolve', briefly in the next track, also later on 'Coalesce', and possibly also sped up into a more explicit rhythm on 'The Size of Our Desires'. Puce Mary has produced a far more composed, richly musical piece with *The Drought*, but as is always the case when some sort of noise is present, or there to be uncovered, it never settles. Its instrumentation wavers, and tilts, its samples never rest into fixed rhythmical comforts, although they do repeat in percussive loops. Hoffmeier's voice is only mildly distorted throughout (or hidden completely as musicalized/noised sound) as it recites lyrics based on physicality, decline, need. In contrast to this potentially organizing voice come the interruptive moments of clattering, of harsh coloured noise, or cuts, jumps and veering deviation.

'Dissolve' opens up the prospect of a machinic, non-human noise body, within which the human (expressed as voice, as controller of soundscape) sits, struggles or tests their limits. The flapping is recorded high in the mix, its proximity and scale a troubling and claustrophobic 'opening' – quite the opposite of opening, in fact, more like an unending, potentially crushing enclosure. These sounds return fleetingly in the following track as trace but also marker of movement, of escaping control. Almost opposite in effect, the noise bursts of 'To Possess is to Control' that come after the recital of the title line are a sign of power, as listeners familiar with power electronics and noise might picture a heavy gestural touch of switch/knob/slider/pedal. The broadbanded noise indicates that control, though, is not total, nor permanent. Even as expression and outcome of control (in the lyrics), the thickness and transience of the dense sound plays out loss of rational control. The lyrics approach the body, hint at sex, but no sex is happening here – if there are bodies, they become abstract, locked in among other devices, in the devices of bodies themselves and subject to the words, not in charge of them. While Hoffmeier recalls Kate Bush's wish to trade places with the other in 'Running Up That Hill', she also makes it more tangibly disruptive as opposed to experiential ('If I could open your body and slip up inside of your skin').

In 'Red Desert', a still flatly intoning voice bemoans loss of real experience and also contact. Beyond that, 'I'm an old woman now', and slowly being separated form the world, caught in physical decline and a filling, possibly failing, memory. The sound of something like a (musical) organ and clattering suggest a melancholy fall, but this is a voice full of a realistic and self-aware sense of diminishing. Strength lies in dwelling within this character. This sucking out of a grounded and secure subjectivity continues in 'The Size of Our Desires' as a tiring and overheated environmental setting expands the desert, just as the water flows away from the coasts of England in J.G. Ballard's 1964 novel *The Drought*. The drought is not just absence of water, but its removal, its drying of what remains, and the ultimately dusty merging of what were distinct and individual things and creatures. Even as the album dries, this track features fleshy percussion, like the last wet objects pounded to hurry their end. So the path is prepared for 'The Transformation', where, in the lyrics, desire leads to liquefaction and dispersal into an entity that is beyond the individual, and is only liquefied desire. As this is not a concept album, we should not track the dryness elsewhere into this point as a necessity, but as noise returns, so too does a rapidly fluttering percussion – without offering hope against aridification, a parallel apocalypse is posed, one that is disrupted, boundary-threatening and flowing with all the noise that has built and fallen away in the course of *The Drought*, an album that is sonically, as it is lyrically, about removal.

Puce Mary's recordings pose a worldview that is mapped sonically through disruption and composition – maybe it's too easy to say it is a type of de-composition, but certainly her work reminds us that noise in the place of music is not all about improvisation but about the sacrifice of freedom to improvise, or at least the limits on losing control, if disruptive noise is to exist as an effect on listeners. The presence of the distorted female voice is a transformative noise on the performance of what has narrowed into being 'noise music'. Puce Mary and Pharmakon exemplify a knotted set of connections between bodies, social realities and expectations, machine use, physicalized sound production and aesthetics with harshness at their core as representation and form. The 'noise body' summoned by either is one that conveys these un-bordering effects of noise, often quite subtly, as they purposely attempt nothing like a 'female aesthetic'. Like Duchamp's 'infrathin', their work is in the realm of the same-yet-different. It is different in its intrusion into what had previously been perceived as a male realm, not just in terms of participation, but in terms of unwittingly essentialist judgements about harsh noise, industrial music etc., which in the guise of gender critique provided exactly the opposite of trouble. The performance of dwelling within noise in these two musicians is not reliant on any type of exceptionalism based on skill, but on their aesthetic choices and practices, use of sound and noise. Within, or maybe, through, mobilization of genre strategies, gender is rethought as mouldable, a practice, any practice.

The Silence

A silence is descending upon the near-future. Amid the clamour of communication lies the prospect of a terrifying apocalypse and a living-on that is defined by the need to stay silent, or to not see. Such are the very similar fates marked out by the films *A Quiet Place* (2018), *Bird Box* (2018) and *The Silence* (2019). These monster-based musings come hot on the heels of murderous films *Don't Breathe* and *Hush* (both 2016) and seem to indicate a new threatening quality to silence, even if silence is what can allow survival (there is also some exploitation of hearing difficulties and non-speaking across these films). But silence is not the danger, it is the world that happens around the silence that is the danger. Silence is never the problem as such, but a marker of it, sometimes a possible solution, sometimes a signal of the impossibility of escape. Perhaps these films are a new avatar of acoustic ecology, where the silence that is good listening reveals the bad sounds of non-natural environments. But perhaps they are also the hope offered by the capacity to listen (or respond) to sounds other than those made by the listeners/ humans/survivors or in encounters with unexplained escapers. This hope would map on to the dream of hearing the world, the salving powers of an isolated immersion, that sound artists, musicians and the simply spiritual have sought, and sought to share with those of us who need help on the path to aural cleansing.

In this chapter, I consider some modes of listening in silence, within it, creating it, encountering it, seeking it. But, instead of cleansing, we can question exactly what is supposed, presumed, attributed when silence becomes a good, as opposed to a perceived state that is far from unbound from the material. By the end, we will hear not just that there is no such thing as silence, but that the hiss of the quiet failure to attain silence is the unexpected noise, the nail on the stairs that your bare foot steps on while evading the composite, thinly imagined monster of *A Quiet Place*.[1]

Silence has long been part of the contours of noise – as Christof Migone says, both form part of the unsound (*Sonic Somatic*, 4).[2] Eugene Thacker writes of strategies of the unsound as taking sound away from hearing and listening ('Sound of the Abyss', 191). Both noise and silence are outside of sound art and music in a way that their specific absence can be brought in to work on and through sound and music. Both have been heard as coming into play in John Cage's ostensibly silent piece *4'33"* from 1952. Both have served as origin and endpoint of all that can be sounded and heard. Both have been re-posited as fullnesses, variants of the subterranean pleroma inflecting 'our' hearing. The introduction of silence into the realm of music appears to allow the emergence of noise (which Douglas Kahn questions in *Noise Water Music*), but how does the purposeful introduction of silence into places of hearing remove silence from existence?[3] There is nothing new in this wish to impose the goodness of listening in tandem with the absence of sound – the quest for silence has always been about hearing, or listening, or reflection, or truth, or something. Even as absence, silence comes freighted with unwanted non-silence. So, after Cage, after the endless revealing of the same, the non-self-same silence, I am going to consider some much more recent and mindful attempts to break out into silence by George Michelsen Foy (*Zero Decibels*), Thich Nhat Hanh (*Silence*) and Erling Kagge (also *Silence*).[4] Whilst it is easy to complain about such worthy attempts to uncover the true silence of the self, world or life, it is only in emptying them that we can come back to the near-music attempt to remove sound. Perhaps annoyingly, I then want to reintroduce variants of quietness as near-silent near-musics, and imagine these as getting much closer to silence than the dogged attempts to move outside of hearing sound can manage.

Once upon a time, in a world where there was no silence, apparently, John Cage had a dream – his dream was to occupy the place where the Muzak Corporation put music (i.e. as soundtracks for commercial spaces) with silence. Why, he mused, could there not be a pause, a place for 'A Silent Prayer', as he expressed when presenting a talk at Vasser College in 1948. John Cage no doubt thought long and often about silence at this point, and he discovered that maybe there was a place where he could finally find true silence. Leo Beranak, who had worked on military applications of acoustic testing in the Second World War, had built the anechoic chamber at Harvard early in his career (in 1943), before becoming professor at MIT. An anechoic chamber is set up to be as quiet, as non-reverberant, as possible. It is full of baffles placed at angles to interrupt all flows of air and the material and forms seem to soak up sound. John Cage found out about this magic chamber and wanted to go there, and, in 1951, he did. When John Cage went into the room he was astounded – the interest and even threat of true silence gave way to two parallel sounds. Upon leaving the chamber, he asked the engineer about this, and was informed that one sound was that of his nervous system functioning and the other was his blood circulation. Whilst doubt has been cast on the likelihood of that being the case, and speculation entertained about what he did hear (not least by fellow composer Pauline Oliveros), what was not in doubt was Cage's view that the world was now entirely changed, as silence was not possible.[5] At least, silence in the presence of humans was not possible (presuming 'we' all hear the same, and understand what silence is in the same way). Life was noise, and noise should be music, or come to the place of music.

Of course, what happened in this fable is both more and less than what is presented by Cage. He himself was clear not only as to the value of the experience, but the value he was extracting from it (he specifies, in 'Indeterminacy', that this is a story he tells often). Even as he discovers there is no such thing as silence, he is putting silence into discourse, bringing it in as an unsound silence, one that will not be heard. The immediate imputation of universal sensation and the physicality of sonic experience are melancholic reductions in the role of processing sound and silence, at least for humans. All humans inhabit culture, and specific moments within it. So the universal experience inferred not only by Cage but also by neuroscience and spiritual thinkers is an actual silencing of difference because difference cannot be silent, it is too disruptive. At least Cage had already got beyond the idea that sound or hearing are special because we 'cannot close our ears'. Cage had shown, unwittingly, that hearing was more distributed and was processed without the intervention of airborne transmission (unless he actually imagined that the microsounds he was making had filtered out of his mouth, or through his pores and then drifted back or clustered around him). Perhaps he had farted out the sounds and they clung to him like odour. In any case, some new kind of listening had been accidentally discovered – one that did not drive Cage beyond sound, but into the ear-based reception of the sound of a musicalized world. Instead his bodily listening served as a moral exemplar, a sign of the world that awaited listening. The world would now be a giant body existing to be sounded.

Silence had not only become both a presence in the world, through Cage's listening so very hard to hear it, it had also vanished just as it came into being, a Boltzmann brain observing the universe and changing it before winking out of existence. Far from the quantum-esque coming into being of silence as absent in the world, Cage put silence to work. Not only would it figure in his discourse and reach into all of the as-yet not-even nascent world of sound studies, it would now become an origin story. John Cage emerged from his capsule to bring the news, Zarathustra-like, that silence was no more, and so had never been. Experimental musicians had mostly not known that what they were missing was silence, let alone that the thing they did not know was missing would come into existence only to become impossible. Such is the complicated genesis of sound in silence. Structurally, silence becomes the beginning of all noise, all sound art, much experimental art, not because it is in any way the actual ur-sound, but because it was made into the beginning, and this beginning reverberated backward to have become that from which sound springs.

On 29 August 1952, in Woodstock, New York, David Tudor was cast as the person caught up in the construction of silence, as he performed the premiere of John Cage's *4'33"*, an all-or-nothing, all-and-nothing statement about the possibility and impossibility of silence in the presence of humans. The piece calls for a performer, with an instrument of their choice, to not play that instrument for four minutes and thirty-three seconds, marking the three movements in some way. As Tudor chose to open and close the lid of the piano in front of which he was seated, the convention has mostly been to mark the movements with a repeated gesture. This work is not the first, or the only 'silent piece', it is not even Cage's only silent piece, but it is, as Craig Dworkin says, 'the classic' (*No Medium*, 145).[6] Its influence is such that it has variously been understood to be the beginning of sound art, of experimental music, of listening, of field recording. It could be construed as the beginning of noise, which it is and it isn't.

As Tudor performed *4'33"*, it would become evident not only that no music was happening, but that sounds were. Without staying in the mode of anecdote, suffice it to say that the sounds that occur in the course of *4'33"* are generated by two arguably different sources: one, the world, and two, the audience who had been expecting to hear music, but now reacts uncomfortably, expressing its unease at the world taking the place of music. Audiences now do precisely the opposite and are competitively silent in response to the canonized piece (as a video recording of the BBC classical proms performance from 2012 shows), and humorously allow themselves to shuffle about, cough and perform audience-ness in breaks between movements. I suppose the world of all-sound can only open up once.[7]

Cage's piece asks the audience to accept the importance of listening, of being present in the world of sound as opposed to letting sounds hit 'our' ears. We are called upon to do this in the place of music. Most of the things that music needs to happen are still here, after all: a composer, a composition, a score, an instrument, a performer, a performance location, a programme of which the piece is part, an audience, a duration, a title. It can be played again, it can be recorded. It is for this reason that I would agree with Douglas Kahn that Cage did not introduce noise in *4'33"*, but instead musicalized the world, or rendered it as music. Cage would not disagree, necessarily, enjoying repeat performances of this or *0'00"*, particularly outdoors. The world is revealed by Cage to be in its capacity to be heard. And this hearing takes place when framed in musical shape, much as Heidegger's conception of the work of art acts as a framing device for the world which comes into being as that which precedes and surrounds the work of art.[8] Kim-Cohen is firm in his critique, stating that 'the piece *4'33"* never strays from the condition of music most admired by the Romantic poets: musical areferentiality' (*In the Blink of an Ear*, 163). So the piece's musicalization, and not its silence, is what creates its disjunction with issues beyond the formal.

If there is noise in *4'33"* it lies in the interplay, always to remain incomplete, between musical expectation (of notes), the sounds heard (non-musical), and the traditions of music-making that are not rejected but extremely respected in it. The noise is not in the sounds made, even if those are of an ideal and fretful conservative audience fearful its ignorance is being exploited.

4'33" implies an opening up, a time where the space you as listener are in is what makes the sound part of the piece occur. Where other music closes listening into a loop or helical relation with its listener, *4'33"* does not so much empower the listener, as a casual reflection might suggest, but expose their listening as the location of production, in a laying out of the existential sense of freedom as something dangerous and potentially unbounded. Over time, it has come to signify these processes of instilling a listening practice and/or experience, and lost the materiality of either a practice or an experience. For Kim-Cohen, *4'33"* has an interest that exceeds or even undercuts all the talk of listening. Far from being tied irrevocably to Cage's fabled journey to the lab, or his love of Zen, or even his interest in Robert Rauschenberg's white paintings from 1951 (*In the Blink of an Ear*, 160–62), it emerges from a sense of the same processes of removal present in Rauschenberg's *Erased de Kooning Drawing* from 1953 (*In the Blink of an Ear*, 164). This means that *4'33"* is not even in the realm of sound, or at least not of sound to be heard or listened to or for. Instead, it signals the possibility of sound work that does not induce the vibration of air humans use for much of their hearing, even if the work of sound is still within it. This would connect Cage to the institutional-critical work of Michael Asher who would 'exhibit' the spaces of empty galleries, sometimes intervening in the structure or infrastructure of those spaces (to the exclusion of all other works) or to Robert Barry's *Closed Gallery* (1969).

Conversely, Tara Rodgers attributes a closing down or silencing to Cage's work, arguing that silence negates identity, keeping non-beneficiaries of existing cultural privilege out, noting that 'despite Cage's own efforts to disrupt hegemonic silences, the centrality of his work in subsequent electronic and experimental music histories has often had the effect of silencing others' ('Toward a Feminist Historiography of Electronic Music', 478).[9] Although there is some slipperiness here as to how much to attribute directly to Cage, who after all was not exactly in the most privileged category in the 1950s, however that might seem today, and given that if he was silencing anyone, it was himself, but the point about the aesthetics of blankness, emptiness and whiteness has also been picked up by both Lloyd Whitesell and Marie Thompson (see Chapter 5 above). What is clear is that the exemplarity of *4'33"* has been part of the patrilineal story of sound art that parallels that of Nam June Paik's Zeus-like head-birthing of video art in the mid-1960s. What is shared between the idea of Cage as an institutional-critical artist and that of his being privileged enough to allow himself the luxury of silence is that the sound (or indeed actual performed silence) of the piece is accepted as secondary to the setting, context, effects and consequences of the work, as Cage himself intended by placing (seeming) emptiness in the place of music.

On its way to becoming a monument to the androgenesis of experimental music, *4'33"* not only aimed to open ears to the sounds of the world, but also to make listening if not audible, then present as practice. Instead of listening as means to an end, it became the outcome. Just as with Pauline Oliveros's practice of deep listening that occurs over a long time and in the presence of musicality and community, Cage's sense of listening was an ecological awareness that implied a resonant community of those who could listen. Listening would then summon the other practice of indeterminacy that Cage valued highly. Frances Dyson argues that Cage was

> looking for – the silence of sound in its a-significatory, non-discursive muteness … In Cage's hands, silence is an extremely full metaphor of lack, not of material sound but of intention/mind/discourse/culture/meaning.
>
> (*Sounding New Media*, 68)

So when the silent pieces seem to reveal the world sonically (or, I would say, as a sonic artefact of listening, brought into pre-existence to have been heard), then what is heard is a silence that is not absence of sound, or really of anything.

The presence of the sounding world allows listeners to attain an '*Ur*-silence' (*Sounding New Media*, 69) which is that of the absence of intentionality. Like Kim-Cohen, Dyson ultimately thinks that Cage's silences are even more silent than silence as absence of sound or of silence as re-presencing of sound. Sound instead occurs as a variant of silence – which carries Cage away from a possible imposition of silence to its always-open potentiality.

The varied ways in which Foy, Hanh and Kagge approach silence is akin to imposition insofar as they wish to make silence happen. Equally, none of them think silence happens by itself – instead the human creates, finds or releases it. Silence is hope, ground, container, clearing and symbol of what lies beyond the mundane. While this suggests a journey into the vacuity of silence as mindfulness, there are nonetheless insights to be had for the study of sound and the making of sound art in these three quests for the always partly suspect cleansing that is silence. What unites these three seekers of the absence of noise is the sometimes unspoken but often overstated value attributed to listening. Listening, after all, has long been taken up by career politicians, and since the facilitation of total and mostly consensual surveillance via internet communications, listening is also the attentiveness that occurs in the tracking of, or even in, the data. Listening does not need ears, or the vibration of sound, but waves of code, some of which are limited enough to be sonic in the human range.

Suffice to say, those who undertake a quest for silence are less than attentive to new modes of listening or indeed cryptosonics. For our intrepid uncoverers of what lies beneath the terrible overload of living, all technology, and possibly all contemporary life is noise to be reduced. Both Foy and Kagge refer to 4'33" (Hanh's meditative aesthetic is probably the closest to Cage, but does not refer to him). Foy does not 'find Cage's ideas original or particularly insightful' (*Zero Decibels*, 63), although he is interested in Cage's 'discoveries' of the non-silence that is embodiment (not Foy's words) in the anechoic chamber (64). Foy is not alone in communing directly with Cage's originary revelations, to the detriment of critical literature, including Cage's own subsequent ideas or what meanings others could attribute to 4'33". Kagge is also suspicious (it would seem we all need to find our own silence …), and, although he likes Cage's 'Lecture on Nothing', he finds Cage's reduction (as he hears it) somehow lacking:

> Cage removed all of the tones in his piece 4'33" and created his silence for four minutes and thirty three seconds. Audiences adore this piece of silence even today. Or rather: the silence minus the noises that the audience makes as it

struggles to stay quiet. Cage had many intellectual thoughts about silence ... But I tend to think about silence as a practical method for uncovering answers to the intriguing puzzle that is yourself.

(Kagge, *Silence*, 105)

It would be harsh to say that Kagge seems not to have heard 4′33″, and relies on a perverse unsound of its occurrence to reflect on it. For one thing, he seems to think it happens in a room where only the present humans would be sound generators; for another, the way he imagines the appreciation of the piece is to imagine something very fixed and properly personal to Cage. Like Kagge, Cage saw silence as a tool, a flawed one, a Zen blade vanishing in the act of cutting. But Cage, for all his possible shortcomings, did not think of either silence or the soundworld as individualized, but as fully ecological. Neither Foy nor Kagge can grasp the importance of framing in 4′33″, the possibility that silence needs some sort of containing in order to be freed, either as unsound, or as the absence that dissipates in the listening.

Foy and Kagge both seek escape to find peace, the self and the meaning of the world. Hanh, closer in spirit to Cage, actually has music in his mindful toolkit, and travels only inward, while holding the noisy world at bay. The stripping away of all culture, in all three cases, is highly apt for Rodgers's critique of silencing of others – what do we actually reject when we close off the noise that disturbs? This is not an abstract question but a very material, always identifiable set of sounds or phenomena. All return the silence-seeker to a centredness that is fundamentally a refusal of otherness, of uncertainty or adaptation. Perhaps the first fully realized simulation of a human by actual AI will create a mindful brain in a vat.

Foy rejects all noise, and finds all contemporary life noisy. Living in New York becomes harder and harder as he finds it more intrusive in all regards, he writes. He writes that, in the course of living in the city, 'noise became intolerable for me' (*Zero Decibels*, 1), but his quest seems only to heighten his sonic panic, as he spends considerable time measuring the decibel levels wherever he goes, and also mapping the change in level between rooms and times of the day:

I started this project with a feeling that I was subjected to constant and overbearing sound and that I needed to escape it ... Every measurement I made brought home the truth of my first, normative impression: that my world was full of noises I could not control ... The cumulative effect of noise was harming my psychological well-being and maybe even my physical health and that of my family.

(*Zero Decibels*, 131)

If you go looking for noise, you will probably find it. While Foy's book does reveal more of what is hinted at in the final sentence quoted above, it is perhaps inevitable that the quest for silence ends up in the parallel uncovering of noise, or at least noises. Foy explores the various kinds of silence people have referred to over the course of history, he examines physical and psychological aspects to human hearing, he includes the cosmic and the anechoic, and yet, or 'yet', there is just more noise. His explanation is that we (always we, undifferentiated), are caught up in what he imagines as 'the noise of useless information' (132).[10]

Foy's increasingly fretful search for silence takes many paths, and consists of many parallel, yet superficially analysed modes in which silence could occur, or places where it might have a chance of soothing him. He is an anti-Cage: far from finding solace in the inevitability of noise where there is human presence, Foy finds he is in a hell of a noise chamber where only the realization that he might be making his own noise (in the form of tinnitus) can mitigate the relentless sound production that is the world. Largely, he does not consider anyone else's world – pausing briefly on the statistics about noise exposure in workplaces, but steering clear of how income, background and milieu might have considerable bearing on just how noisy your world is. This agitated book also reminds 'us' of the heroism of the noise-afflicted individual, as very few are seeking silence – and 'the reason for this is simple: thinking independently and creatively is perilous' (*Zero Decibels*, 139). To sum up, if the various books on silence offer different models of engaging the world as quietness, then this variant is one of individualism – the tormented yet gutsy creative will find their way out or not, regardless of specific context because 'we' share the fundamentals not only of biology, but of culture, ideas and tolerance of noisiness. We become us by virtue of 'our' universal Ear.

Erling Kagge is an individualist seeker of silence in the course of seeking adventure (he has walked to both poles, climbed Everest and now written a pocket-sized coffee-table book). This would-be Last Man confesses that 'I had a primal need for silence' (Kagge, *Silence*, 1) and that the contemporary world is making it increasingly hard to find: 'We live in *the age of noise*. Silence is almost extinct' (37, emphasis in original). Like Foy, Kagge despairs of humanity's loss of immediacy, caught up in mediated inputs, outputs, communications and information. But perhaps Kagge's search for silence confirms that we do indeed live in an age of noise and we should be thankful for it, because the angst-laden 'lightness' he brings to his philosophical musings is ultimately not that far from the validation of listening, of openness to new sound, to the sound of the world, and therefore the world itself. Critics of Cage's silence are searching for the same thing, a new kind of listening, a better ear. Kagge is no less a quester for truth through cleansed listening than any acoustic ecologist, or any gently anti-anthropocentrist – and silence is moral, whether indicative of something grave (*Silence*, 33) or something improving (34). As Attali noted over forty years ago, and Marshall McLuhan a decade prior to that, what is new will always seem noisy to some. Technological and social change come across as threatening, and the known acquires an unwarranted evidentiary simplicity.

If, as Kagge suggests, silence is nearly extinct, is silence itself a privileged endangered creature being destroyed in the human-created mass extinction of the present? How would silence 'go' extinct? The most obvious way is that it has been shoved out by rival sound-entities, whose noise clutters the space (or niche) that silence needed for its existence. This is certainly the sense Kagge intends, in line with Foy's haunted, slow revelation that the silence he seeks is no longer there. But perhaps there are other ways that the extinction of silence needs thinking. In any case, its capacities, characteristics, habits would no longer serve a survival purpose – either humans no longer need to hear clearly, or humans have moved beyond a co-evolutionary dependence on silence. Maybe silence no longer needs 'us' and its non-inaudibility bespeaks its escape. Maybe silence was a prey animal of humans and has been over-farmed, over-hunted.

Silence in the wild, in the state of nature, seems much more complex than Kagge conceives. He offers the following about the presence and prospect of silence: 'nature spoke to me, in the guise of silence. The quieter I became, the more I heard' (14). It would be easy to just say that Kagge, despite his easy manner with well-known philosophical ideas, does not have a very clear idea of whether silence is active, passive, a result, a cause, a thing that pre-exists or a thing that is brought into being, and that actually, he is not even talking about silence. But he is saying so much less than that, he begins to create an unwittingly curious and multiple silence. So, Nature speaks to him – but has no voice, as in fact, it speaks in order that Kagge not actually hear, but become a hearer. Nature, for Kagge, is silent, and that is its communication. As it speaks, saying nothing, it erases the prospect of anything being said, as silence spreads in the act of speaking. To labour the point, the production of speech by nature is the empty sound of silence. This is not the end of this story, as nature speaks only in the *guise* of silence, so must we instead think that nature seeks to speak, but needs the cover, the code of silence? As Kagge hears the speech of silence, and he becomes quieter, resonating with the non-message, then he begins to hear. But what is there to hear? Only more silence, especially as nature's silence has stilled him so he can hear, and what he hears is 'more'. So is he missing nature's message now, which after all was silence? Or has he gone so far into nature that silence fills him – this in fact is where he wants to go, or has found that he has travelled to, in any case, as 'the most interesting silence is the one that lies within' (25)?

It is unclear whether this silence is inherent – particularly as it requires finding, with nature achieving personification to spread itself like an unvirus as one unlikely method of its transmission. I think Kagge's silence is something within each of 'us'. Everyone, he estimates, has their own silence, but that does not mean it is present, and as a result, neither are you, until you find your silence such that you can get 'inside what you are doing' (51) and 'create your own silence' (57). He actually writes that 'you must' create this silence (ibid.). Principally, that must be because the world is in some way hiding it from you, even as nature tries really hard to say nothing to you so you can finally not hear it. But it is also an admonition. Like a sonic existentialist, Kagge thinks every individual can attain silence, a silence that is there, in some way, inside and outside but not accessible.[11] Silence is a duty, and your correct listening is both reward and appropriate behaviour.

Although Kagge addresses us all (as part of a universal self-same humanity that for some reason achieves what it wants through doing exactly what he thinks is good, in a softly categorical imperative way), he addresses every one of 'us' as an individual, for it is as an individual that you will find silence. Silence is about being self-contained (though possibly also containing the silent speech of nature), and, following the logic of creating one's own silence, Kagge writes that 'everyone possesses their own [silence]' (102). Unwittingly Kantian, Kagge's silence is something that traverses the subject, and therefore has to go via an individual mind/spirit/essence etc. But this essence seems very empty, given that nature is perhaps not even silent but needs silence to even come into being, to give it inaudible ectoplasmic (and non-cochlear) form, and that 'our' existence seems only to follow from an encounter with silence.

Still, once silence has been made, by the individual, for the individual, it becomes an object 'I' can own, a possession. Fully capitalist in its access, if it has not been hunt-and-gather-ed, it is 'an experience that can be had for free' (i.e. it has a market value, albeit of zero) (66). It is also part of 'the potential wealth of being an island for yourself' (78). Silence is therefore meritocratic, and the product of labour. The labour of attaining silence, and therefore some sort of full subjectivity (which even without this slightly perverse reading of Kagge's book is never actually presented as having any positive characteristics) is something available equally to all of us. But, as Kagge acknowledges in passing, wealthy people live in quieter places (68). In other words, far from being a choice we can all work for and receive as a reward, silence is much more likely when the actual economic divides favour the silence-seeker. So the labour is not equal, and, in fact, some must labour so that others can attain silence. Perhaps the threatened extinction of silence is due to its being extracted from workers alienated from the fruits of their silent labour. Silence has been stripped from the sonic economy and flown to oligarch enclaves, or to inaccessible locations that can be attained through a combination of wealth, technology and skill built up in a highly developed economy. Even walking solo across the Antarctic is the opposite of free from cost, a fabulously wealthy frugality, within which silence can speak into the spirit of the quester.

A clear politics emerges from Kagge's exploration of silence, one that has some awareness of nature, but nature is only a consequential part of human existence, i.e. it is not really there if humans are not within it, 'hearing' the silence within which it shrouds itself for those very humans. It is also a type of liberalism, interested in the common good, but unquestioning as to the inequalities that belie his universalist statements and advice. Philosophically, Kagge wishes to demonstrate that he is a philosopher, but his own philosophy is less clear, and more curious. Is there anyone inside the body-machine that walks around looking for silence? What would it do once silence is found? Above all, a sense of realization, tranquillity and completion seem to be the result of the attaining of silence. This is not an uncovering of a silence – even if it is inside everyone, potentially, it needs to be worked at, not revealed. Silence then becomes a space for an emptied subjectivity to simply be. This pragmatism is unsurprisingly close to Buddhist ideas of the value of silence as one of many paths to get beyond the illusion of things. The silence-d person is not made silent, but has silence brought into them, and is now ready to exist, away from all the terrible noise of the world, of others, of a world where silence is not equally available to all.

But silence can be demonstrated, for Kagge, via the art of Edvard Munch, Mark Rothko or Marina Abramović. What seems an interesting final choice is less so when the reader discovers that Kagge is referring to Abramović's *The Artist is Present* in New York's MoMa (2010), a sort of stadium-rock version of performance art. Over three months, people came and sat opposite Abramović, and this silent communication offers Kagge a final chance to think of silence in the course of an interaction (*Silence*, 112–14), but he still wants to concentrate on her own experience rather than the creation of mutual silence. His ideas on music are odd, but still hold out the prospect of silence working through music (into the individual, where silence actually seems to happen once implanted). His first example is about withholding some sounds in pop music, so it is about using only a few tracks of a multitrack recording capacity, but his second example is the most advanced thought in the whole book, as he refers to the silence of the drop in electronic dance music (of which the thing called EDM is just one variant). It is not just his choice of example that is good, but what that example does: silence is anticipation of non-silence as a song builds up and up, only to pause and then crash back in, ideally with massive newly introduced bass. Silence as expectation is a transferable concept, something that can filter back into Cage, into Oliveros's version of deep listening and into the (genre expectation of) thwarting of expectation within harsh noise music.

The idea of the drop suggests a more noise-ful inversion, one where music becomes the anticipation of its absence, and for this we can travel back down another path of primordial art gestures and think of Yves Klein's *Symphonie monoton*.[12] In this piece, an equal amount of single tone music would be followed by an equivalent time of silence. Later this would be solidified as twenty minutes of each. The music and silence become equivalent in a way that clearly states that music underlies silence and vice versa, at least as raised in the performance of this symphony. Not only unsound, but also unmusic. The ending of harsh noise wall is the same – the world is rethought as the absence of the solidity of thick noise, largely unchanging, an absence of music, silence or even noise. The ending is the revealing of what was underneath the 'noise' all along, once noise has brought this underneath into being as that which is not currently occurring. Finally, through the medium of music, Kagge's quest has acquired a method, location and communality that takes him out of the mind-body/world divides he mostly inhabits. The aesthetics of almost absent silence show an openness that all the heavily wrought self-discovery hides, and shows professionalized praisers of listening that music and its consumption has always already been a vital part of human assumptions about hearing and an active mode of apprehending the world, as Cage suspected in *4'33"*.

If silence in Kagge's world is about something for the subject to have or to encounter, then in Thich Nhat Hanh's mindful view, silence is that which allows the self to encounter the self. So silence becomes a privileged intermediary. His view of silence is as full of trouble about the outside world as the impressions held by Foy or Kagge, but he knows his method and his enemy from the start.

We must, he thinks, cultivate silence to escape the terrible incursion of noise. We are lost, he says, 'because our outer and inner environment is filled with noise' (Hanh, *Silence*, 147), and so we need to 'quiet all the noise within us' (*Silence*, 5). This noise is the noise of intrusive culture (33). Only when we introduce silence, which will resonate with our inner silence – 'our true mind is silent of all words and all notions' (76) – will we even realize that we have been filled with noise up until that point (5–6, 36).

Not only have we been filled with noise, avers Hanh, but this noise has made a vacuum inside us (4, 24), and 'we may feel an inner void, a sense of isolation, of sorrow, of restlessness' (24). All things to be sought in the form of harsh noise and harsh noise wall in particular, but to be avoided here, as moral bad hygiene. There is no surprise that a Buddhist advocate of mindfulness has these particular reckonings, but there are still interesting consequences of the precise mishmash of ideas on offer. Silence lies within us, indeed, 'we' are nothing but being in silence, it would seem, and yet the void inside 'us' created by the existence of culture, other people, new things, many things, urban society, things that interrupt our auto-communing, is false. It is hard to see why – surely this void is exactly the difficulty in finding inner dwelling 'we' 'must' have on the way to understanding? Mindfulness demands of us a presencing that cannot stomach a voiding. For one thing, the noise of the world means 'we can't hear beauty's call' (*Silence*, 1). Like Kagge's silently clothed nature, Hanh's beauty is revealed only in silence. This would seem to bring Hanh in line with Cage, but close attention (perhaps a noisy attention as opposed to mindfully accepting consumption) opens up the prospect that Hanh wants us to travel in the opposite direction to that signalled by Cage in his silent pieces.

Hanh wishes to close off the noises that prevent mindfulness, that hinder self-communion, but he still wants everyone to be listening, to be attentive enough to silence, or to create silence, so that a kind of warm bath of being can happen. One of the ways into silence is through music, specifically a bell. Hanh introduces this practice early on in his exposition, saying that 'mindfulness is often described as a bell that reminds us to stop and silently listen' (4), and he means this to work through the use of an actual bell, as outlined later on. 'In Buddhism, the sound of the bell is considered to be the voice of the Buddha' (101). Upon hearing the bell, we are to stop what we are doing, breathe and be (102–03). The bell sonifies the presence of Buddhist thought, the Buddha in the guise not of silence, but of the bell. This chime is the bringer of silence, an intervention of music to provide a bridge out of noise and into silence. Where Cage sought to open up the world of sound, the world as sound, and thereby musicalized the world while making it an object for hearing, Hanh uses music to close off the world. The bell is the sound that opens the self to silence and silence for the self. The warm mindfulness of Hanh's brand of Buddhism has taken a turn into pure formalism, only not of art or music, but of being, as all we have left is a destimulated self, closed off from all that could disturb (i.e. from contemporary culture), turning on itself in cognizant pleasure, but not learning anything. Or experiencing anything other than itself. The 'fullness' of mindfulness is a new void to replace the supposed void Hanh thought had been inflated inside us by noisiness of the world.

Hanh's world is all about stilling, being 'able to still all the noise inside of you' (12). An emptied Cartesian model presents the body as absent, a skin-void that allows noise to permeate – both body and mind need to be stopped (158) for happiness to be possible, so that we can be present to the world. Except that for this presence to happen, it seems as though everything needs to be stopped from interfering. There seems to be very little that is not interference. Even stopping seems to require intervention. In the end, Hanh's mindfulness is a slightly desperate and unwittingly melancholy recognition of the non-existence of silence, not just in the way Cage 'found' but more profoundly, as even in making silence come into being, it slips away, or the thing it was designed to bring about slips away as another noise. Perhaps it's harsh to imagine Hanh's *Silence* should offer a coherent model for subjectivity through listening, sound or silence, but it does, albeit not in the way it intends.

Hanh regards silence as health-promoting, a way to have a morally and physically better experience, as the toxicity of living in the contemporary world will be swept away once the real or metaphorical bell has sounded. This kind of health is to be avoided. Deeper than any health disciplining, the type of silence that mindfulness can live on parasitically is one that avoids the world, rejects change, shuns newness and otherness in favour of a circular mono-communality. For all the listeners who wish for silence to be able to hear, and then properly listen, the lesson from the silence seekers is that to control listening is a demand that the world become less noisy. Far from being an ecological thought, such silencing is toxic, the equivalent of ecotourism, a return to self via eco-refreshment, and the creation of a sonic niche that is outside of any interactional ecology.

The wish to receive sound that is uncluttered, unfreighted or that at least partakes of some sort of fidelity is an apt utopianism, but one that needs to avoid finding silence, which is such a sonic outlier its only possible manifestation is in its own absence. The apparent perfection of the digital signal as presented via CD or minidisc contains silence, even glories in it, but this is a silence that is not to be heard. It is a silence that underlies all the sounds that are properly present to be found by the laser-reading device. The code that silences all else needs to remain inaudible. That is not to say that silence cannot play the part of silence that seeks to be noise, and this is primarily when silence presents itself as the presence of silence itself, at other times this can be through a silence that encounters its own failure, at still others, silence as a sort of abject quietness (for example in the form of tape hiss, vinyl crackle, the clunk of an eight-track cartridge, the whizzing sound of a CD skipping through multiple silent tracks).

Whilst the world of listening has to some extent moved beyond 'the digital', at least as a point that needs to be singled out as bearing a phenomenological novelty or potential, the inception of digitality, outside of music production (from instrument to studio) and inside of the consumer-listener environment, did change the positioning of silence. Underpinning all the sound of a CD, the silence that cannot be heard is the silencing of noise – but all formats, as Jonathan Sterne has noted in *MP3*, from the telephone thinking of Shannon and Weaver to the continued ubiquity of MP3, carry noise, use noise. This is the case even as the coding builds an impermeable sonic object that seems to the median ear to be peacefully surrounded by a protective moat of silence.[13] The CD not only offered the fidelity of sound but fidelity of time – the reflective and uncontoured (to human eyes) playing surface used its appearance as a suggestive metonym for its sonic surfacelessness. No sooner was the clarity of the new format accepted than artists played with it, introducing what had been seen as format failure (crackling vinyl, muted radio/microphone 'low' fidelity sound) as evocative atmosphere. Was the retooling of 'warm' analogue format noise a whitening of black noise? Taking the multifarious modes of vinyl playing technology that spread even as Philips and Sony worked on their new crisp, classical-friendly discs, 1990s crackles and pops changed experimentation into media retro/archaeological returns. Such play, just like glitch, relies on the claims for precision of the thing being scratched, crackled, Popped.

In silencing the world of material intrusions typical of ageing vinyl, the CD was designed to focus on the music, and retroactively make everyone realize just how badly affected their listening had been. Decades later, different species of media file occupy distinct niches, as high-detail code formats please high-end listeners, remasters and reinvigorated vinyl tap the median listener, and MP3 and associated formats offer a loss of detail in favour of focus. In terms of silence, you can make very high-end silence, or go for the opposite. In file size, quality counts here as much as anywhere else, with great differences in the quality of silence according to file type.[14] An empty CD is not silent, it's an unused object. A silent CD will have a time for the track or tracks to play, and will have, at some level, the sound of silence. Inserting silence into a recording, or making a silent track, are both very straightforward. Once we are past the ontological banalities of looking for silence, or letting it happen, then how we encounter it counts, and for this reason the onset of digitality represents an interesting change in silence.

As the CD became a 'mature' format, artists began to play with the track-reading conventions established for players, and introduced silent tracks, often with the silence merely extending the track as recognized by the CD player with a period of silence followed by a period of music. This infuriating practice was used by artists from Nirvana to the Pet Shop Boys. The latter made signifying use of the silence on *Very* (1993)'s final track 'Go West', which ended, then moved into two minutes' silence, only for the usually vocally silent Chris Lowe to sing the brief 'Postscript (I Believe in Ecstasy)', a powerful, tranquil paean to sexuality and excess after an album that combined despair at the spread of HIV/AIDS with a utopian art-house drive.

Introducing silence at the end of an album only to introduce a 'bonus' was presumably designed for people listening on the then-new CD Walkmans (maybe someone can make a sound art project based on the short memory jog-function, as applied to silent parts of CDs) who would forget the album was still playing and then receive a pleasurable jolt as the bonus kicked in. Or, maybe it was designed to force out diehard stereo listeners, who finally had a clock to chart the progress of a track, and awaited slackjawed as the silent minutes unfolded, the slowest transport ever. I think that the silent track on mainstream rock and pop albums was not aiming for the latter listener, let alone one who had discovered how long they needed to wait for the next track to kick in, and that the ante-closure silent track on CD served to act as validation for the rest of the silence achieved by the greatness of digital recording and production – this is what you have been listening to as the enabling mechanism of the sounds of the rest of the album. Unlike Cage's view, or that of any of the meditators above, silence would not reveal anything other than itself as enabling condition for something better. This was a silence designed to show that filling silence was now fully enabled. The same can, of course, be said of gaps between tracks (which for many years has been standardized at two seconds, at least for home recording). Silence becomes default, where once it might have been primary.

Digital, formatted silence is not the same as the acoustic presencing of silence in commemorative events or in the playing of *4'33"*.[15] It is also not always the same thing, and can have very different meaning, create different affects, as Craig Dworkin shows extensively in *No Medium*. But once it is in a digital consumer format, whether physical, an option in software or app, or streamed, it has some elements that have become characteristic, arguably of digitality itself, though that is surely of very little interest today except to people who have no music knowledge post-1990. Silence on the CD or audiofile is not the same as on vinyl (or tape, or in concert, or in a field or a train station). That silence in digital form takes space, evidences its existence and does not change over time, even if the listening of it can change. A CD, or minidisc, could be damaged, but let's stick to what is designed to happen. The sound is pristine, maybe even high fidelity, and surely we could in theory use the empty track to hear the rest of the world around it, just as with Cage's silent pieces. I think that the properly silent track is not the same as these works, and acts instead to undermine listening, and that is why, paradoxically, maybe, it is the silent digital track that leads into a more estranging sense of how silence acts materially.

In 2002, The New Blockaders released a new silent track on the four CD compilation *Gesamtnichstwerk* ('total absence work', an undoing of the idea of a total art work – *Gesamtkunstwerk*). 'Null Bei Ohr' deflects the medical injunction to take 'nil by mouth' to the ear, and so refers to the hygienic element in silence, in listening that is not determined by content. But digital silence (over twenty minutes) is even emptier than all other types. Like *4'33"*, though, we are left with the temporal element, as the clock on the CD player marks time, and also the visual element (in this case, the clock again, like David Tudor at the piano in 1952). The silent CD track brings out the peripheral aspects of silent music, making it clear how much is not only the 'world of sound' but also the world that is entirely separate to the sounds being made. In this case, a reiterable experience made possible by programming a CD player or computer to play, so we can watch the progress of a track. All other interventions are possible, but this track resists, unlike most others (well, unlike all the others with sound in). This track becomes the materiality of the object, and its interaction with an audio machine, as well as the other material parts of the release such as the cover, box, inserts, text, image, title and so on. Like all other tracks, only more itself. Unlike Cage's opening (of music, ears, concert space) to the world, 'Null Bei Ohr' is about stopping that sound, its purpose a heightening or lowering of the mission of the CD format to reduce noise. It is a mission to take noise to a point of reduction such that it becomes noise again.

Streaming formats are wary of noise, although plenty of silent tracks are there and Vulfpeck seemingly gamed Spotify's massively exploitative 'royalties' algorithm by getting people to play their *Sleepify* (2014) album whilst sleeping. At least this goes against the moral virtue of listening to world-revealing silence, while revealing just how much Spotify encourages listening and/or profiteering, but at the same time you will notice that streaming services do not include the fifty-two tracks of silence on Ministry's *Dark Side of the Spoon* (1999) – these silences have become exclusive to the material format. Like 'Null Bei Ohr', these silences gain some of their suggestive power through proximity to much louder (infinitely louder) tracks – industrial metal in the case of Ministry, metal-based industrial noise in the case of The New Blockaders. In different ways, both illustrate the parallel role of the CD clock or music programme counter in the visualizing and framing the experience of silence.

Now to the case of noise on tape, which is where The New Blockaders first released the silent 'Epater les Bourgeois' (with the title borrowed from Baudelaire's injunction to shock the sensibilities of the then-nascent mid-nineteenth-century middle classes). This blank tape, which received no recording of silence, and so consisting only of the sounds generated by the tape itself, was remade for the *Gesamtnichtswerk* compilation. Here, the tape is recorded and mixed for digital.[16] The track is substantially different as the CD is not being presented as any empty format to be heard as such, but is actually a new content, an actual recording. The gentle hiss is almost melodic, a fifteen-minute ghost ambience of what was nothing, or at least 'no work'. There is a very long fade in and an equivalent fade to close the piece, thus supplying a new structure. Previously, the tape version would have started with one type of absence, revealing the sound of the lead-in tape, then rapidly moving to the proper recording surface with an audible jump. The 2002 CD version proposes a smooth incline up to and down from the plateau of not entirely flat white noise. Like 'Null Bei Ohr', 'Epater les Bourgeois' (CD version, for the digital-conforming listener of 2002 as opposed to the Walkman chic of 1985) reveals the materiality of the format, and in this case doubles that moment of unveiling: instead of no-recording, there is material (the tape), a recording process and a product with recorded sound on (the CD). Not only is there material, there is also labour, and production. All for nearly nothing. This is the point – instead of Cage's beatific rendering of the idea that there is no such thing as silence, this is the pathetic failure to even do nothing – the impossibility of cutting off the world. It is also pathos for the listener, who rather than being praised is being placed in the position of patsy – there is not even nothing to hear, here. Just the spectacle of there not being quite nothing to hear, and that is meagre, noisy fare.

Francisco López first released *Paris Hiss* in 1997, having made it through a process of recording one blank tape playing onto another, in a dual tape deck, 'for hundreds of generations', producing a surprisingly tranquil, but not featureless soundscape of white-ish noise. Re-released in 2011, it remains a tape piece, and so not only reveals the materiality of marked chemicals on the tape surface, but also the different responses from different tape players (which would also be the case if you simply played a blank tape at high volume on different machines). In a way that parallels The New Blockaders, work has become no work – the more that has been done to the sound, the less effect it has had.[17]

One reference point is Alvin Lucier's *I Am Sitting in a Room* (1969), where Lucier interacts with a tape recording of his own voice in a specific room. Lucier would speak his text, recording it on tape, then play the recording back and record it over and over until the words crumble into a sonic mush, and as content slips away, the sound proper to the space takes over. In López's case, the artefactual element does not add in order to reveal something else (the room in Lucier's case), instead it blocks specificity in favour of a categorical sound of recording on (a) tape as 'tape recording'. The peaks and troughs of higher volume, apparent textural change and tunnel-like sonic spaces are produced statistically, a sonic Gaussian white noise processing, if not quite white noise in its own right.

Such apparent change (the change is real, but the processing of that in human hearing is not consistent across listeners, or from one listening to the next), even after the difference that can be induced by the use of different cassette players, is akin to that of the full frequency sound of harsh noise wall. This is a type of noise predicated on the absence of change, yet its change is continual if microscopic, then playback devices and cartilage receivers do the rest and supply macroscopic features (if not structure). I had this in mind when I bought a cassette by Vomir, *Pas de vie éternelle, mais seulement un emmerdement permanent* [sic] (2010), only to find there was no recorded sound on it. I had listened in a high state of anticipation, awaiting the loud and sudden onslaught of unheralded noise, only to hear nothing. I then tried turning it up very loud, and heard a variant of the sound all tapes make that have no recording on their surface, a gentle white-ish hiss. Vomir (Romain Perrot) confirmed that there was supposed to be sound on it. To fix this anomaly, or rather to use it positively, I bounced the tape from cassette player to laptop and back (not hundreds of times, about eight in total, but at maximum volume every time). The result is the Vomir/Safe release *Pas de vie éternelle …* (2013) where 'Vomir supplied no sound, Safe did nothing'. All of these 'silent' tapes work as strategies against the opening up of the world in favour of localized and hermetic noise that is nonetheless a transcribing of actual sonic phenomena, a highly materialized and speculative type of silence that is not in any way silent, but a liminal quietness. Even the Vomir/Safe tape is in this sense quiet, as it occupies the place of silence, in a kind of Quiet/Silence, always refusing the orderedness and propriety of a listening space where a centred human can take in the exterior world.

Recent horror films imagine the strangeness of not being able to talk and make all the other daily human sounds, in order to posit a core humanity that nonetheless resists and rebuilds even in what is shown as sensory deprivation. The use of not-silence, the integration of the sounds of the recording process and material is not a surface effect, not even a haunting, but the filling-in of aural space that is where noise must go to stop not just the occurrence of music but also of noise.

Part Three

Unmoored

Neither noise nor music are immune to the material – and given the context of economic disruption of the last two decades, known to neo-liberal entrepreneurs as disruptive innovation, the context that noise refers to has changed dramatically, and not just as a result of inhabiting a post-pandemic, post-shut-down (if it even is post). The idea of noise in the setting of the economic-material is perhaps counter-intuitive and centres on the realization that making music free has not had liberating effects, other than for 'capital'. Now that music is mostly free, where experimentation has not vanished, there is now no money, so if the progressive position for experimental music is to refuse the market, 'we' have won, and now musicians are not even exploited but somewhere beneath that zone. This, of course, replicates the situation across business, industry and work (between 2000 and 2020, at least, the 'gig economy' phase). Noise is a commonplace in algorithmic and speculative markets (as Adriana Knouf outlines in *How Noise Matters to Finance*).[1] The first chapter in this section compares the value attributed to improvisation as a social good to the stripping out of reward for musicians. Improvisation has been taken to create community, in opposition to the culture industry, but I argue that we need to consider valuation as something more complex, beyond those simple categories. The second chapter thinks about how music consumers spend more on music than ever, but it is on, say, headphones, as opposed to what is now thought of as 'content'. Instead of content providers receiving money in return for their musical content, auditors produce themselves as listening spectacle.

The third chapter questions what might have been considered a good thing by many listening and playing in the margins, and that is the valorization of vinyl, which has gone from being a defendably superior form and interesting niche object for the experimentally minded to being the least subtle exploitative device of twenty-first-century music economies. The final chapter in this part, on tape, is less about its resurgence and revalorization as a marker of DIY authenticity than about its breath-like, living, altering quality. Tape's materiality is restored as form, even while, as commodity, it has started to transit from avant-garde exchangeable to 'cult' mainstream via soundtracks *Guardians of the Galaxy* (vols 1 and 2, 2014 and 2017, respectively) and *Stranger Things* (2018).

Playing Economies

1 producing

When improvisation spreads stealthily through music in the 1950s and 1960s, it is ferrying the aspirations of many parallel, political ideals. From free jazz to The Grateful Dead, from the labs at Darmstadt and elsewhere to the smashed pianos of Fluxus, from guitars shaking off the blues to the wilful amateurs of Cornelius Cardew, the Scratch Orchestra and the like, utopias shadow the idea of freedom as *expressed* in music that leaves composition behind. Sometimes this was more conscious, as in the Association for the Advancement of Creative Musicians (AACM), other times implicit to the point of absent intention and awareness.[2] But at every point, improvising implies a breaking-free, a move outside of stifling structure, instruction, precision, correctness, moral goodness and upright participation. Machines and bodies would be exceeded, driven outside of normal tolerances and function, and creativity would be rethought as the mobilization of truly inventive chance where 'musicians who specialise in creating something in real time cut through manipulation and the star system' writes Ben Watson (*Derek Bailey*, 3).[3] The hands, ears and appendages of the improviser, or experimenter, would be a conduit, both for themselves and a wider communal expression.

The improviser is never alone, never in the position of being the universe of all sound, for she or he is letting their constructedness play. The illusion of freedom is replaced by something more profound, a freedom of restraint, even as it feels like an unchaining. The improviser is also often to be found among others – a community of the fellow free; a community that is rethinking the idea of itself continually, hopefully. Its key hope is the potential for interaction, an intersubjective entity forming from the purest kind of democracy, continually

Earlier version published as *Playing Economies* (Glasgow: Centre for Contemporary Arts, 2011).

reforming: 'it's the one practice that has managed to preserve that revolt as activity and experience rather than image' (Watson, *Derek Bailey*, 4). Fred Moten goes further, seeing improvisation as defiantly radical and a specific expression of oppressed marginality being seized and turned on the structures of composed and taken-for-granted order and convention. Improvisation will act 'as the breakdown of the rigid opposition that Adorno makes between improvisation and writing' (*Black and Blur*, 81) such that 'improvisation [is] precisely that material graphesis that makes the organized whole a possibility' (82) and '*is the unacknowledged grapho-spatiality of material writing* – the arrangement of people at the scene as audiovisual condition and effect' (82, emphasis in original). I return to Moten at the end of this chapter, and although I will be reflecting on the value of improvisation along the way, in the context of the living-on in the end of the music industry, I am not questioning the value of improvising, but I do want to highlight that improvising is *given* value in experimental music, a value that is seen as superior, more radical, freer and separate to the confines of something like a culture industry.

In the 1960s (or perhaps ever since Ornette Coleman's *Free Jazz*, recorded in December of 1960) genres that did not habitually encourage improvisation were disrupted (the avant-garde rethinking of music after John Cage, for example), and those that did provided excess after excess in an improvisational potlatch. Jazz gives way to itself, opening up its own 'tradition' of improvising, in the shape of Coleman, John Coltrane, Archie Shepp, Cecil Taylor, Alice Coltrane … and the content of material, musical freedom as a sign and vanguard of community liberation, shifts inward in subsequent improvised music. At some point, the strength of free playing is precisely that it indicates or hints at other social changes, but its key is its own utopian construction (in a group improvisation).

Whether in progressive rock, 'krautrock', post-jazz, free music, soul jams or in the generating processes in electronic music, improvising is permanently haunted by its roots in 1960s protest and alternative social models. Ostensibly, this has led to improvisation being filled by left-leaning individuals, operating leftist organizations with a social model based on equality and the promotion of liberation. This model has become more complex in recent times, as it takes on board a strong desire to offer new types of explicitly politically aware social practice. Gillian Siddall and Ellen Waterman exemplify this position, in *Negotiated Moments*, arguing that, more than being an inherently radical practice, the practice of improvisation opens 'a negotiation (of power, of subjectivity) at the nexus of discursive and material bodies' ('Introduction').[4]

Like many avant-garde movements, this has never permeated as far as popular music, let alone the popular, large-scale or 'mass' audience. Maybe it never can or could, and maybe that is not a problem. But what has happened instead is that the ideals of liberationist aesthetics have permeated the avant-garde sound/music/noise world. At the very least, those constituencies see themselves as being outside the culture industry identified and repeatedly critiqued by Theodor Adorno, often attacking jazz specifically (many have attacked Adorno, but see Moten, *Black and Blur*, 81–85). Some type of improvisation is a default value in experimental music – and other than the occasional re-emergence of bilious virtuosity breaking up that ethic, is accepted unproblematically.

However, for all its noble qualities, improvising needs to be questioned. It needs to be questioned as a form and backdrop to economy – it is not inherently a 'good', or a non-commodity 'good'. In its own terms, it sets up an economy of play that steps outside the constraints of composition. If we take it that a group of musicians or artists experimenting live has a value, then we need to recognize that value is present, not dispensed with, even if we consider this worth a radical one. We might imagine that value as taking the forms of authenticity, integrity, presence, responsiveness, listening. All of these look to be something more, something better than just being music played by musicians. In Marxist terms, there would be a value generated that eludes exchange value. The act of improvisation will not just be a matter of taste, but an engaged art, an art that has, or better, is, a philosophy, a practical one. It is these presumptions that allow the possibility of imagining the live 'composition' as a social model (which could even be 'militantly dialectical', as Ben Watson has it [*Derek Bailey*, 9]), and, equally, that a social model can appear in the unfolding of a sound piece.

We might have built, or acquired, an image of improvisation that supposes it is always formally communal, left-ish or leftist, when we are mistaking where it came from with what it does or aspires to be in its practice. Is improvising (or experimenting, for that matter) inherently democratic and forward-looking? The claim is that the community it establishes is democracy in action, in negotiation, as example, as vanguard or as cradling, because it does not stop changing, adapting to the actions of all of its members. We play, hear, see freedom and a play beyond rules, even if rules establish themselves by consent over the course of the time the society (the performance) persists. It seems a paradigmatic anarchistic social model: no hierarchy, no rules that cannot be altered, removed, bent. And the surrounding economic reality of DIY gigs, releases, writings seems to confirm this. This is not incidental, but a direct consequence of the material locations and history of free or free-er musics. Improvisation extends beyond the playing of musical pieces into the organization of concerts, associations, groups, venues. The idea of DIY filters through the artistic avant-garde, via the Los Angeles Free Music Society (with Smegma at its core), into punk, hip hop, industrial music and all experimental genres or variants of genres ever since.

But – is this utopian modelling the only one we can imagine? After all, this would-be community operates in a world dominated by capitalism. A world of industry, finance, products, incomes, even before we get to the question of exploitation and hierarchy. Improvisation wants to be something else, the somewhere else of utopia. But something of the market endures in this resistance: the players of a group improvisation could be envisaged as an organically structured and maintained market, where competition leads to a unified outcome, and social order arises from consensual combinations of individual endeavour. In working like (Marx's) 'primitive communism', it paves the way for its own becoming-market, a becoming never mentioned, as far as I recall, by Deleuze and Guattari in their proliferating lists of becoming-other, but far from excluded from their world-view. Like Adam Smith's original conceit of the 'invisible hand', the improvising group creates social goods (the piece, the group, the event) incidentally, and this through individual choices and practices.[5]

Where is the community gathered into being by the experimenting or improvising group? The where is constructed in practice (of public live creation, not rehearsal) and varies widely. The prospect that is underplayed is that the group that improvises is creating itself as a society in a way that does not include the audience. At one level, this just means an improvisation that has somehow failed. At another level, the parallel societies feed into one another – it is not a problem that performers and other listeners who are present do not form a holistic unity. On the two occasions I saw the group AMM, I was never brought into their world in any over-explicit moment of 'we're all in this together', but the room did feel like a pulsating, maybe swimming, organism. But, even here, the three players were developing a community that was overtly separate from the audience, however much the two parts of the room were sharing. So, whatever we think of a particular encounter of this sort, the question has to be raised as to whether the players' interactions has made of them a corporation. Or some sort of guild, perhaps.

That brings us back to a model of artisans, and maybe that is how to look at group improvisation – craft production. Neither is this transparently good or bad, democratic or otherwise, as the idea of craft as skill can lead to the problems of virtuosity (domination through superior musical capital), whilst it does connect to the cottage industry model that is both in and outside of 'the' market economy. The cottage industry model of music-making and distribution spreads, out of necessity, from the experimental to all music, as the monopolies decay (to be replaced by other monopolies, other exploitations). The music industry of the past seventy years or so is fading fast, but has privatized the idea of exploiting the musician. The self-sufficient music production model sits between these extremes. In the last few years, the growth of exploitative listening through stockpiling on hard drives has been re-monopolized. If we take Marx's model of imagining all industries as part of one massive 'capitalist industry' and apply it to the music industry, we can see that only the names have changed – the interregnum of torrenting merely stopped the artist's surplus value being extracted and they now have all value extracted at source.

So, 'real world' economics have become something that cannot be ignored in the name of the authentic otherwordly muse. Only the self-sufficient in financial terms will be permitted to be music-makers in the future as the utopia of music on demand takes effect. Improvising musicians, avant-gardists of all stripes have long taken the hit for their autonomy and will to freedom. But in the midst of that material reality, the idea that the freedom made it worthwhile endures, and it does so in the belief that formal freedom is a type of social as well as musical liberty.

There is nothing more communal about improvisation, when compared to other group musics. A highly structured music played by a group still creates group communality, and, often, more of a sense of community among the audience. The rock group that plays its planned tracks is just as much a generator of community as a group playing from scratch. Or it can be. The fact that music created in the now, in the setting of a live event, is often less hierarchical than the tuneplayers is a result of friction and noise. To expand: the group making its piece now, and only now (and the document of such an event only heightens the sense that the event was a now, was a thing present and is now a trace) must not be based on mutual connectivity to the point of complete consensus. As an elective community, any musical group creates itself as society, but if we allow noise, dissonance, fighting, then what we have is something like a 'negative community', one based on its differences. This is not to sanction playing that is effectively shouting over all the rest, but the core of the actually anarchist community in music is the possibility of failure, of communication breakdown, of fracture. That this can end in perfectly harmonious playing (not literally, I mean in the sense of connections being made) is not at all strange, it is the playing in the threat of absent community that can bring communality. Then what we have is a community of absence. Loss of self, loss of mission, trust pushed to limits.

2 commodity

If experimental musicians involved in (any sort of) improvised sound-making are social actors, some sort of economic modellers, then the objects made in avant-garde sound are the objects of trade, objects that carry ghost values of the music-making, price values to cover costs, maybe profits and rich signifying values. We can trade these things not only through making, selling, giving away, buying, acquiring them in marketplaces, but also in their rarity (a central part of what it is to be a commodity), strangeness or artistic authenticity (through handmade recordings, objects, artwork). In 2005, Nick Smith wrote about the commodity fetishism and desire he saw in noise, citing the massive fifty-CD Merzbow box set, and also the symbolic acquisition of deviance through finding the harshest music possible.[6] Although he might have overstated the case, it is an inevitable outcome of the love of *material* in noise and experimental music that objects acquire multiple layers of value. Increasingly, music is dematerializing, losing the need for physical supports, so it makes sense for cottage industries to go the other way and assert the claim of actual stuff. Stuff where the format matters makes a difference to the product, to the point of being an integral part of the music/sound. The dematerialization is highly practical, some sort of economically pragmatic progress, and the result of companies insisting on high profit levels on material forms – new formats are still being invented to maintain those gains – Blu-ray came into being to keep the consumer price of a movie at something like 20 euro, 3D movies to keep you at the cinema, 4k to keep the cinema in front of your eyes at home … and also to reduce the chances of copying the originals well enough to be the same as them.

Dematerialization is an ideology in its own right, that is, a way of thinking and acting that obscures actual practices while pretending to be neutral. Material production processes are now hidden and/or devalued, whether we are talking about major corporations or bedroom recorders. Material gains are apparently gone, when they have moved – to technology and telecoms companies, as well as those who profit from 'free music'. Nick Smith was on to something when he noted the collecting fetish in the unacknowledged psychic economy of noise listening, but so much more is going on that the conscious production of fetish objects has to be seen as resistance. Ideally, these will become proper fetishes, not the diminished para-Freudiana they might well be. Noise music mostly appears in the form of limited editions, with many variations in format, packaging, availability (e.g. at gigs only), and this is what can feed reification. Music that occurs in the terrain of noise has specific strategies through which it becomes excessive in a way that thwarts the collector's desire to dominate artist and fellow listeners through privileged control, and simply ends in failure, or in absurdity. Japanese artist Merzbow proliferates his releases like weeds – and every one has the potential to be 'more of the same', blasts of white noise or something unexpected, including diversions into rhythms, beats, digital instead of analogue. As the first of these carries the potential of colossal variation, both possibilities conspire to keep the listener interested to pick up more. And yet there is so much, you can only be defeated as Merzbow recordings pop in and out of existence on a plethora of labels from all around the world – and this devaluation is the difference between collecting 'noise' and collecting classic rock box sets. The website discogs.com suggests the possibility of knowledge mastery at least, but perhaps also heightens the sense of failure to keep up with the collecting frenzy. What psychoanalytic thinking might designate as the necessity of incompleteness for the collector is recast by both material and informational proliferation as project failure.

Harsh noise wall artist Vomir releases prodigiously and almost all of the material could have been chipped off the same noise mountain or cake, some come in crumbs, others chunks, but all relentlessly similar with no clear logic why they are the length or format they come in. So in these two cases, the form of the sound, its noisiness, informs the material side. The material object cannot just be removed, just as a conceptual artwork can be adequately described, but still not be the set of objects collected in the physical work of, say, Joseph Kosuth's *One and Three Chairs* (1965). This is not to praise the authentic aura of an original, but to not deny the deep importance of material to noise. This is not quite the same with improvised performances when they appear on recordings. There the function is to serve both as document and as knowing secondary level material, heightening the authenticity of the moment of creation, the passing time the performance occurred in.

Both noise and the improvised music of many subgenres seek to dwell in the transitory, the fleeting, the sounds themselves only ever being structured live. The recording reflects this in presenting the absence of the moment of making as its content. The community that builds itself in performance is also one continuously threatened by and embracing the prospect of disappearance, of perpetual change, and this is exactly the way in which the commodity form(s) of music are challenged and undermined whilst not being removed or ignored.

Maybe experimental music needs to be making its contestation in the apparently immaterial and free zones of communications. Was uploading a form of noise? It would seem obvious that downloading, as an acquisition of sounds, was a type of stockpiling, classic capitalistic behaviour. But the uploader was or is often a utopian, a sharer. A noise in the system of product creation, ownership and fetishization of ownership. The noise might be more in the pile-up of sound stuff – there is so much, and so much to hand, that it will not matter if music-making stops.[7] The breakdown of music economies might be strange, but the marketization of music, the possibility of being some sort of professional is surely the historical anomaly. And why would an avant-garde improviser or noise musician want to be paid, when they claim to be subverting and/or transgressing the expectations and norms of music practice? So they are expected by non-paying publics to maintain their vocation and supply the sound stuff because in some way they are driven to make it. As mentioned earlier, the day-to-day reality of the experimental musician is one where the music has never really supplied much in the way of income, and no one has ever waited to 'make it' by being found by a major label. That said, once music is distributed entirely free, the musician is effectively being asked to pay the listener for their attention, in the hope that one day this relationship will be requited by the listener paying to see the act live. This has proved to no longer be the case, except for the most established and most mainstream of stars, those whose stats bend the curve of the 'industry' to suggest it is in rude health. Further excess economies have come to replace the 'hope economy' of people paying for live music, in the shape of online followers and approvals. Once again, music and musicians have eluded the pitfalls of being paid within the culture industry.

The alienation proper to basic market trading (the separating of producer/labourer from product/work) is transformed, in the situation where music is expected to be free by its consumers and distributors, to properly capitalist exploitation where value is extracted from the performer. This applies as much to 'pirate' services that facilitate the spending of money in the vicinity of music as to the corporations of the recent past. If noise and/or improvisation is to drive community through music, it would need to restore a more equal relationship on the basis of a new social contract where listeners do not separate themselves from the sound-makers. Networks where this occurs are many – and many listeners at experimental events are also performers. As an actual functioning means of social connectedness and modelling, it is pretty good. But more attention can always be paid to how this is established in and around releases, performances, distribution and relations between all those involved in performances.

As music disappears from its position of centrality for those who would listen, and those who would make an industry of it, noise comes into its own and so does improvisation. The thought of either of these being opposed to material and economic situations has to be ignored: entwinedness and possible subversions are much more interesting. Instead of imagining inherent or essentialist characteristics of a type of music, or a type of access to it, the paradoxical, noisy relation of experimental music to its own market and/or objects and privileged locations is what requires attention, and will repay it.

The utopia of certainties, however it imagines its ideology, is vintage, a properly pathos-filled desire. Which will fail, as it is so easily appropriated. Let's remind ourselves of the failures in noise and improvisation, and how the attempt to overcome them, in the almost-full certainty that this too will fail, is a permanent, paradoxical and utopian outlook suggested by content, form, practice of those musics. Failure is not something bad, but the only thing that simply is not wrong. To overstate slightly, this is to try not to fail in expressing the value of failure. This, then, is nothing, but in a good way, or at least, slightly not as bad as it could have been. There is nothing defeatist in the advocacy of failure, it is just more difficult (and therefore more appropriate for avant-garde makings). It is also connected, caught within as well as without. Failure is the noise in the commendable fallacy of a pure activism, a re-imagining of a pure music thanks to dematerialization or cosy community.

Noisy music-making has its hands dirty, and will put its curious and grubby fingers into whatever it comes across. It has no time for the virtues of clean and too-clear vistas. It is formal wariness. This is what Mattin has in mind in his contribution to 'Anti-self: experience-less noise'.[8] This is what Moten has in mind when advocating the non-community from out of outside – one where the community does not congratulate itself on harmonious unity but where it exists as non-being in opposition to official being, and without excluding, as the other is removed from otherness when there is a 'we' of non-self-identical performers, whose coexistence is a non-*real*-ization:

> Society is not friendly association with others; it's friendly association without others, in the absence of the other, in the exhaustion of relational individuality, in consent not to be a single being.

> (Moten, *Black and Blur*, 282–83)

Noise is no different – such association is noise, the noise of communal forming that is more like an in- or de- forming, even as it grows. The economy of this is not tenable, not constrained by choices made that expropriate musical making, musical labour, whether noisy or not, and it is not part of *the* economy or the restricted economy of financial, asset or approval rating processes. Neither is it the melancholy acceptance/heroic assumption of a life outside of remuneration, response and generative community.

The Spectacle of Listening

There's a lot of listening happening today. A lot of attention paid to hearing, to sound, to openness, to empathic communication, to shared soundworlds. Some of this attention happens in the zone of sound studies, pleased that at least some part of the world around it has finally grasped McLuhan's sense that the future would be full of sound, and that the acoustic would be the privileged way of imagining space and social interaction: 'ours is a brand new world of allatonceness. "Time" has ceased, "space" has vanished. We now live in a global village ... a simultaneous happening. We are back in acoustic space' (*Medium is the Massage*, 63).[1] Without wishing to distinguish too much between listening and hearing, can we say that hearing more sound is better? Presumably, as writers never tire of pretending, the ears cannot be closed, so react passively, even submissively, to sound produced by someone else. Acoustic ecology tries to rectify this terrifying presence of McLuhan's allatonceness, and restore the measure of listening, in place of unwilled hearing.

Much of the hearing is of music, the organization of time through sound. Only now this is consumer space/time being structured by centrally generated sound. If not that, then the surprisingly healthy medium of radio, notwithstanding government attempts to restrict the gift-like promise of its medium or long-wave travels. Digital radio might be available everywhere there is some sort of internet, but within a territory it allows state broadcasters to regulate and monitor users, ensuring flow of resources in the form of licences. TV 'catch-up' services are the explicit rendering of the reterritorialization of viewing and listening rights. Or it might come in the form of the noise of people, or even sounds they produce in a private and mobile sound territory emanated by their phone. As retail leaves the cities, maybe all this sound will dissipate, replaced by audio green shoots, perhaps in the clarity of hearing a nearby river or a conversation that doesn't seem too aggressive/too different/too new/too foreign/too fucking loud.

Earlier version presented at *Tuning Speculation II*, Toronto 2014, and also on excentrics.org.

But audio predators stalk urban streets, mumbling, shouting, laughing, their eyes glazed. The urban niche occupied by the illuminated drunk is now taken by the invasive phone-wielder, holding their upturned shell, peering into it, talking one-sidedly, while the circuit's completion remains unrevealed to the passive listener, the unwitting consumer. There are no objective sounds in the city, only sounds in relation to listeners, contextually constructed listening devices interacting in a mass bone oscillation. It is tempting to say that if there is more for us to hear, then it would be good for us to listen, to apply conscious ears where before not all hearing was actually heard. In passing: Jonathan Sterne has often pointed to the connection that should be made more between sound studies and disability studies, rather than everyone drifting through a world where full hearing is presumed. I do not presume all our ears are open, equally, or in the same way, or to the same things – any listening involves selection, loss of messages. Any hearing involves diminution of other potentials. All the while, things are also simply not heard because they fall outside the capturing point of significance. I think listening has become so good, so prevalent, so welcome, that it has turned into a personal commodity, a demonstration. Have people ever listened so much? To so much music and chat? Has it ever been so obvious?

So we need to go back, even beyond the habitual passage by the door of John Cage, and think of listening as something worthy of seeing. There is, of course, a massive history of music in painting, and indeed of listening to orators, to lovers, to words from superior beings: a history of attention conveyed through showing and looking.[2] For all the interest in Vermeer's *The Guitar Player* (c. 1672), announcing the self-reflective humanist subject and a reconception of music as secular philosophy, it is worth having a quick look at Manet's *Concert aux Tuileries* from 1862, a foundational modernist work, in which there is very little sign of the music, or indeed of listening, as Manet's sitters and other figures attend to being seen by concert-going public and painter alike. For modern music in Paris was about attendance, about music as a social condensation. Also, if we look at his *Café Concert* (1878), we can see a very specific (and gender- and class-located) listening at play – distraction, but also the role of music in permitting distraction, in allowing observation as well as audition. In the social gathering of the café (highlighted by Benjamin in his 'Berlin Chronicle'), we do not look at the performers, or dedicate multisensory reception to the production of music, but only listen, as looking is dedicated to the surrounding members of your class.[3]

Richard Leppert tells us that audiences only became silent (accompanying the rise of Romanticism in music) in response to social change (in 'The Social Discipline of Listening'), expressed in new public concert formats, with their sound-making contribution restricted to points in between those of the musicians. Whilst this heightens the discipline of 'proper' listening, it does also build tension and drive the possibility of a potentially tumultuous and acoustically unpredictable moment of excess. Avant-garde movements of the twentieth century tried shaking up audiences in many ways, but did anyone try harder than Cage in presenting the silence of 4'33" in 1952? The audience becomes a heightened listening machine, and in the minutes of silent non-playing it makes many of the sounds that will fill the acoustic space. More importantly, it makes the piece through its listening. In one fell swoop, Cage had changed the borders between music and non-music, silence and sound, performer and audience, and opened up the world as a producer of an essential musicality of all things. But what he also did was create a skilled, trained audience, establishing a practice of close listening, of open ears, ready to receive the world, and, as this skill was one generated by you the listener, you could display this skill through your stasis (or, your knowing movement), your listening face. Your understanding of the history of the world being opened up could play gently across your ever-so-slightly moving head, which is trying to capture slight variations in sound.

At roughly the same time, Yves Klein produced his *Monotone Symphony*. Unlike Cage's piece, Klein's symphony addresses the divide between music and silence, summons all music into one note and then dismisses it. Cage fills the world with sound, Klein empties it, a void where once was sound. Maybe that's what we see in this audience for the piece, but actually what we have are competing models of attention. The last twenty years have seen the slow, hesitant spread of the silent disco, where a room full of people shuffle around, singing to themselves as they listen on headphones instead of over a PA – as if participating in a sound art event, or learning about exhibits in a gallery. The privatization of a nightclub to the point of listening to your choice of different music tracks is, then, not very different to other technological developments around what used to accurately be called a personal stereo. Today, it is probable that the silent workout has replaced the silent disco, as in-ear speakers transmit listening that will convey the body and show how sound carries the fit or fittening body.

Shortly before Cage and Klein invited audiences to becomes the focus through their listening, IBOPE (Sao Paolo, starting in 1942) began measuring radio audiences, raising the question, further on, as surveys became more targeted, not just of listening quantity but also quality – what kind of listening was going on? From the 1950s on, subcultures developed their own practices of listening performance. Rock 'n' roll audiences made the breakthrough for the display of listening as ecstatic communion, a situation both threatening and commercializable. As rock diverged into different genres, the way in which listening was done would alter, and would be depicted differently according to genre-based practices, such as looking at art, or dancing, contemplating, throwing yourself around. All of these practices signify your commitment to being a certain sort of listener in a given context, but it is when this context goes private on a mass scale that things change, and the 1980s saw this in the shape of the Walkman, amid more public developments such as the boombox or ghettoblaster, enabling a portable version of the block party, and also the mobile phone. All of these are about the transit of sound through the city, all involve machinery that can be seen when in use, or merely through being transported; all therefore reterritorialize sound on the individual and heighten the possibility for displaying the act of listening.[4] For now it is the act of listening in itself that is on show, whereas concert performances had established behavioural genre conventions (the cassette or eight-track-equipped car was a way of transforming the visual of the car into sound, displaying not the listening itself, but that listening could happen).

Such would be a simple media archaeology of technologized listening as display, a bit like running a metal detector over a huge lump of metal rock. Without even mentioning Mike Judge's innovative programme that showed Beavis and Butthead watching music videos, listening constantly alters, and what is being displayed when we look at listening alters, and does so significantly when the Walkman is relaunched as the iPod.[5] Up to this point, what we experienced as viewers of listening was its visible aspect, not yet its mobilization as display. Hi-fi headphones were for the secret pleasure of the audiophile, and full of the microscopic variation that Baudrillard identifies in his 1968 book *The System of Objects*, or that Bret Easton Ellis observes in *American Psycho*. These new buds would be the sign of adherence to a cult – white, slightly streamlined compared to the now mass-produced and cheaply sold standard earphones that came with the Discman, the shuffling, jittery upgrade of the cassette Walkman. The white buds have remained a defining Apple object, even amid a new bloom of variety, once Apple saw it was missing out on the colours and mock-aerodynamics of fitness buds (Powerbeats Pro are now 'available in black', as if such a possibility had never existed and the white buds were all that has ever been) – different for every discipline, for every self-improving and no doubt mindful set of exercises. So earphones have come to offer new possibilities for status identification – the white ones initially signalling belonging to the rebellious now tech-giant Apple, and, more relevantly, still today the access to a big volume of data that you now had on your iTunes drone device. Of course, this access no longer needs to signify the stockpiling capacity, as it is access to streaming and internet acquisition that counts, and twinning machines so your listening can be viewed everywhere by what comically refers to itself as a (streaming) service provider.

In a way the iPod seems very much like the end of an old model of music collecting and listening, but I don't think we should be misled – the stockpile is rampant. Its days as a commodifiable marker of torrent compiling skill, monolithic piling of material and broker of 'freed' music are possibly over amid the entropic sprawl of 'everything all the time at once'. Things have moved on: for the double life of the home audiophile has blossomed, through fertile variegation, and now includes real headphones, noticeably large, head-protecting devices that dramatically improve the standard of iMachines, as Sterne notes in *MP3* (237). But are they for listening? Multicoloured, advertising their design purposes like 'upstart' wines brazenly telling you the grape they are made from instead of their heritage or terroir, and sitting largely and expensively on many heads. Audiophile websites and other media are not impressed, and I'm sure in some way they are right: Beats by Dre are an update on 1970s desirable design-focused Bang and Olufsen, or the Christmas tree excess of 1980s/90s cheap stereo systems. But I'm not interested in their reproductive quality – the point is that allegiance, expenditure, quality and embrace of the industry standard, in all its trimmings, is on show. In fact, Beats and its imitators (or its purchasers for $3 billion, in the case of the industry standard of industry standards, Apple) turn the tide on what was the widening of public sounding of devices – from early mobile phones, to the normalizing of their use, to their use on public transport as audio display machines, a properly pathetic miniaturizing of the boombox. Now the headphone is the display, and the same can be seen in concerts – with the development of a range of in-ear sound delivery objects came a parallel surge in noise-reducing buds, and loud concerts feature the ostentatious display of their use, mimicking the use of onstage earphones used for checking vocal pitch or as more general monitors, or, in some cases, to preserve hearing when close to amplification.

What is this rendering visible of the act of listening about? Is it an assertion of the value of music (or more general listening) in an era that seeks to cheapen it through easy availability? A land grab of listening by tech companies? Sterne observes that the presence in the world of the easily exchanged MP3 format might have removed finance from some parts of the music industry, but it has proved extremely profitable for patent holders, manufacturers and retailers of MP3 and net-friendly devices, telecoms companies and, now, headphone makers. Unwittingly, it is Chris Ruen's anti-downloading polemic, *Freeloading*, that gives us a sense of what the extent of this increase in financial value of music must be.[6] He says that average spending on CDs and other material formats dropped from $71 in 2000 to $26 by 2009, a colossal tailing-off, as opposed to any sort of long tail (*Freeloading*, 8). But, actually, it tells us just how little was ever being spent because the higher figure is one from the year of greatest turnover and profit from musical recorded commodities. The amount being spent on devices, on wireless internet connections, even when we discount the profits made by 'pirates' who are more accurately to be thought of as skip chasers, opportunists, lazy foragers or profit-seeking 'disruptive innovators', means that listening machinery as a whole accounts for huge expenditure in 'listening to music'.[7]

Looking beyond the glee of those who manoeuvred themselves into the right market position by establishing industry-standard formats, it seems that demand is truly there – people want to pay. As pro-downloaders guess of their fellows, they do want to pay for something. Sadly, they would rather not pay the 'content provider', and if they don't get round to paying, they used to go to a concert and pay for that (some used to believe that downloading individuals spent more on music, as Ben Goldacre claimed, in the course of his talking down the losses made by the music industry in the early 2000s).[8] In fact, streaming means that plenty of people get paid, but if streamers actually bought more music there would have been an exponential growth in sales of music itself, as opposed to a reduction to a fraction of the 'golden years'. But concert sales and whatever music is still being sold is increasingly only of meaning to already established or in-house media corporation artists. People want to spend money on listening, not on music. In fact, this reterritorialization, its radical machine capitalism, is a sort of resistance to dematerialization: the headphone becomes a way of refusing the absence of objects – listeners have not been weaned nearly as much as we think. Only their fetish is no longer in sound: if that sound is in file form or format, then the desirable object (playback machine, headphone, new phone, watch) is (in) a container that retains value, unlike a purchase of actual music, which is essentially valueless a few days after – or before – release. Much more than triumphalist vinyl junkies, Beats-cradled listeners have erected a barrier to piracy by renovating the commodity. Unfortunately, that also means they have something worth stealing, as early adopters of iPods found through identifying their ownership via the white buds.

Can listening be stolen? Music-making can be, music production can be, but what exactly is worth stealing in 2020 other than listening devices – preferably ones that can have other functions? Can listening be seen and recommodified as spectacle – in your own 'home'? You can give instruction and have music played to you by a generic and basic AI, or have a shuffled playlist delivered in a range of devices, even by your fridge. Maybe the moving display that are (or were?) in-ear and conspicuously over-ear 'phones will be replaced by the audiovisual or transmedia spectacle of hearing people asking an AI to play them something and then responding. The spectacle of audiovisuality has been taken over by the extremely young on public transport who terrify commuters with repetitive and harshly electronic games and TV shows. They are the ones who have brought back listening and noisy hearing to the realm of commodified viewing of others' listening.

The Restoration: Vinyl and the Dying Market

After years of silence about vinyl in the mainstream press, you can barely hear yourself over the excitement generated by the massive and seemingly continual upsurge in record sales.[1] For so long the province of fans and listeners boxed into the slightly sinister category of 'audiophile', vinyl is breaking free, coming out. All the people who were puzzled by its persistence as a format, if indeed they knew it was still there, who had followed industry instructions to abandon the LP and embrace the CD and then the (legal) download, and now the sanctioned formats of streaming, rush to the 'record store' to buy LPs to file alongside box sets. Younger listener/purchasers eschew the dematerialized and low-grade MP3 and associated formats in favour of an object that comes complete with the fetish fun of actually handing over money. Finally, the sonic, visual and moral value of the format that was the vessel for the golden era expansion of the music industry can be recognized as an evolutionary highpoint.

These should be happy times for the vinyl advocate, and Dominik Bartmanski and Ian Woodward's 2014 book *Vinyl* celebrates the new type of materialist avant-garde that comes not from being first but from surviving long enough in a set of niches to emerge as a potentially dominant species in the ecoaudiomarket.[2] Independent producers, music fans, DJs, underground labels and shops kept the format alive, through 12-inch singles in particular, keeping the record presses in business in the lean times (*Vinyl*, 21–23, 166).

The spread of the CD in 1982–83 saw off vinyl and cassette to become the dominant format by the end of the 1980s. In the UK at that time, a new album cost more or less double the price to buy (typically £11.99 compared to £5.49–£6.99), and cost significantly less to produce, so the profit acceleration was considerable. Not only that, but listeners could be coaxed into buying a supposedly superior version of something they already had. Tower Records,

Earlier version posted on excentrics.org.

then a dominant international player in selling music, led the stores' attack on vinyl by removing LPs from sale in the course of 1990 (Tower stores today are heavily loaded with vinyl products). I think that in addition to responding to an upsurge in demand for records, music retailers and record companies have identified something very specific: a way to exploit a dying market that has unexpected consequences outside the mainstream industry once we consider the independent, small-scale, DIY and/or experimental parts of music production, and is far from being a beacon for a newly responsible and auditorially superior relationship of purchaser to artist or label.

The revival is a given, it even has its own Wikipedia page.[3] Appealing to the twin demographics of trend-followers and stuck-clock readers of 'the' press, the vinyl resurgence is well charted. The mid-2010s saw the beginning of a tiresome chorus of writers amazed at vinyl's resurrection, and saw Pink Floyd's *The Endless River* (2014) confirm the trend of a move (back) to vinyl and an increase in sales (Pink Floyd are also repeating the permanent presence of *Dark Side of the Moon* [1973] in 1970s charts at the end of the 2010s). In 2015, pop and rock drove sales to the best levels for many years. Much like global warming, year-on-year vinyl sales just keep rising, a force of nature taking its vengeance. In the US, even the boom year of 2014 was outstripped by 30 per cent, and since then *Forbes* has returned to the rich well of over-reporting on vinyl success every few months, and US sales are now around the 10 million mark.[4] The *Guardian* has been more cautious in its regular reporting about what the percentage surge meant in sales relative to the rest of market, likewise on cassettes, which have been infiltrating the noise world for over a decade, and this is now being noticed across the international press.[5]

Midway through 2015, and then again in 2018, it was being noted that vinyl sales were more profitable than paid downloads.[6] What is clear is that vinyl's percentage rise in numerical sales is immense, and as part of music sales its share is increasing, but still tiny. When seen in the broader context of streaming, downloads, ringtones and other tie-ins, it is basically as irrelevant as it has been for three decades. We need more detail about what is happening here, and that detail is not there in the rare sharing of a triumph between capitalist corporations and would be on-trend listener communities.

Where the 1980s saw CDs priced at double the cost of a vinyl LP, and then bloating in length to 'justify' the hike, a new-release vinyl LP is likely to cost up to three times the price of the CD. Heritage music albums, that millions of people bought on CD, possibly more than once, in the form of remasters, deluxe versions, box sets, are now available for the same price as new releases, so in many cases are up to six times more expensive than the CD version. Of course, the records are much more expensive to make, and cannot be churned out at home off a laptop, so are seen as valuable objects. Perhaps the high oil price of recent years has helped keep costs high. But, above all, a driver of price is the difficulty in getting a record pressed. Many vinyl production units were closed down as a result of the success of the CD format, so massive bottlenecks arise on the tiny number of extant machines. New vinyl presses and machines have slowly been introduced to match demand – and this is not decreasing the price. Just as high oil prices make deepwater mining and tar sand dredging profitable, it is the high profits that drive vinyl production. The first consequence of the revival has been that production prices go up and stay up. The second is that access for small-run production becomes nigh on impossible. The third is that rarity of product is maintained, so the high price appears to reflect an internal value.

Another area of detail lies in what people are actually buying. Every major album comes out on vinyl now – and band fetishists of all ages will buy products made by their idols. But the sales of new pop on vinyl are still quite limited compared to rock. And rock is dominated by heritage acts, who previously peddled the line that CD was the only format that was worth using. The heritage act is therefore capable of producing format novelty in three ways: a new album that matches the material quality of those from the 1970s; old albums that never appeared on vinyl from the 1980s or 1990s that are genuinely new objects (though often not mastered adequately for vinyl); or, most pernicious of all, the famous album restored to its proper medium, that can tickle not just a musical nostalgia, but a nostalgia for the act of initial purchase. When I first saw racks of Motörhead albums in Dublin's Tower Records, I fell into some sort of irony/paradox/deconstruction overload. As I flicked through the racks of shiny reissues of all genres, I felt the rising, returning surge of earlier initial encounters (the moment of first buying these albums, but now, right now), not as melancholy but as consumerist farce. This was nothing to do with the excitement of new music – instead of the new object, the ideal fetish object: new but exactly like the one you liked already. Time to get out.

Classic rock acts (and all classic albums in general) constitute a major part of the vinyl revival, monetizing albums yet again, on the back of format authenticity, but it is not just rock. Any major album can now use the authenticity of the niche, and through a few thousand high-price units steal the clothes of the subculture that subsisted at or mostly below those levels. In short, major record producers looked at artists who were immune to market change, but also those who were weathering the storm, and saw the model of the diehard fan, the cult, that had been developed through net communities for avant-garde and struggling touring bands alike, and transposed it to a new income stream for the middle ground. At least, people foolish enough to ditch vinyl albums, or eschew them in favour of the CD, are paying for some of this revival.

The intermediate phase between new underground music that stuck with vinyl and the cash core of £30 albums is the specialist reissue label (such as 4 Men With Beards, or Sundazed). In a way, the new 'revival' attacks those labels more than they directly affect anyone else: in the 1990s, during the nadir of vinyl's commercial viability, numerous independent curators, collectors and fans, in tandem with the crate-digging aesthetic, sought to reissue rare albums that were either unavailable or in such limited numbers as to be prohibitively expensive. Instead of prices in the hundreds, the lost folk or funk album from the 1970s, maybe with extra tracks, could be yours through websites, record fairs and bolder indie shops for £20. These records were like irruptions from parallel universes, not the reappearance of a cathected/connected past, but old/new, an amalgam of times and technologies. The major label's own reprint offshoots transformed this democratizing of access (which also had the virtue of passing on royalties to artists) into a centralizing economy, where, without rights negotiation, further money at high profit rates per unit could *raise* the price of a solid classic. The more archaeological labels continue to operate, as do specialists in global sounds, or in the new marker of experimental listening capital, the soundtrack, and will at least be stocked in a shop amid the classics.

We haven't even got to the coloured vinyl, heavyweight, now double, now triple, now boxed, now re-ordered, remastered, re-produced variants. Like the specialist reprint corner, the visibly rare and attentive object common in avant-garde genres was a mode ripe for mainstream colonization. Combine all these desirable traits in the Queen back catalogue on (admittedly well-chosen) different colour vinyls for *c.* £285, while waiting for Record Store Day (Queen fans who paid a lot more once it was sold out may be frustrated that it was being reissued in 2019, thus diminishing unit rarity value). But in the diminishing marketplace for music (at least in terms of exchanging currency for music), artists in all spheres have upped the prices through producing limited-run objects, reasoning that they should get part of the profit that mostly accrues to second-hand sellers.

Record Store Day has helped the profile of vinyl immensely. This is not the place to comment on its policy with regard to independent music stores (all sales to be paid for in advance, unusual in any period, in this particular business, but lethal in a time of market decline), rather to note how it has fuelled prices in collectable items, with its special limited runs sold out rapidly and sold on again on eBay or discogs. Reissues sell particularly well, odd combinations, and cover versions, too. I do like the appearance of songs on 45 rpm that did not get issued that way the first time. But what I find very curious is the massive retail cost of mainstream records brought out as instant collectors' items, particularly the 7-inch singles.

Singles commonly retail for £10–£15, around €15 in the rest of Europe. Mostly, these have been brought out in runs of 500, some as many as 5,000. When I would get a run of 300 singles pressed in coloured vinyl, with a colour cover, it cost about 5 euro a copy. That would mean a surplus of 10 euro per copy. Of course, it costs way less than that for a 'proper' record company, as once you make 500, the price is more like 3.50 per unit. At 5,000, it is something like €2 at most. So, it seems miraculous that a single by a million-selling 1960s artist, on a client label of a major, in any way 'needs' to sell for six times the cost of production, when small-scale independent labels are lucky to get 1.5 times the much larger outlay.

In fact, very few smaller labels will be bringing out many records, because the dearth of record presses, the high profitability for major and the bigger indie labels, and Record Store Day have meant that many presses will no longer print small runs (GZ media, kept alive by indie, noise, experimental and techno labels in the 'dark years' no longer do runs of less than 500, and now strongly promote their capacity to make ultra-high-quality editions targeting already-established artists). If they do, many months of the year are no-go zones (in the run up to April Record Store Day and, increasingly, for its secondary version in November). Of course, new record presses have been slowly arriving (at massive cost), and one day the last drops of heritage may eventually be squeezed out, but in the meantime the record revival is a way of returning the music industry to aristocratic hierarchy (in parallel to streaming's tendency to centre listeners on what is most popular or 'relevant' to them).

The internet of the late 1990s and early 2000s had enabled highly specialized music production to reach low-level, long-tail sustainability, with record sales feeding touring and vice versa. These niches have been decimated, even though the amount being spent on music is still massive. What has happened is that independent, underground or just more obscure artists have been bled out by the concentration of wealth on the one hand, and the complete absence of financial exchange on the other. When Chris Ruen argued that free access to music meant less would be made (*Freeloading*, 23 and throughout), it seemed true. It would not just be cash-hungry bands that refused to bring out albums, but those who had been purchasers would stop subsidizing private capitalist music hoarders. Since 2012, however, the rules have entirely changed, and money is flowing through exploitative streaming services just as it did in the good old industry days, and into the hands of record companies as well as telecoms, device-makers and so on. Far from being destroyed by the new sharing of music, the music industry culled one set of companies and new ones took over, now using new models of non-tax payment, negligible investment outlay except in cash-harvesting tech, and low to zero royalties, while still charging customers. In the meantime, the underground is hit to a much greater extent by the loss of a key defining mode of delivery, the vinyl record, as part of the supposed success of the format. The resurgence of vinyl is a pinnacle of exploitation of musician and listener alike (no worse than streaming, of course, as far as musicians or as labels are concerned).[7]

Vinyl is a great success, and far more lucrative than its market share suggests, because it mobilizes the niches where previously it only looked to the main phase listening population. It manipulates niche strategies and logics to control a small but increasingly valuable consumer base that is easily targeted. The fading commercial viability of music was ripe for takeover, and it has happened while fans and critics of downloading alike were looking at the past models and busy moralizing about them. Music can properly be described as a dying market because the 'industry' as it was is gone, but what remains is a new scavenger market, not restricted to the upward momentum of prices on eBay, but one where the last remaining opportunities can be seized on by the already financially stable and lean remnants of major companies.

The last days of music as commodity that attracts money will not be about democratization, or anarchic social models, but the manipulation of practices established by such communities (independent labels, musicians and producers in all genres). Some of these small labels will continue to do well, just as authors and publishers still gain something from the monopolization of the written word by one online retailer. Hopefully, the dying market fight for the mainstream will finally expire, and a new equilibrium will arise. In the meantime, the battleground for resources needs to move away from sterile debates about whether music should be free or not, and reflect on where the money is going, where the cultural capital feeds wealth accumulation. Look at how vinyl works in its great resurgence, and you will see a direct mirror, as always with the music business, of current economic trends. Music may circulate for free, but massive profits are being made as new income streams harden into unstoppable flows to the 1 per cent. A few cassette sales or exchanges of releases when bands play concerts for little or no financial exchange are not going to balance this communism for the rich. Music has ended up an exemplary harbinger for change, but, in complete opposition to what Attali said, what was seen in premonitory form was in fact the extractive global capitalism of the broader economy.[8]

11

The Hallucinatory Life of Tape

I

It would be easy to see tape as part of a sequence in the development of increasingly perfect means of reproducing recorded sound. It would take its place after wax cylinders, shellac records, wire; alongside vinyl of varying formats; itself diversifying into four-track, eight-track, elcaset, compact, mini or micro cassettes; and before the digital perfection of CD, minidisc and ultimately digital sound without hard media. Such a view could be substantiated or contextualized within a story of cultural production, of technologies in a wider sense, or of a drive to progress, whether commercially or artistically driven, as Sterne has said, with regard to the situation of sound reproduction and recording in the late nineteenth and early twentieth centuries, and highlights a critical complicity that has built up around 'modernity as modernism' and 'modernity as modernisation' (Sterne, *The Audible Past*, 9–10).

We cannot lose this story of progress, for not only has it been told, it has been heard, many times, before and even now, surrounding the machinery of listening and production, pre-empting it on many occasions (*The Audible Past*, 288). But at the same time, other narratives occur, spawned even within the thrust of perfection. Many critics have come to question perfection as ever having been possible in audio media, and have observed that apparent flaws are often enabling devices for normal functioning.[1] As well as this counter to the sense of perpetual improvement, there is also the question of residue: as the 'perfect sound' leaves one media for another, the now surpassed, superseded media is supposed to die. If it does, its passing can be mourned, and preserved; if it doesn't, then it can be helped, kept on a life-support machine and hopefully

This chapter first appeared, in an earlier version, and still appears, on *Culturemachine*, where it was part of Gary Genosko and Paul Hegarty (eds), *Recordings* (2007), https://culturemachine.net/recordings/.

nursed back to health (like vinyl?). Within the dying of media comes the passing or slow dying of individual units – tapes, records, cylinders, cartridges – all of which decay, and in so doing seem to take on characteristics of having lived. Once digital media arrive as 'other', as cyborg sound, the analogue seems to breathe, however rasping the sound. Nostalgia and melancholy imbue formats in general and individual items with *pneuma* (the essential life force or breath of everything in the universe, according to the Stoics).

These narratives of progress and melancholy are twinned, each necessitating the other. As Sterne notes, the 'obvious' function of early sound recording in preserving individuals' voices, or the voices of dying cultures, was not so obvious at the time because of being unrealizable. In addition, the very preservation meant a 'sound recording did as much to promote ephemerality as it did to promote permanence in auditory life' (*The Audible Past*, 288). Not only was the thing being recorded a pre-emption of its demise and transitoriness (318, 330), the fact of only capturing small moments on fragile media meant that 'the sound recording itself also embodie[d] fragmented time' (310).

Tape works within this narrative of temporality through technology and, of course, has its own material conditions of production and location in consumer culture. Once I have looked at that briefly, I will expand on the idea that tape has its own narrative, its own way of structuring narrative, that is intimately caught up not so much with the economic materiality of its production, but the materiality of its form. This implies a centrality of one narrative: that tape is uniquely oriented to narration, and that this is a narration intimately caught up with human belief in life as an accumulative narrative. Fragmentation, the possibility of cutting and breaking, shadows this, and consistency and failure *inform* each other. Around this, tape coheres in specific modes: the mixtape, the cut tape and the decaying tape.

II

Tape was developed as a viable recording format in 1930s Germany, made its way into recording in late 1940s America, and crossed from professional to domestic use with the invention of the cassette (Philips, 1963), which closed the tape in and made it highly portable. This portability was fully realized with the Sony Walkman (1979). This brought tape to the highpoint of its commercial success, which would fade only with the definitive implantation of the CD as prime consumer format, in the early 1990s (although it had to fight off the minidisc). In the early twenty-first century, it persisted in the form of digital audio tape (DAT) in recording studios, but even here, at least for portable recording, hard disc recorders and industry standard software have more or less edged it out.

Tape's rise is a story of usefulness, portability and durability. Field recordings, studio work, editing all seemed easier. Even if early tape was not of a great standard, it was much easier to duplicate from the outset. Multitrack recording became a normal procedure, as 'for the first time in history, audio could be manipulated as a *physical entity*' (Clancy and Miller, 'CALL Technology for Listening and Speaking', 492).[2] Initially, this involved literally cutting the tape up and reorganizing, through reconnecting the separated bits. John Cage (in his *Fontana Mix* [1958]) and William Burroughs both saw the immense potential in new work from fragments of pre-existing recordings. Radio studios appeared all around Europe and in the United States from the late 1950s, with tape the preferred medium not only of storage but of manipulation. *Musique concrète* had worked with lathe-cut vinyl, and now could open its samples to collage and fragmentation.[3]

In addition to claims of heightened functionality, tape was a way of re-organizing existing material, and so takes centre stage in a history of sampling and ownership of material (culminating, for tape, in the mixtape). It becomes an explicit means of intervention, altering what we think 'intervention' is and who controls it: 'the records, samples and various other sonic material the DJ uses to construct their mix act as a sort of externalized memory that breaks down previous notions of intellectual property and copyright that Western Society has used in the past' (Miller, 'Algorithms', 353).[4] Sterne questions technological determinism that would say a particular technology altered thought or society, arguing that the technology is part of a wider technology, or Foucauldian *épistémè*, but media also carry unexpected outcomes, uses and abuses (in the same way feathers evolved 'because' of the need to keep warm and then turned out to be useful for flying). Something about tape's linearity suggests both fragmentation and the possibility of a restoration of order, ownership, control. Tape is manipulable in ways cylinders and vinyl are not, whilst holding out for continuity. As can be seen in Burroughs and Brion Gysin's cut-ups, tape is a modernist medium: you can fragment, split up, position yourself as losing identity in a fragmentation, and the result will be the appearance of a new, albeit fragmentary, whole.

With the cassette, ownership of material, or of creativity, is stretched further. Where sound experimentalists sought hidden new works that would break out from residues of the existing world, home tape recorders offered the prospect of avoiding the need to purchase pre-recorded musical commodities. It also meant you could record your own material. This combination of compilation and DIY recording is thought of as 'cassette culture' (see Moore, *Mix Tape*), a way around the culture industry, a reappropriation of the means of production. Its apogee is the personal 'mixtape' (itself now commodified in the form of getting already established musicians to prepare their selections for mass-produced CDs).

III

The mixtape is both personal and an expression of technological will to power – an intervention that occurs not outside but against and within power relations that structure music listening. Mostly, though, the mixtape is heralded as a personal expression, even if that communication is based on appropriation. Matias Viegener writes that the mixtape speaks, on behalf of its creator: 'I am no mere consumer of pop culture, it says, but also a producer of it' (in Moore, *Mix Tape*, 35).[5] Indeed, as Moore suggests, the tape is mostly about the maker: 'is there a desire to convert your lover into you?' (43). The mixtape compiles bits of recordings from the producer's collection, and tries to target its audience of one, either through didacticism, showing off, trying to match up interests.[6] It conveys something of the character of the person making it, in theory, as well as being a display of commodity ownership, as opposed to copyright ownership, through creative juxtaposition. This investment (including when the tape is destined for your own use) means the mix takes on the character of a snapshot, and like Barthes's idea of the photographic image, it suggests narratives beyond it.

For Rob Sheffield, '[the mixtape] does a better job of storing up memories than actual brain tissue can do. Every mix tape tells a story. Put them together and they add up to a story of a life' (*Love is a Mix Tape*, 26). Sheffield's book is not an analysis, but a sentimental (without being overly sentimental) memoir of his time with his wife, who died young and suddenly, and is told via a series of mixtapes. The tapes are indexical of other narratives: his life, the life of his wife, a record of his listening at the time, the state of US indie music at various points in the late 1980s and early 1990s, the metanarrative that such a tape can make links to narratives ostensibly external to it (Nick Hornby also suggested the capacity of the mixtape to make these links in his novel *High Fidelity*).[7] When he begins, slightly purply, he writes that 'tonight I feel like my whole body is made up of memories. I'm a mix tape, a cassette that's been rewound so many times you can hear the fingerprints smudged on the tape' (Sheffield, *Love is a Mix Tape*, 12). The tape is not only index, it is charged with being a carrier of being, slowly exhaling that imbued *pneuma* with each playing.

The materiality of the tape seems incidental, its functionality compressing its specificity (this seems to be heightened with tape compared to other media). The composer Alvin Lucier is dismissive of tape (despite making a very significant contribution both to sound art through tape and to a form of narrative working through tape itself, see below):

> I didn't choose tape, I had to, because in order to recycle sounds into a space, I had to have them accessible in some form. Tape, then, wasn't a medium in which to compose sounds, it was a conveyor, a means to record them and play them back one after another in chronological order.
>
> (quoted in Chadabe, *Electric Sound*, 76)

The mixtape is deemed so unreliant on its carrier that it can be separated off, by means of a sub-Cartesian surgical procedure, and reappear as a mixtape, only this time on CD. Moore states simply that CD is the current form of the mixtape (*Mix Tape*, 12). Sheffield, despite basing a whole book on tapes as a way of narrating life stories, writes: 'most mix tapes are CDs now, yet people still call them mix tapes. I can load up my iPod with weeks' worth of music and set it on shuffle to play a different mix every time. I can borrow somebody else's iPod and pack it with songs I think they'd like' (Sheffield, *Love is a Mix Tape*, 24).[8] But, other than using a still-expensive genuine CD recorder, burning CDs removes all possibility of live intervention as the whole stack of files is prepared before recording starts. There is a nostalgic reference in the persistence of the term 'mixtape', but I think above all it is a *forgetting* of tape. The CD respects the materiality and the completeness of the cassette, but maybe today the mixtape playlist, while being sourced more impersonally, is open-ended, open to adaptation. In short, even the stream can be harnessed in a more traditional mode than the CD allows.

Sheffield's statements about the work of a mixtape bear further scrutiny: beyond the simplistic idea of one self-contained, self-aware subject depositing a fractal avatar of him- or herself on tape, to be consumed, communed with by the second self-aware, self-contained subject, we can think of all of these apparently autonomous moments as being caught in circuits of fetishism, all partaking of some mystical essence. Tape, and its mixtape manifestation, are uniquely positioned, as media, to function and/or structure experience this way. Sheffield notes that the mixtape stores up memories better than brain tissue. In saying this, he is coming from the point of view of reliability, of preservation. He does not look into how the mixtape works, so does not see how right his point is: as a fragmentary but connected multiplicity, the mixtape works as a more accurate version of brain functioning and structure (not just an actualization of connections made unconsciously in preparing a tape) that justifies the comparison, and the belief in the more obvious level he explicitly notes. Mixtapes do not tell stories, or, despite Sheffield's explicit view on this, present themselves as unities each with a single story: they are looser, about connectedness, processes of association, not completed tales with a clear ending, moral and purpose.

He also imagines himself as a tape, a body made of tape. Despite his and Moore's protestations, I do not think the same imaginary can occur with a CD, or collection of soundfiles. Tape has a resonance with the body, with life, just as early recording and vinyl resonates with death foretold. This is not to say that tape is more truthful, more organic or better for all that. Nor that it excludes death. Instead, it does death differently, and returns life to its residuality, to being a by-product of destruction and decay, as it dwells within (and continually returns to) that slow dying.

IV

The belief in the transparency of recording media held by *musique concrète* practitioners was not shared by Adorno. Lucier, Pierre Schaeffer and to some extent Cage saw tape, even, or especially, when cut and re-edited, as almost absent as medium, feeling they were dealing with sound itself.[9] Adorno looked to the record as a social object, gathering the family as a social unit around the gramophone player (Adorno, 'The Curves of the Needle', 272).[10] Music itself was trapped, reified, just like a photograph. The record presents neither the time of music (as an authentic structuring of time) nor a static representation of that actual time of playing, but something odder, with 'time as evanescence, enduring in mute music' (Adorno, 'The Form of the Phonograph Record', 279).[11] The record is not listened to all the time, and even if you did do that, it would be to the cost of all other records. The actual form of the record itself helps construct these functions. In terms of the social reiteration of the family it structures, it is not just the joint presence around the hearth, but also, he says, because it reflects our wish to see ourselves reflected, and brought into some kind of permanence in so doing:

What the gramophone listener actually wants to hear is himself, and the artist merely offers him a substitute for the sounding-image of his own person, which he would like to safeguard as a possession. The only reason that he accords the record such value is because he himself could also be just as well preserved.

(Adorno, 'The Curves of the Needle', 274)

Adorno is reasonably neutral in making this particular statement, but it is surrounded by the continual insistence on the inauthenticity of such behaviour, and its part in helping the culture industry replace what he sees as real cultural activity. But it also tells us of a relation between subject and technology that is itself a 'technology of self'. The record plays out selfhood and a relation to time that continually returns to mortality, and this despite its aim to distract us from thought (in Adorno's view). The record itself conjures mortality through the spiral of the groove:

[the theologian] may also tend to hold that the truth-content of art only arises to the extent that the appearance of liveliness has abandoned it; that artworks only become 'true', fragments of the true language, once life has left them; perhaps even only through their decline and that of art itself. It would be, then, that in a seriousness that is hard to measure, the form of the phonograph record could find its true meaning: the scriptal spiral that disappears in the centre, in the opening of the middle, but in return survives in time.

(Adorno, 'The Form of the Phonograph Record', 280)

Adorno uses the figure of 'the theologian' to indicate a return of archaic thinking summoned by reflection of the medium of the record, and, far from criticizing this, seems to be suggesting the record encourages this, whether this is a good thing or not, and therefore provides a legitimate technology for thinking the self. We should not be misled into thinking Adorno wants us to meditate on the inevitability of death being like a record reaching its end, but instead recall Nietzsche's eternal return, and, again, not in the banality of getting up and putting the record on again. Instead, the record at every moment contains its ending but cannot close it off (except perhaps in a locked groove, but this would be another version of eternal return anyway); and every time it ends it contains the possibility of coming to be.

Tape can be read similarly, in terms of the ending of a tape, and both record and tape offer the possibility of restoration or a living-on when turning sides, but not all tape offers the spectacle of its own demise and/or living-on. Open-reel tapes can show you how long is left and even unspool without destroying the tape. Cassettes offer a murkier version of this. But we should recall that, for Adorno, the record does not invoke mortality in the form of an eternal return because we can see how long is left, or that there will be an end at some point. In the record, it is the inevitability of tracing a path that can only end in nothing that does the work of this phenomenological machine. The tape, however, carries the promise of a continual loop, with death a break in that, rather than something coming. Tape does not have the tragic being-unto-death as an explicit part of its working, and instead signals decay and/or disruption.

Beckett's play *Krapp's Last Tape* of 1958 sees the eponymous Krapp mostly sitting at a table replaying tapes of himself talking. From the numbering system he uses, it is clear that huge chunks of his life must be here, on tape. But what we hear contains little or no content, in terms of events, consisting, instead, of observations, a large number of which concern the process of recording, of living-on as recording. The only identity he has is through recording, and this identity is very little, as identities go. This is life as reduction, but where reduction is the only means available for anything to almost be, or seem to have been. The 'last tape' of the title signals that the life, as the tape, as this tape, will end. But the ending has already occurred, in the form of the silence that ends the principal tape listened to, from '30 years ago', which plays on through the end of the play, so can never end, as the silent tape runs on, rather than finishing (Beckett, *Krapp's Last Tape*, 223).[12] The Krapp present before us is already gone, already integrated into tape and the decay it *contains*. Not only that, but the Krapp in front of us has yet to come, as the 'action' is set in the near future.

Krapp and Beckett are aware of the metaphysics of tape, beyond its ability to commemorate, store, simulate etc. Krapp often refers with delight to the spool, or even 'the spooool' (216). Tape is not just a metaphor for life, but a reflection, an equivalent, alternative version: the continual spooling of tape the safety of human linear living, but always carrying the threat of interruption, of ending unexpectedly, just as much as it might end at a clearly signalled moment. Krapp himself interrupts the tape on several occasions, fast-forwarding, sometimes pausing, but always as a reaction rather than because of some worldly interruption. Even as he 'cuts' the tape, he is forming and re-forming his relation to it, and himself as relation to it.

Krapp is also working through a model of memory where, despite the apparent linearity or sequence of tapes and comments he has compiled, access is more intuitive, more arbitrary. Beyond these fairly obvious philosophical ideas lies the question of the subject's relation to recording, of how the spool structures consciousness and access to same. The spool itself suggests a core, a point (birth? death? deconstructed subjectivity? the excluded middle?) around which life accumulates at an even pace. At the end, a linear narrative will have come to be, through the tape's winding. This winding of the tape itself separates tape from the winding on a record: there is less of a possible mind/ body divide, as the ravelling is simultaneously of both sound and tape. Krapp's glee around the 'spooool!' suggests that he spools around the spindle of the body of tapes that is him, adding another possibility to the meaning of the central spool (around which the tape winds): here the spool (not the tape itself spooling) is the life, a life now only an absence turning amidst something else that seems to acquire solidity (and this the most ephemeral element, as it is words spoken in the past).

V

Krapp, and tape, Krapp and tape, and the playing of tape, the playing of Krapp and the listening of Krapp combine into something more, or significantly less, than a subject (Krapp) listening to an object (his voice, the tape) through another machine (the recorder/player). This then approaches Deleuze and Guattari's body without organs, or, even more closely, Lyotard's 'libidinal band'. Lyotard himself is keen to distinguish this 'band' (a sort of Moebius strip combining bodies, sounds, movements, objects etc. into a continually circulating surface)[13] from other 'bandes' or tapes: the libidinal is not inscribed or marked into something else, because such marking 'implies an aspect [catégorie] of accumulation, storing up, and material memory, and, which is more of the same, diachrony' (Lyotard, *Economie libidinale* [Libidinal Economy], 25).[14] But neither is tape – Krapp's, or anyone else's. Tape is constantly moving along a path that crosses with listening and recording subjects, such that these become tape, at some level, and will now have always been, less the controllers than that which has been wound, will be wound. Becoming tape is neither becoming something that is recorded on, nor just *like* a tape. It is a process that begins with the mechanical realization of technological sound reproduction. From that point on, mirroring, recording, simulating, storing, preserving are all not merely life (or the keeping alive of what is now dead) but a full interaction of death and life as dual processes, one held off by the promise of the infinite reel, the other held off by the promise of the ending that will come at a given moment.

Krapp is a model of intervention that gets immersed, losing agency even as action/activity occurs, but Burroughs seems to offer a way of mobilizing tape against itself. Deleuze and Guattari point to resistance happening through breakdown, disruption and interference (*Anti-Oedipus*, 31).[15] Burroughs himself uses 'tape recorder technology' as 'part of a larger project, which he conceives of most often not in terms of experiment or play but of warfare' (Lydenberg, 'Sound Identity Fading Out', 414).[16] Like so many others, Burroughs does not attribute any agency or specificity explicitly to the medium of tape, but Lydenberg is too hasty in merely seeing tape as a means to an end, a transparent support – making tape just like the paper Burroughs cuts up elsewhere. This means that voice is the medium (as writing is) (426), and it too can be cut up like written words. But we can read Burroughs's use of tape as something much richer, and the role of tape as more important than we might suspect. Burroughs and Gysin developed the cut-up in the 1950s, as tape was spreading as a medium. The cut-up is not only ideally suited to tape, it is as if they emerge as parallel and adjacent parts of the same technology. Each takes the failing of language to reveal new meanings and suggest new possibilities. Later, in the 1960s, through to the 1980s, Burroughs writes often on the revolutionary potential of tape recorders and the manipulation of recordings, particularly live ones recontextualized (Lydenberg's chapter offers a comprehensive summary of those writings). Unlike cut-ups in text form, tape recordings or, more accurately, tape and tape recorders, can react to new settings and events. Burroughs recommends directing public events through near-subliminal juxtaposition of, say, political speeches and the sounds of animals or riots. The key to this is not just to multiply sound sources and confuse a gathering, but to cut different recordings in order that new meanings and imperatives can be heard. Ideally, you would intersperse sounds from around you with other recordings, and this would be done through fast-forwarding and recording over parts of the existing track. This process is not just the same as the cut-up, it is a more profound version, that can only exist on (more accurately *as* or *via*) tape. Arguably, the whole model of disruption through cut-up relies on a metaphysics of tape, as outlined above, where the linear must always be asserted, but intervention or interference is a constant risk for that linearity and a necessity (because without it, no recording).[17]

At one level, Burroughs's tapes and textual cut-ups are very much an extension of the project of the classic modernist novel, where fragmentation is the new truth. At another, though, Burroughs's fragmentation never even resolves as an answer: instead we have many answers, many assertions, multiple assessments, all undermining one another. The fragmentation that occurs through tape is resolutely anti-linear: i.e. it does not ignore linearity, but replaces it with a parodic version, whether through splicing or picking random moments of a tape in which to insert new recordings. Tape will always exceed the intention of its operator, as unnoticed sounds make their way on to the tape (Burroughs, 'Electronic Revolution', 137).[18] As this occurs, the listener is running his own tape recording, which has been edited in real time: 'the sound has been erased according to a scanning pattern which is automatic' (ibid.). Far more than Lyotard suspects, his 'band' translates into tape, at least when tape reveals its non-functioning, limits, ends etc., that it relies on for functionality.

VI

As is well known, Burroughs regards language as a virus that has invaded humanity, making humans dual creatures, alienated from a more interesting (not necessarily truer) universe. Language is a parasite, benefiting from human activity and directing it. Tape could be seen as a way in which language solidifies its hold, imposing a simple linearity on experience. Hence, the cut-up as a way of disrupting this. The cutting-up of tape is not just the written cut-up by other means – it is a deeper operation, not because it operates with voice instead of writing, but precisely because it operates through a prosthetic living, a prosthetic speaking, both of which emphasize that there is only ever prosthesis when it comes to the ideas or conditions of living. The cut-up intervenes directly in the symbiotic evolution of recording and the human.[19] It refuses the immunity of inoculation (i.e. living with recording, accepting linear, spool-based life) and replaces it with a constant test situation. Disrupting the 'natural' progress of recording methods in order to illustrate the chance elements and the 'flaws' in systems that allow operation, cutting up tape, literally or otherwise, takes tape into the realm of recombinant DNA. This might seem an obvious and only metaphorical connection, but the working of DNA occurs very much within the thinking induced by tape as medium.[20]

A superficial connection also exists between the double helix of the DNA molecule and a reel of tape, but more interesting is the connection suggested by the presence of mitochondrial DNA, which Lyn Margulis suggests is an 'endosymbiotic' element, having initially invaded the cell hundreds of millions of years ago.[21] DNA is affected by this extraneous but contained other, and once together the structures need each other. Cutting and splicing is not a new phase, but does alert us to the interdependency of linearity 'objectively stored' in recorded form and the sense of continuity and living on in expectation of a linear end, and that this is not inevitably how it was always going to turn out, nor is recording a progressive evolution toward the best, but a more non-linear and fully *hazardous* path.

At a literal level, this can be seen in the succession of forms of recording media. For commercial reasons, inferior media have often succeeded over 'superior' ones (VHS over Betamax, MP3 over other digital formats). This is not always due to the choices made by corporations and struggles between them, but due to unexpected popularity of formats, or rejection of others (such as disc-based video formats). In hindsight, this is always justified as the outcome of a rational competition, based on utility and fitness. But the only fitness is survival (survival does not prove superiority), everything else is ideology and hindsight (even if this is all we have). Therefore, we do not need to reject an evolutionist history of recording, but reconfigure it. In addition to recording media helping us to recall Darwin's thought of what fitness actually means, we need to refer to the idea of ecosystems: individual 'species' do not struggle against everything else. If nothing else, the highly corporatized history of recording means that the capitalist economy prevents a war of all against all it claims to want, in favour of the equally Hobbesian Leviathan of oligopoly. Any apparent competition cements incorporated power and profit. All formats, in machine and 'digital' phases, feed into the success of player-machines. Tape cohabits with vinyl, helping establish a dominant form of, or for, stereo equipment. It has an uneasy relation to the eight-track cartridge, as these look to the same resources, but eight-track can be adapted to play tapes through a further cartridge. More recently, cassette players in cars are given a life-saving prosthesis to connect to CD players, and then to iPods, in the form of a mimetic cartridge empty of tape. Cassette as coral.

Tape has yet to become redundant – it has even recovered from its endangered status – and just as new species do not abolish 'older' ones, tapes live on, infesting houses and cars, their primary exoskeleton preserving slowly rotting insides. Survival rates are often higher without the decorative coverings that house the cassette. Decay is a fundamental part of tape's existence, due to the presence of oxides that initially fixed the recording. But, crucially, the inside and outside do not necessarily die at the same pace.

VII

Tape's ironic fate is that recordings made on it need preserving on new media. This is not necessarily due to the quality of playback, but the *effect* of playback on the medium. Restoration and preservation offer new niches for what at least were tape recordings. Awareness of tape ecology has moved on considerably since the BBC threw out huge portions of master tapes, or recorded over them some thirty years ago. But outside of this transfer of tape into simulation, with its apologies for variable levels and quality, and heritage-style references to the initial conditions of recording, tape persists differently, or its life is examined differently.

Like the alien in the eponymous film series, tape lives on in space despite attempts to destroy it. The Voyager spacecraft run tape recording systems which record plasma, plasma wave and low energy charge particles. This digital tape is based on 1963 technology and was launched in 1977. It continued to work for over thirty years, and it was only due to communication limits that it was to be switched off in 2010.[22] This tape has lasted so well thanks to being outside of earth's atmosphere, but perhaps also because of its specific mode of functioning, which is to be permanently recording, transmitting and erasing, whilst in continual movement.[23] The Voyager tapes constitute a far more human artefact than the more famous gold disc with its images, sound recordings etc., which is also on board, for aliens to find. The tape's operation will reveal much more of how humans predominantly construct their existence. Whilst the tapes interact with us (through transmission of data), it is as if some human presence lingers at the outer limits of the Solar System. But the tape has not only travelled many multiples of miles further than humanity, it will persist cryogenically. Ideally, an error might restart it at some point, as it records and sends data, futilely, as far as we are concerned, through increasingly emptier space.

VIII

Alvin Lucier explored the saprophytic possibilities of tape in his *I am sitting in a room* (1969), but seems oblivious to the specificity of tape in producing this effect. A more satisfying and less conceptualized work that looks at tape recording in decay is William Basinski's *The Disintegration Loops* from 2001. Whilst engaging in the preservation mode, archiving old recordings, Basinski soon realized that the tape loop itself was disintegrating: as it played round and round, the iron oxide particles were gradually turning to dust and dropping into the tape machine, leaving bare plastic spots on the tape, and silence in these corresponding sections of the new recording (*The Disintegration Loops*, liner notes). This creates a seemingly elegiac piece, as the tape plays itself decaying through the medium of the sound decaying (in terms of the new recording). It is not just being saved or preserved, though, because the saving is performing the destruction. This recording is not just about endings, then, but process, decay and the necessity of decay potential in allowing tape to act as recorder.

Over sixty-three minutes the track 'd|p 1.1' gradually solidifies into clusters of increasingly noise-filled lumps as the structure loses definition. The warm, short phrases give way very quickly to their own breakdown. Specific pressure points appear, and those sections of the loop lead the decay. But for long periods the tape seems to be only very sedately disintegrating (this is probably just as much due to this listener getting used to a process and imagining it as constant). The erosion is geological, water dripping on rock, but more accurately it is biological.[24] The tape is the reiteration of its basic process until it can no longer sustain it, and having declined at a much more rapid pace (after forty minutes, and again toward the end). So there is the catastrophe of sudden collapse, as the disintegration is not fully constant. The music is gradually submerged in its own decay, its definition lost. Only a suggestion of its momentum/rhythm persists. Sounds get less distinct. *The Disintegration Loops* mark their own passing, make their own passing happen, and, for Basinski listening in 2001, they mark the passing of his past, and of the lives of people killed in the World Trade Center attacks. They can only do this through tape, and through tape as transferred to another medium. As well as marking the conditions in which tape can work, 'd|p 1.1' marks the passing of tape, but not its end, rather its mutation and persistence in its failing.

Part Four

Undermined

The final section of the book addresses a range of specific examples, beginning with a chapter that stays with the materiality of sound production and listening, through locating Joy Division's 'sound effects' (devised by Martin Hannett) as the essential device that connects them to late 1970s gloom, and how, in so connecting, these sounds undermine the value attached to 'proper' production values. The next two chapters deal with what are now virtually legacy experimental/noise acts: the chapter on Organum centres on their 7-inch releases, as a way into thinking noise as the uncanny. David Jackman, as the person behind Organum, plays with the difference between 'David Jackman' and 'Organum', whilst experimenting with the materiality of the single, especially the 45 rpm record. The uncanny spatiality of Organum's records is transposed into a skewed temporality of 'versioning'. The following chapter, on Nurse With Wound and The New Blockaders, is not only about their work, but also the idea of influence and the cover version. Since the first version of this chapter was published, it has featured on the inner sleeve on Nurse With Wound's re-imagining of The New Blockaders's debut album, adding to the idea of noise as 'version'. The penultimate chapter is about metal, but it is more directly about Dante's epic poem *Commedia*, particularly its opening volume *Inferno*. It uses black metal theory and metal to look at the sonic comparison of heaven and hell made by Dante, and to say that his model is ultimately a heretical one. In the context of noise as a whole, this essay is not so much about noisy music or even the cacophony in Dante's book, but how metal and Dante can be read together through a perverse hearing. The closing chapter, on harsh noise and harsh noise wall, extends the exuberant metalification of netherworlds into the often thwarted desire to consume noise so as to make it familiar, digestible and ultimately excretable. All noise needs emptying, including attempts to make it palatable as a positive gesture. The painfully inevitable return to harsh noise wall completes a running thread where noise not only reveals the nothingness around it, it dissolves its own truths. If 'we' can all leave here with no positive model of a noise that just is, or is generative through a positive process, or is a tool in some way, then 'we' will all have got nowhere.

Supplementing (in) Joy Division, *Unknown Pleasures*

The culture industry has always liked to 'do it clean', to make the surface smooth and shiny, so that the object and commodity can disguise themselves in the apparently pure listening experience of a properly produced piece of music. Studio intervention grew to be commonplace, particularly when labels looked for (and marketed) a specific sound, or when executive producers sought to maximize the appeal of a new pop release. But even in the 1960s, such practices became more formalized, allowing star producers and sound directors to emerge, such as Berry Gordy or Phil Spector. The more interventionist the producer (or non-artist involved in the recording process), the greater the danger of noise entering the circuit. Whilst this topic – the studio as noise-generating input – has rich potential in its own right, here the focus is on one producer, one record, and, within that, two tiny instantiations of production that reveal the supplementarity of production, and thereby introduce noise into all production.

If most record companies looked to smooth the surface of the sounds of their records so it sounded like nothing had happened, so it sounded like an artist's inner soul appeared by magic on a piece of plastic and entered the ear and then the heart of the communicant listener, this was not true everywhere. From the end of the 1960s on, dub was at the forefront of musical experimentation through production. More than the studio wizards and string-drenchers of pop and rock, more than the psychedelic border nudging in psych and early prog rock, dub's method consisted of a

> deconstructive manner in which [these] engineers remixed reggae songs, applying sound processing technology in unusual ways to create a unique pop music language of fragmented song forms and reverberating soundscapes.
>
> (Veal, *Dub: Soundscapes and Shattered Songs in Jamaican Reggae*, 2)[1]

Earlier version presented at *Atrocity Exhibition: A Symposium on Joy Division*, in 2015.

Dub made the sound of material production audible, and removed the conceits of the song itself, of the authentic musician, or the factory-style production of hits, in a complex renegotiation of sounds where artists often got lost, layered and pasted away, or transformed completely. While dub played with the structure of sound, and did feed into punk to some extent (as Veal notes), it certainly could be heard in post-punk, which came after a powerful surge in popularity of reggae in Europe. This is not what Joy Division had in mind when engaging Martin Hannett after some disappointing studio experiences (notably with the 'Ideal for Living' EP made whilst still going under the name Warsaw).

The role of producer Martin Hannett in the making of their first album, *Unknown Pleasures*, from 1979, is controversial, not least due to the band's 'mixed' views on it. Hannett's sound is a perversion of the smoothing of mainstream rock producers so active in the 1970s, but it is still some sort of 'scaping', an attempt to mould disparate and angry songs into a unified sonic entity. Hannett took it upon himself to be very proactive in the recording, mix and soundworld of the album – so much so that Peter Hook and Bernard Sumner could barely recognize the sound they heard when Joy Division played. As Hook says,

> Ian [Curtis] and Steve [Morris] loved it. Me and Barney [Sumner] hated it. We thought it was too weak ... All the things I now love about the album – the spacey, echoey ambient sound of it – were all the things I hated about it when I first heard it.
>
> (Hook, *Unknown Pleasures*, 156)[2]

Sumner's own account in *Chapter and Verse* is similar, emphasizing how he thought that Hannett had taken away Joy Division's power, and on numerous occasions over the years both musicians have confirmed their initial view and also how they came to understand Hannett's produceriness.[3] Even with the benefit of long hindsight, Sumner insists that Hannett was looking 'to twist the sound of the album from its original inception [*sic*] closer to his own vision'.[4] Although Morris has said that 'at the time I couldn't see the point of [Hannett's production additions]', Curtis and Morris appreciated the unexpected elements and the sonic experimentation, with both keen on the industrial sound and music of Throbbing Gristle.[5]

What was seen by some (not least, by half of the band) as an emasculation is seen by others, and by critical posterity, to be a key part of the album's success. Hannett took the sounds of Joy Division, took them apart (for example recording the parts of the drum kit separately), added electronic instruments and effects – most notably in the relentless use of digital delay. He also added some sound effects, which seem not to have been taken very seriously, either by the band or by listeners. Partly this is due to some suspicions about their presence, partly a wariness to attribute too much of a role to Hannett, and, above all, because what they do is something oddly complex in how they refer the sound of *Unknown Pleasures* back to the misery of the Britain of 1978–79. What they say is something separate to biographical or machinic accounts of intentionality, and something more technological, more artefactual and more ruinous.

The role of the producer in rock music was a vexed one in the late 1970s. Seen by record companies as the enforcer of commercial potential, seen by bands as no more than another part of the engineering process, there was also suspicion of the role precisely because of exceeding either of these. There were superstar producers, fifth members of well-known bands, enforcers of label aesthetics, hit-makers, moulders of stars but, principally, the task of producing was one of disciplining sound and individuals. As the 1970s progressed, major rock bands expanded their songs not only in time but also vertically, in the number of tracks taken up in the recordings. Stadium, glam, prog, heavy rock, all built their bombast and augmented group-level virtuosity through the use of the studio. In the course of this, it was not only complexity that emerged but also clarity. Nowhere was production smoother than in the hands of engineer Alan Parsons, knob-twiddling Pink Floyd into a frictionless blanket on *Dark Side of the Moon*, or in the shiny debauchery of West Coast rock. Conscious use of production 'values' also helped define dub, disco and the vapid noodlings of proto-ambient electronic music. Only punk stood firm (it thought) against the planing away of rock's apparently authentic values. This return of 'authenticity' – a back-to-basics approach, as also advocated by the right-wing Conservative party in Britain – of restoring the energy and aggressive attack of the unmediated, was central to punk's myth-making and its popularity.

High production values also came at a financial cost: studio equipment, time, employees, arrays of new instrumentation to use in tiny flourishes … and this was often happening far from Britain as rock stars sought to flee phenomenally high tax rates. Certainly, this golden commercial age for music led to profiteering and also the distancing of the most popular musicians from their fans. Punk would establish a different way: simple tunes, simple technique (if any), loudness and, above all, a rejection of what came before it. That this, too, was not exactly true does not matter, what counts is the way in which a rejectionist ideology acted as a musical technology, just as much as any distortion pedal or shouting.

Punk's trading of authenticity as a commodity is well known, and we would be wrong to think of it as only Malcolm McLaren's fault. For Stewart Home, punk was all about the sell-out, the letdown, the failure.[6] Authenticity was a false value to pin on punk. What is peculiar about Hannett's production of Joy Division is how an overt level of 'falsity' of something extraneous is able to bring the music toward a more authentic expression. In this it is a perfect supplement, the equivalent of the ivory false teeth that sixteenth-century essayist Michel de Montaigne says bring about physical beauty, and that Derrida takes to be the only way truths, origins, meanings circulate.[7] In other words, we are stuck with supplements, not to the detriment of authenticity, but because of it and in order to have it. It is tempting to say Hannett, or any producer keen on their own ideas, merely 'brings something out' of what is already there, but it is that 'bringing out' that puts the 'what is already there' into place, and so this exists retrospectively, as if it was always already there. Perhaps this is what Ian Curtis heard, and why over time the lyrics and song structures move toward the spatialization favoured by Hannett.

The 'what is already there' is also a gesture to the material, as well as to materialism and materialist critique. The material or sound matter are sounds that stand in for that which exists outside music, and brought in to give credence to their connection to a real they displace.[8] This threatens the authenticity of music even as it adds to it, as it troubles the border between artistic creation and contingent or submitted reality. On *Unknown Pleasures*, the introjection of sounds – the lift in 'Insight', or glass smashing in 'I Remember Nothing' – are carriers not just of a message of 'the real', but also of the materialist context of music – i.e. modern music (or any, perhaps) does not emerge fully formed in an explosion of energy that expresses feeling or sense, instead any such effect is the product of the studio, even when ostensibly rejected in lo-fi, live or in some way limited form (like 'unplugging'). This is made present to the listener (including the band), with the audible intervention of the producer, particularly when it concerns sounds that are non-musical in origin and then moved into being part of a composition (more so in 'I Remember Nothing' with the reiteration of the sounds of smashing). This intervention shows the rootedness in the material culture of the recording process and industry. These are in turn caught up in an economically materialist world where costs and profit accrue before, during and after the studio session.

Material here is therefore threefold: the matter of sound, the material and proximate context of the recording activity, and the embedding of both of these in what is sometimes presumed to be the base of materialism, the capitalist economy. I think the sounds of lifts and glass smashing accrue a fourth term, and that is the base materialism suggested by Georges Bataille in the late 1920s, as a way of rethinking the material world beyond Marxist critique but in a way that still undermined mainstream presumptions of the inherent goodness and rectitude of matter and materialism.[9] Base materialism reminds us of all that is low, of the process of lowering music into sound or even noise, and the reassertion of base motivations within the 'good' materialism of the restricted, merely financial economy.

Base materialism does not ignore economic critique – far from it – but its mode of critique is seemingly more abstract, a parodying or a troubling of correct social order, as opposed to the literalist and therefore, paradoxically, actually more abstract denunciations of punk when it has a message. Joy Division played with signs, sought to transgress acceptable norms, and Hannett's *musique concrète* is part of this, a play of the referent.

This referential world, of 1970s Britain, in the grip of economic struggle and gloom, is there in Joy Division's writing, playing, visuals and concepts, but it is too tempting to see their music as rising above, floating free of it. Or to see it, on the other hand, as a straightforward reflection on the malaise of a society losing its bearing as a once-dominant colonizing power, as the new realities of globalization and challenges to earlier conservative habits take hold. Between these two amorphous ways of connecting the music to the real world of 1979 is a more direct one, and this connection occurs in the presence of the extraneous sounds in 'Insight' and 'I Remember Nothing'.

I am not interested in the abstraction of the referential Britain into the lyrics of *Unknown Pleasures,* or even its musical form, but its supplemental not-quite presence in those tracks – especially as the band were not paying too much attention to what was around them except in their direct vicinity. The industrial unrest that is there to be heard in *Unknown Pleasures* was something of which Sumner says, in Derrida style, 'we weren't to know that at the time' (*Chapter and Verse,* loc 1671). In the winter of 1978–79, British society was in thrall to economic civil war, at the same time as tension was rising in working-class areas, leading to mass riots in 1981, after numerous instances of racist and counter-racist fighting before. In the winter of 1978, massive pay demands by trades unions representing the public sector ended up with the army on the street, in a weird counter-revolution of enforced scab service provision, in their green goddess fire engines, or ready to inter the unburied dead, or ensure the distribution of fuel to hospitals and other key social, economic or military sites.

Government and workers were caught up in an inflationary spiral potlatch, with massive price rises leading to equally impressive wage demands (or vice versa, as conservatives would have it). While the memory of oil and petrol shortages (from 1973 on) that enlivened some people's childhoods with the three-day week, power cuts and bonus school holidays was still fresh, in fact petrol should have been the answer: Britain was now swimming in the stuff, with North Sea oil available for governmental and government-sponsored plunder. In the two-month period between recording and releasing *Unknown Pleasures*, Margaret Thatcher's Conservative party was voted in to power and became the vanguard of communism for the rich, redistribution of wealth upward, through deregulation and privatization and lower tax rates for high-income earners. But the end was already happening before that. From afar, it seems the only logic-based explanation for the collapse of a leading industrial nation lies in a malignant conspiracy of unions and governments to remove the people from the world of work. Unemployment rose rapidly, and all the wage gains were wiped out in inflation and never stopped the deeper problem of relative deprivation.

In other words, from whichever political position you can adopt, inequality was on the rise, and this led to divisions within trades where there were varying levels of skill requirement, and between sets of workers in different roles or sectors, all pitted against each other. Areas of urban society were progressively isolated, caught up in cycles of reducing hours, skill mismatch, and just not being part of the culture of a city. Housing estates and tower blocks would increasingly house a hopeless population kept at arm's length from gains of some sectors. Vast expanses of post-war utopian rebuilding were already collapsing, or in need of demolition (e.g. asbestos). Manchester was somewhere between these moments of dereliction – building the high rises even as it was becoming clear elsewhere that this model for living was not working. The services which were to link these planned communities to the rest of the city dwellers fell away, even a Labour government saw no value in extending an equal level of protection to its poor, to its immigrant areas or to those entering the brave new world of structural redundancy.

The lift in 'Insight' is more (or less) than a real machine in a recording studio – it takes on acousmatic form, that is, separate from its source, and takes on signification beyond the 'sound as puzzle' of the sound effect. The fading in of the track, over the functioning of the lift, shows Joy Division emerging from the brutalist dream of concrete as new natural material, of height as the new land, or the displacement of property into stacking, holding patterns. The sliding of the lift indicates the smooth operation of high-rise living, but its presence and the prospect of its failing haunts dwellers of the upper storeys. Bernard Sumner, Paul Morley and Jon Savage have all commented on *Unknown Pleasures* inhabiting a place from where the decay of social utopias arises crisp and clear, but it gets further in to that rotting utopia through the sound of something other than music, 'defining not only a city but a time' (Savage, *Heart and Soul*, liner notes).[10] The lyrics describe an overcoming of alienation or, better still, a conscious dwelling in alienation such that even if you are 'not afraid any more', you still 'keep your eyes on the door'. Neither ethereal nor mired in reiterations of the shouted complaint, 'Insight' embeds singer, band and listener around the lift-shaft of an upward-looking new society that instead runs monotonously, a machine at the heart of dwelling, or that falters in a premonition of the post-work world that lies ahead of 1979. The lift is the device that promises liberation but in 'Insight' it brings us in, its cage door closing us into the song.

The narrator of 'Insight' asserts the potency of his memory, and that through the capacity to build narrative he learns about his surroundings, about others and himself. All of which is necessary, perhaps every day, to stave off the permanent present of being outside of work time, itself a process of destruction of the subject. This, of course, is exactly the mode of time in 'I Remember Nothing', a total living in time that offers no forward movement, a total self-absence. This song is a perfect expression of living in growing entropy. Information transfer fades, becoming nothing, and all we are left with is the sense of order declining into irretrievable fragments – in the falling glass, in the softening grasp of memory in the lyrics, in the long tail of the heat death of the song. It is amid breaking glass that the opening line brings us in ('we were strangers'), and it is through more breaking glass that we leave. Or, in fact, try to, but cannot, as the sounds continue right to the end, closing off this us, this non-socio-us, of strangers. The abstraction of the lyrics takes them out of exclusively autobiographical confines and into the new enclosure of urban living that can no longer be dwelling in light of the diffraction of some sort of 'post war settlement' into distorted, monadic units of not-quite-living, ideal as entrapment, made ever more pressing in the light of economic failure, whether individual, group or society-wide.

The glass in 'I Remember Nothing' is easily heard as the sound of chaos at the borders of housing, as disaffection in an urban setting, but, more than this, it counters the ideal aesthetic of a musical, song-based mode of attack on society, in favour of a concrete sound, an intrusion of the real, an extrusion of the real as that which is brought into music only to be signalled as the outside, even more forcefully. The glass, like the lift, is actual context, expressed materially, as opposed to abstractly, and as this happens, the real itself abstracts, only to be seen through the prism of understanding that cannot function as a self-identical construction of memory. In all this to and fro of a material real, the studio acts as 'a microcosm of the society in which it exists' (Veal, *Dub*, 23). At the cost of those exposed to the material world as exploitation, the sound material's operation of a real as absent signals the coming of post-materiality, a post-capitalism that is worse than capitalism for ejecting the erstwhile exploited into being the not-even-exploitable. The lift is the beginning, the foreclosing; the glass that smashes is the replacement of vision with entropic object in no need of humanity.

Less Familiar: The Near-Music of David Jackman and Organum

Since the late 1970s, David Jackman, either under his own name or that of Organum, has been producing a steady stream of strange records that sit uneasily between noise, industrial, ambient and contemporary classical. Unlike many practitioners in or near those genres, his records approach musicality continually, often then to deny expectations even more thoroughly than 'extreme' noise musicians. Jackman's releases work through the uncanny and 'the double', as identified by Sigmund Freud (after Otto Rank), and this occurs within the musical pieces, between them and in the very material through which they appear – and this last with particular reference to his 7-inch vinyl releases.[1]

The uncanny comes replete with a host of negative connotations, 'it is undoubtedly related to what is frightening – to what arouses dread and horror', and is something that causes 'repulsion and distress' (Freud, 'The Uncanny', 219).[2] More precisely, 'the uncanny is that class of the frightening which leads back to what is known of old and long familiar' (220). These are certainly feelings that we might have when encountering Jackman's music, but it is the making material, the making visible, as well as the making audible, that creates this effect. Jackman tells us even more about Freud's theorization of the uncanny when we consider the latter's near-deconstruction of these first two layers of the uncanny, through its connection with the familiar, the homely:

> '*heimlich*' is not unambiguous, but belongs to two sets of ideas ... on the one hand it means what is familiar and agreeable, and on the other, what is concealed and kept out of sight. '*Unheimlich*' is customarily used, we are told, as the contrary only of the first signification of '*heimlich*'. [According to Schelling] everything is *unheimlich* that ought to have remained secret and hidden but has come to light.
>
> ('The Uncanny', 224–25)

This chapter has appeared, in earlier but similar form (in French), in *Revue & Corrigé* (December 2017), 22–29.

Freud's argument is encapsulated in the oddness of the very thought of the uncanny, which in turns comes to structure the more straightforwardly haunting manifestations. This is precisely the process set in play by Jackman in the way he contorts our expectations of what a material release should present as its content, making the form a double of the content, an unsettling other that nestles within the properly musical.

The Tower

It begins quickly, a high drone fading up, ascending into layers of clatter, scrape and squeal. Soon, a rapid mechanical flutter starts up a non-percussive hint of period, of a structured time for the sounds to happen in. We are in the midst of percussion, or, more accurately, percussiveness, but in the absence of striking – any striking is feathery, an elongated sawing or bowing; the flutter jars, and raises and lowers in volume, as does the insistent drone that sits at the centre of all of this, rather than providing a base, or acting as a surrogate for melody. Then, after just over a couple of minutes, it tails off, without ever having established a narrative, or coming to a resolution. This is followed by a harsher return of essentially the same range of sounds, the scrape and drone more concerted, so that even in the lack of tangible narrative drive, a sense – a feeling, perhaps, or even a dread – of purpose arises. There is literally more edge in the scraping of this 'soundscape', and it is more firmly punctuated by sharp changes in volume, creating a sense of pitching and yawing. Finally, the sounds drag themselves away. These are parts one and two of Organum's 'Tower of Silence', side one of the 1985 release of the same name.

There is an oddness about Organum's music that goes beyond instrumentation. By the time David Jackman was recording and releasing works (the late 1970s), so-called non-musical objects had featured in many experimental pieces and had even become something of a staple of improvised music. Arguably, 'industrial' music was already putting forward its less benevolent version of John Cage's view of the possibility of bringing all sound into music, where all material could be re-mobilized as part of an aural commentary about fragmenting, declining societies. At the same time, Jackman, and artists such as Nurse With Wound, The Haters or The New Blockaders, began adopting similar musical strategies, but without having a metanarrative to shape how these 'non-musical' materials would signify. Jackman himself is wary of the 'industrial' tag, but I think we can hear evidence of the same musical move that Throbbing Gristle or SPK made – at least insofar as the incorporation of objects and playing 'techniques' that lay outside musical expectation was not to result in a simple colonization of sounds into the safe home of music.

Organum's music is part of a specific moment in the breakdown of generic divides that comes out of that key moment in Western 'popular' music, that is after punk, after free improvisation, after the hybridization of rock with other styles. Jackman's quietness about his music, and the difficulty of associating it with categories or genres even at their most radical, even at their most flexible (such as that of noise), has, I think, led to his work being more marginal than that of many of his peers who have been placed within categories, or had new ones grow up around them. Beyond this, there is something unsettlingly timeless about Jackman's records, as if they do not belong in any time, or even to the time in which they emerge. There is something disquieting about their near-musicality – made up of an absence of many of the things supposed to define music, combined with the clear similarity it bears to music. It is not noise, not even the use of noise, but there is something noisy about how it relates to music and the perceptions of musicality induced while listening to an Organum record. This uncanniness is not only what makes Jackman worth listening to and thinking around, but means that his releases constitute an argument (or statement) about the nature and beginnings of music.[3] The aural qualities of the recordings are part of this, but the material objects they arrive on, the seeming arbitrariness of lengths of pieces, the gnomic titles and the near-absence of information or explanation are also significant. These are combined with covers that are mostly either devoid of content or waylay the listener/viewer with possibilities that parallel the sounds rather than directively shelter these with pictorial or written deciphering keys.[4]

The tower of the *Tower of Silence* is a jagged irregular structure, a quiet affront to the structuring that music needs in order to occur, to in turn structure time. This challenge to structure persists across much of Organum's work, particularly the early material and 7-inch singles that pepper his output. From Pythagorean ideas of the universe being structured in proportions that could be thought of as musical, to music being a subset of the mathematical proportions of the universe, the ratio – the connecting structure – is what makes music be music. This is not a universally held perception, despite its claims to be such, but it has dominated Western cultural understandings of music, and indeed much that lies outside music. Even in the West, the idea of what music is or could be has not been stable. Music is also deemed to be connected to human production of structured sounds – seen positively by Rousseau, and negatively by Kant (to be slightly reductive about these two writers).[5] That it ties into what is human (for Rousseau it represents the birth of human language and culture) is part of its belonging to a sense of measure, of fitting and being something that creates 'fit', rightness. For Jacques Attali, this process of humanizing sounds into music is a reduction of the sacred power it had before being separated off as an autonomous art (*Noise*, 24–26; again, referring to a Western cultural idea of what music is).

So we have measure, the human, and structure as defining parts of what music is. The twentieth century saw numerous attempts to remake and rethink music, pushing the limits of those criteria and/or reducing their number to adjust notions of what was needed for a series of actions to be thought of as music. Structure cannot be fully left behind, particularly if we see music as being made up by more than one of the above ideas. Cage's complaint about Varèse is that the latter does not want to let go of the idea of 'organized sound' being a set of sounds organized by the composer (see Cage, *Silence*, 69, 83–84).[6] For Cage, 'organized sound' can and should be something much broader, offering infinite possibilities for music to happen, as the 'organizing' is done by listening (as well as by strategies that set off chance processes to generate the musical piece). There is still structure, and if the outcome is not familiar in terms of sound content, it is still a 'making familiar', a bringing-closer, a bringing into structure. Noise music, in many forms, attempts to dismantle or destroy the edifice of music – Masami Akita's Merzbow directly refers to Kurt Schwitters's *Merzbau* (the original, in Hanover, begun in 1923) wherein the Dada artist reconfigured the interior of a house with an ever-growing array of objects attached to the previously solid and linear walls and ceiling of the house. Just as this 'Merz' stuff became part of a remoulded house, so noise music can never stay noise, because it will become non-noise, either a new type of music or something that merges with the familiar. Organum does not try to reconfigure, extend or destroy the house of music, or its building, but tries to be another music, an other music that seems so similar to music it works at the foundations of music as if at a set of loose teeth. 'Tower of Silence' does feature a storm, sinking boats and a subsiding house (as well as a collapsing steeple) in Jackman's cover art, but Organum's music is not the destruction of the temple, rather it is something that occupies musical space (more accurately, musical time) differently.

Music, beyond and beneath its 'measures', occupies time – brought to a logical conclusion in John Cage's time pieces, the best known of which is *4'33"* – and in very material ways Organum comments on the idea of music as organized sound in time. As time is occupied by the sounds of music (or 'noise'), so the listener has their time structured by their listening, making a 'space' of dwelling. This can either be the commonplace dwelling of just being in a familiar space, or the phenomenological dwelling of Martin Heidegger, where to think on the problem of dwelling is to dwell on what it is to inhabit the earth and to know that Being is bounded by death, which exists as a perpetually absent framing. Dwelling, too, often falls into everyday living, and this is actually a refusal to knowingly dwell.[7] Meanwhile, dwelling, once thought, turns out to be a problem rather than a solution for the question of Being, because dwelling is fundamentally without ground, without meaning, and is *uncanny*.[8]

Organum's music is properly uncanny, properly dwelling in that it allows only troubled habitation. It not only illustrates, but enacts the *unheimlich* that lies within the *heimlich* from the start. It haunts and is haunted at the same time, its near-familiarity unsettling. It does this because it is so nearly music, so close to being something we recognize. It occurs in recognizable institutional forms – as recordings. It organizes sounds into finite chunks of time, and often features recognizably musical instruments. But like the double, the ghost, the automaton, it is subtly something other than music (Freud, 'The Uncanny', 226).

The single

'Pulp' (1984) surrounds rumbling, thumping objects with a ringing oscillation, not so much accompanying them, but adding a frame through which to perceive them, and bring them close to music. It is hard to think of either element as accompanying the other – the more musical sound does not work as a background or as an organizing layer, but as a hearing tool, even a recording device, making 'Pulp' into a sort of archaeological object within which something has been captured. Despite the relentless activity, it does not attempt to go anywhere (the droning element quelling the ostensibly highly mobile percussiveness). Something has happened which may or may not have meant anything, and what we have here is a gnomic residue. This is not the simple result of the sounds contained within 'Pulp', but also an outcome of its appearance as a single, with the two sides being parts one and two.

This single is a collaboration with The New Blockaders, most of whose releases, especially around this time (1984) are crunching, noise-filled 'soundscapes'. Typically, a record by The New Blockaders suggests human reappropriation of residual sound, objects, even spaces, and, as it develops, that first hearing gives way to a sense of an absence of intervention, as if what had happened is that someone stumbled upon the noises and brought them back as 'The New Blockaders'. On this and their other collaborations, the distinctiveness of The New Blockaders's sound falls into the Organum soundworld, dragged to music, and with the collaborative singles it seems less like an extract of some other 'musical universe' and more like self-contained zones of extra-musicality, much like Gordon Matta-Clark's *Reality Properties, Fake Estates* of 1973–74, where the artist-architect bought sections of land that fell between freehold properties, and re-presented these apparently peripheral areas as an autonomous and interconnected space.

'Pulp' is about three minutes per side, not enough time for the listener to acclimatize to the new conditions. Replaying does not provide more answers but seals the piece back in on itself, as if holding off learning.[9] Staying with The New Blockaders/Organum collaboration, there are two further 7-inch releases, 'Raze' and 'Der Graben', both incredibly short, both with A and B sides that differ only marginally. Organum have made many short records, but to what extent are these records singles? The expectations of a single are that the track, on the A side at least, is capable of autonomous existence.[10] Brevity is not unexpected, but is largely a characteristic of highly narrative music (whatever the limits or strengths of the lyrical narrative of songs released as singles), or even a statement in itself – such as in the late 1970s and early 1980s, as punk, metal and early 'hardcore' favoured short singles. This was a return to the short instrumental singles of the 1960s, or even to the brief outbursts of the rock 'n' roll single. Organum is not coming from any of those areas, but from a background of improvised music work such as AMM, the workshop approach of 1970s free music, and, despite Jackman's misgivings on this, from some of the strategies of industrial music. Any of these forms, at their most essential, required time for the 'noise' of their recordings or performances to unfold, as they were often involved in an undoing – an undoing Jackman really is not bothered with. He has set up elsewhere.

There were 'industrial' singles in the late 1970s and early 1980s, and in the intervening decades since those collaborations with The New Blockaders, a large amount of 'noise' or experimental music has come out on 7-inch single, or has actively used the format of a release, its musical and material expectations, to disruptive effect. Very few singles are as consistently non-dramatic as Jackman's 45 rpm records, with their emptying the sounds of their overt construction and or sense, whilst making those sounds into something that is static, as opposed to the apparent urgency of the short time window available to the 7-inch single.[11] In one way, David Jackman's regular resort to the 7-inch does refer closely to the late 1970s heyday of independent labels, both rhetorically (displaying autonomy) and materially (relative affordability of production and purchase). But it is still more like a withholding, a refusal even, that sees Jackman release small runs of records, which, individually, can hold little, and on which he puts less. These are singles, then, from somewhere history unfolds differently, where even exploiting a particular medium throws up anomalies.

'Raze pt.1' (1994) is 1.31 minutes of malfunctioning machinery, blanketed in hiss with indeterminate metallic squeals, ending with a sudden, crisp note, as the sounds emerge from muffled discord into a momentarily glimpsed, clean, clear future, or a moment of release, that is immediately shut off. 'Raze pt.2' is harsher, because less murky – here there is separation between grinding and squealing mechanics and distorted electronic sounds, but still, at 1.31, its time is up. It too ends in a vaguely resonant moment, but even more briefly. Lastly, here, of The New Blockaders and Organum's collaborations, is 'Der Graben' (2002), which is again in two parts, and of the same sort of duration as 'Raze', at 1.37 per side/part. This is quite similar to 'Raze', but more frenetic, more noisy, perversely, because the sounds are more distinguishable – so the competing of layers of drones and the raking of whatever is being used as percussion are constantly being sifted, and add up to a more overtly internally dissonant piece than either 'Raze' or 'Pulp'. Of the three releases, it is most like a 'single' – even supplying an ending of sorts as the sounds drop out except for a few last squeals. Side two ('Der Graben' again, not specifically identified as part two) is more broken up, with blunter percussion more to the fore, and the reverberating electronics building with greater evidence. Essentially, these are the same piece, re-presented, mixed or manipulated (more on Jackman's use of 'the same' piece below). All of these collaborations work through the device of bringing noises (not 'noise' as such) into the domain of music, but as representatives of some other music – lost ritual objects, perhaps.

The idea of archaic or lost ritual hovers around *Horii* (1986) from the start, its title and imagery suggestive of Egyptian mythology, but also a kind of ur-mythology beyond that, which the music stands for, as if Ancient Egyptians had had a premonition of Organum's direct access to the lost well-spring of their beliefs. The track 'Horii', though, is one of Jackman's least puzzling pieces – its framing overdetermines its potential content, a sense backed up by the track itself, which occupies a lengthy side for a 12-inch EP, at over twelve minutes. Typically, it does not develop as a strong musical narrative, but there is narration at work, through the instrumentation, and the final fade-out. Ominous wind instrument sounds combine with slow creaking and scraping, themselves very close to recognizable musical tones. From time to time, and at varying volumes, a fanning rises and falls within the rest. The whole summons an atmosphere of the arcane, an ambience that is close to other musical minimalisms (in addition to Jackman's visual proximity to sculptural minimalism in the harsh simplicity of his artwork), and closes, through a very staged fade, tailing off meaningfully. Something here is coming to a close, as the last sounds clatter down and, for once, the narrative reaches closure. Freud is careful to distinguish the distinction between representing the uncanny (even to ourselves) and experiencing it: 'we should differentiate between the uncanny that we actually experience and the uncanny that we merely picture or read about' ('The Uncanny', 247). The latter is only a diminished form, taking place at a distance rather than being too close for comfort. An Organum record is not ever going to be free of the risk of such a representational arcane, but 'Horii' is directly evocative, and it seems to be *about* mystery, at one remove from it.[12]

The same cannot be side of its reverse, the authentically enigmatic 'Keloid', which uses sounds, time and the material surface of the record to become other, through not being the simple 'otherness' hinted at by 'Horii'. 'Keloid' is a steady howl of a drone, riddled with screech and grate. It lasts 1.10, and is the only track on the 33 rpm side two of *Horii*. This side surprises even when looked at, and then by almost being over even before the player of the record becomes a listener. But it not only has as much value as 'Horii', it has an excessive value, where expression is threatened. 'Keloid' is separated off from 'Horii' through being on side two, but it seems more profoundly separated through sound. Many Jackman or Organum works refer to each other closely through shared material, but if there is sharing here, it is not only hidden away, it is resisted. 'Keloid' is further isolated on the vinyl itself, occupying a tiny part of the side. The run-off takes up the bulk of the side and lasts twenty-five seconds in its own right – this is just as much part of how this release works: 'Keloid' is the inner sanctum behind the display of the arcane of 'Horii', and the sacred that cannot be adequately looked on. It is not banned, but seen distorted, unfocused, despite being a condensed, almost crystal-like object. The shine and thin trenching of the run-off emphasizes the excess of that 1.10 burst, continually being left behind, always to be lost, just like the listener's attention, which is consciously foregone, at least on first encounter with this side.[13]

This obsessive return to denseness, to almost frenetic reductions of a potentially immense range of sounds, and shortness are to be found, as noted earlier, on punk singles, but here they are above all to be thought of as *luxury*: they work as rigorous refusals of the use-value of vinyl's length, of the working-out of improvisation or ambience alike, and, most 'materially', are literally expensive per minute. This all feeds into how Organum is something that leaves music, that shows us what music is, without leaving music fully behind.

The double

If Organum's music works as a double for music, this is not just because its sounds are odd, or even because its physical containers take unexpected form, but also because there is doubling within Jackman's records, whether in working through the same sound stuff on sides one and two of a single, or by having a single with Organum on one side, Jackman on the other, or indeed by repeating the same music. As most of these 7-inch records consist of two tracks identified as part one and the other as part two, or just listed under the same title, the listener is forced to make a connection in a way two tracks identified through separate titles do not require (and this is partly because the 7-inch single has, historically, largely featured a leading track, with the B side not having the same status). Organum's case also differs from singles that feature remixes, as these serve to highlight differences, those differences being unearthed from within the material, and concurrently presenting the maximum potential divergence from the same base material. It also differs from other pieces that use numbered parts, as these generally indicate progression, narrative, and would often feature very explicit returns or reprises. Experimental musicians' use of the 7-inch has offered huge variations on this, but, even there, there is widespread use of 'part one' and 'part two' simply because the track has been divided (as with long tracks struggling to fit the single form, like King Crimson's 'In the Court of Crimson King' [1969], artificially given two parts for its single release).

Organum's singles are specifically not doing those things, and deconstruct how the single works by so nearly doing what it is supposed to. Crucially, what Jackman does is strip away those possibilities, creating a claustrophobic object that matches its musical content. Many of his 7-inch singles rely on minimal differences between 'part one' and 'part two'. Progression from first to second part is negated, and 'part two' no longer functions as its title suggests. The high degree of similarity also corrodes the idea that one version is the original. Turning over to side two lures the listener into finding differences, but these carry no intrinsic significance in terms of hierarchy or development, other than the listener being forced to make that happen. So, 'Drome' (1989), another encapsulation of Organum's near-music, built of whirring fan sounds and voice-like wind instrumentation moored in percussive squealing, does have a harsher B side – with higher EQ making for slightly more discordance; the clatter of the fan gets lost, the ending alters, a calm tailing off signals a genuine conclusion. Having dredged these differences, though, the key is that the pieces are essentially the same (this can also be said of the collaborations with The New Blockaders referred to above), perhaps with different processing. But the A side cannot be taken as the original, it just tends to be the side that is played first and whose status then has to be questioned once a relation to side two is established. 'Part one' of an Organum single is never the raw compared to the cooked of 'part two'.[14] The original is never present, and the alteration that supplies an illusion, a hint, of narrative is something also lost, in between the sides, as the player of the record turns it over, and waits in expectation of development, alteration, so the listener and the precise time taken for listening are the only potential locations for narrative. At the same time as Organum leads us to question what is going on in music – its tiny alterations are no less alterations for that – its minimalizing of gestural composition a way of highlighting precisely the way that that process works for all music.

Jackman replicates the strange structuring of 'Horii' on the single 'Crusade' (1994). This is pretty much as close to 'noise music' as Jackman gets, with heavy throbbing, roaring and embedded white noise waves lurching over its 2.18 length, punctuated by the surfacing of two piercing moments. It ends in whatever the precise opposite of a grinding halt is, in clean emptying, or possibly the closing-off of what has just gone. The second side (on the record identified only as 'Crusade', or perhaps part of 'Crusade' as the title of the release as a whole) has more of an enveloping throb as it bursts into its own ending after 0.46, but it sounds exactly as if it were a slice of the A side. Its shortness is the materialization of the content's excess – a sacrificial music, offering up 'Crusade' as an infinitely reducible moment of violence, and sacrificial too of the beautiful transparent record through 'under-use' (which also, pleasingly, makes it near-impossible to see how short the B side will be). The shock of Jackman's near-noise is not in its 'extreme' sound, but in how it mobilizes that in time, and in how the pieces relate to each other. This, then, is Freud's uncanny, as seen in the troubling double, where 'there is constant recurrence of the same thing' ('The Uncanny', 234), but this same thing is a something else that claims to be the same, the true, the actual.

Organum and Jackman's 7-inch singles present the uncanny in what are often taken to be distantly secondary parts of the music's presentation, enabling a process of reflection on how every part of structuring, every part of the material process, is brought out, is functional. This is only possible through making each of those 'layers' estranged from the idea of 'the single' and from the possibility of narrative in a sequential piece in numbered parts.

The other double

For reasons not entirely clear, some releases come out under the name of David Jackman. These are ostensibly the more clearly musical works, but this distinction has been blurring, particularly with Organum's turn in the early 2000s to a more resonant minimalism on the *Sanctus*, *Amen* and *Omega* CDs. As if aware of this, the 'Penguins Eat Fish' 7-inch raises this dual identity as a question with the track of that title by Organum, and its B side, 'Little Dark Wing', by David Jackman. 'Penguins Eat Fish' brings together numerous of Jackman's musical concerns: the sounds of military activity, this time in the form of drums and brass in the style of a march, albeit, one for the lost; amid the howls and scrapes of Organum, there are slow piano chords that do not quite centre the rest. This track seems to already confuse the identities of Organum and Jackman. Is this track a collaboration between them? The second side of the single, 'Little Dark Wing', consists of piano chords, and few of them – the majority of the 2.24 duration is actually taken up by the residue of those chords, as they fade. As with all Jackman or Organum music, we are taken back to the beginning condition of music: if the main part of this piece is residue, at what point do we find the non-residue? The hitting of the chords by the fingers? The transmission of that hit through the machinery of the piano? If so, at what point could we stop and say, yes, here is where it begins? The intention prior to placing the hands? The arbitrary moment of placing the hands? To the thought of some sort of 'essence' of 'Little Dark Wing' in the mind? To a Platonic 'essence' from which all these others are mere derivations? This piece brings out this peculiar condition music habits, or, at its best, perpetually comes to inhabit, never quite getting there. This is not really music, but the sound of music being made.

How, though, do the two sides relate? The separation of Jackman's musical identities might well be designed to remove any possible relatedness, but actually it heightens the question of what the relation is, even as it would hope to diminish it. Piano features on both sides, so perhaps the second side is a distillation, something approaching an essence. As Western culture has mostly forgotten that the piano is just as much machine, just as much technology as any other device for making music, or something like it, we might imagine this is a more personal *expression*. From this, it would then seem as if this is closer to the person named David Jackman, rather than the entity who signs this record. But as 'seen' above, what is expressed is very little, and thoroughly problematizes the idea of a controlling, self-present source. By 'sharing' a single between Organum and David Jackman, Jackman pushes the possibility of a source ever further away, shuttling between its possibility and its absence. The eerie effect is that of the double:

> This relation [of doubledness] is accentuated by mental processes leaping from one of these characters to another – by what we should call telepathy –, so that the one possesses knowledge, feelings and experience in common with the other. Or it is marked by the fact that the subject identifies himself with someone else, so that he is in doubt as to which his self is, or substitutes the extraneous self for his own. In other words, there is a doubling, dividing and interchanging of the self.
>
> (Freud, 'The Uncanny', 234)

At this point in Freud's essay the ambiguity of the double is at its height – it is creative and threatening, both an excess and a potential removal of identity. All of this uncertainty plays out in this 'shared' single, and infiltrates the wider production of Organum and David Jackman. In fact, it is not really tenable to identify a consistent and distinct identity for David Jackman's records as compared to those of Organum.[15] 'The Edge of Nothing', for example, whilst performing its own doubling (6.29 on each side of a 10-inch single, and very hard to discern differences), has the scrapes, pulsings and intense near-stasis of many of Organum's releases. The 'Flak' 10-inch has one side of near-music, and another of more or less straight samples of aircraft. Once more, we are brought back to music that works as a questioning of music: how different is it to arrange any sound into structures, as opposed to tuned or tempered sounds?

Both David Jackman and Organum bring us to the same point where music is about to come into being or be destroyed, but, on the 'singles' at least, David Jackman offers a 'becoming-musical' and Organum a 'becoming-noise'. They are continually becoming (they never approach a completion of those 'objectives') and occupy a similar space, only marginally different. Ronald Bogue writes (in *Deleuze's Wake*) of a 'becoming-metal' of death metal music, where Deleuze and Guattari's ideas of 'becoming-woman', 'becoming-animal' and so on illustrate the workings of death metal.[16] This becoming is not an attainment – the triumph of identity – but the replacement of identity with becoming. Process overcomes fixity, and this is brought out as the fundamental condition of all identity and appearance of same. Death metal is its own becoming in Bogue's 'becoming-metal' 'that at times makes possible the formation of a sonic plane of consistency of affective intensities and differential speeds' (*Deleuze's Wake*, 108). Jackman's music inhabits similar spaces, and only fleetingly. This is a key difference between his music, and, for example, that of Morton Feldman, who also takes us into the moment where music may or may not happen, but over a long time, in the course of which a certain sense of dwelling, of territory to be inhabited, is recoverable. Better still, we could imagine a becoming-David-Jackman, where this identity is put on hold every time it is asserted, or put into play as music that has been signed/named by its 'author'. As Jackman goes from Organum to David Jackman, on 'Penguins Eat Fish'/'Little Dark Wing', he becomes, not himself, but David Jackman as becoming-David-Jackman … always losing identity to raise it as question, precisely mirroring, or doubling, the activity of the music itself.

The double dissolves the same

The Organum single 'Iuel/Wolf' (1990) plays on this diminishing of difference to the point of absurdity: it is a double single where both records are the same, musically at least. The centre labels are the only variation: one is black on silver, the other silver on black. The images, too, reverse – that is, the image for 'Iuel' on the 'first' single becomes the image for 'Wolf' on the second single. The only possible difference can come from the aging of the records, from how many times the record is played, and in the case of my 'Iuel/Wolf', the silver-centred one seems older, as if the black-centred one was left to be the copy, the spare. Which of these is the original? The silver one becomes the original, later, as the parallel issue (with the same catalogue number) carries the silver label: so 'record one' only acquires its identity first by surviving some sort of struggle between it and what will become 'record two', and then only in hindsight becoming the original, the 'one', by virtue of not being the record that makes this the case (the 'second' issue of the silver label version by itself). But there is nothing to say that the 'real' one did not lose out to the double, which takes its place as if it were the real one.

Organum's singles have played out the troubling nature of the double, in the form of tracks with the same name and/or duration on the one single, where traditionally we would expect an entire rejection of the double, in the form of a more important A side and a secondary B side (double A sides are not a doubling, but an even more secure defence against the mysterious powers of the double, as each side sees its individual identity affirmed). With 'Iuel/Wolf', though, the mirror has moved, and this double is even more threatening – what does it want, this near-copy? The tracks themselves work in more of a continuum than in other cases, as 'Wolf', despite having a separate title, could well be a continuation or further exploration of 'Iuel'. This latter is based on woodwinds and drones, with some scratchiness later on, whilst 'Wolf' intertwines scraping and drones from the start, and then has a sequence of piano blasts through the second half.

According to Otto Rank, in *The Double*, many cultures have prohibitions on twins, either according them great power, or regarding them as threatening – often one must be killed. This is the usual position of a record, where simply repeating the same is not allowed, it says too much about possible doublings in all music. Here, Organum has made a record with a more conventional structure for a single, only to present a double not only for one track, but for the entire single. The visual difference actually heightens this sameness, otherwise we would just regard it as two copies of the same record stuck together, which, whilst unusual, would be to create a comradeship these two 'Iuel/Wolf's do not have.

So we approach the very same, in the fullest doubling of all, as ultimately this difference tends to zero – still difference, but with a value of zero. This is what we find with Jackman's CD *Verhalte dich ruhig*, which, unindicated, has two tracks, which are exactly the same. Sweeps of strings, with piano and woodwinds, create a 'cinematic' atmosphere, an almost landscape, or we could hear, at moments, brass or wind phrases signalling some kind of 'new dawn' realization. But it is not as straightforward as that. The track constantly returns and goes over the same atonal motifs every two minutes or so, with the result that neither a landscape nor a moment of calm epiphany can actually be summoned or retained. Instead we are caught within a universe of the endless repetition of the same, but where each repetition is only for the first time (as the track does advance, it is not stuck). This undoing of a stereotypically suggestive 'soundtrack' is never allowed to come to completion, and its only alteration may be some ultra-minimal alteration of pitch, creating a further disorientation if listened to as the background ambience it initially seems to want to be.

The whole is then repeated, exactly the same, but not (it is track 2, even if not listed as such), further emphasizing the impossibility of dwelling in or occupying a space where being unfolds into identity and sameness, such that it can be known, lived as normal. Originally, *Verhalte dich ruhig* was released on cassette, so we can imagine a practical side to the repetition, just as the ill-fated format of the cassette single would repeat so as not to waste Walkman batteries in rewinding. This CD, arguably, could be seen as simply replicating the cassette, as a material accident. An accident of this sort seems very unlikely, in light of Organum/David Jackman's obsessive return to the idea of the double as form. Here Jackman is mirroring only himself, in the guise of his becoming-David-Jackman, but the structure is an exact (too exact?) doubling of 'Iuel/Wolf'. The CD is not the same as the cassette, though, if we think materially. On the cassette, there is a familiar mirroring, with one track in opposition to the other. Here the reflecting glass is gone, and both pieces sit next to each other. One does come first, but if they are exactly the same, why shouldn't the second be the original? In fact, there can never be an original here, and the doubling infiltrates the track so fully, it can only undo itself as it more becomes itself (as it is always already double, always already itself, but two).

Verhalte dich ruhig is a very difficult listen, and this makes the experience of listening twice to 'the' track something more uncanny, closer to the uncanny as something hidden that has been brought to light. Something (it is precisely this vague wrongness that keeps the uncanny near) about the 'always doubled' track creates an uneasiness that is more or less physical, whilst at the same time it is so close to music that a further uneasiness is caused as to why it creates uneasiness. Ultimately, this is Jackman returning us to the origins of music, where it was never self-contained, nor simply itself.

There is a *sound block* that no longer has a point of origin, since it is always and already in the middle of the line, and no longer has horizontal and vertical coordinates, since it creates its own coordinates; and no longer forms a localizable connection from one point to another, since it is 'nonpulsed time': a deterritorialized rhythmic block that has abandoned points, coordinates, and measure, like a drunken boat that melds with the line or draws a plane of consistency. Speeds and slownesses inject themselves into musical form, sometimes impelling it to proliferation, linear microproliferation, and sometimes to extinction, sonorous abolition, involution, or both at once. (Deleuze and Guattari, *A Thousand Plateaus*, 296)

The uncanny double of death (the prospect of non-music, of some other music) haunts the being of this music even (and continually) as it establishes itself. But just as uncanny is the music becoming itself, out of nowhere, with and despite its doubling (with and despite its doubling as itself being the only possibility it has). Briefly, repetitively, internally and externally. The becoming is not only never quite-achieved (so remains unbecoming), but it becomes through endlessly creating what it is not (in the form of near-same tracks, exact copies, tiny and hermetic sonic intrusions into this world of music). The double infiltrates Jackman's music until it becomes the n-1 of 1,000 Plateaus, where the core dissolves leaving only (only!) the processes that made it.

BUNK: Origins and Copies in Nurse With Wound and The New Blockaders

Experimental music, like art history, has developed a canon of key artists, movements and works. But can noise have a canon? Can we fix what 'noise/ music' is? I would argue that we cannot, even if we have to acknowledge a history of what has been identified as moments of noise. Noise raises the question of an avant-garde as such. Even to recognize something as avant-garde (or noise) is to reduce its noisiness, its disruption. This does not need to paralyse us, for it leads us precisely to the idea that noise is not something timeless, but is rooted in time, despite itself. Noise music is something that operates within the paradox of the avant-garde which has *no proper time to be*: it is always ahead, or behind (in being slotted into a canon).

Noise is a negativity: defined in opposition (and therefore connection) to something else, for example, meaning, music, structure, skill, beauty etc. Historically, it has been thought of as literally negative: 'that's just noise'. But, as we know, what is noise at one historical or cultural moment or location is not so elsewhere. This looks like a simple binary with an ordered term on one side and a supposedly radical disorder on the other. But the noise is in how noise and music relate, the noise is the differential (or *différantial*). The thing that is regarded as noise can cross the line, and the process of being judged to be one side or the other, or the assessment that noise has happened in the crossing into the mainstream (or out again) is where noise happens. Or does not quite happen. Before I venture into the morass of a deconstructive noisiness, not for

BUNK is the title given to a series of works by proto-Pop artist Eduardo Paolozzi made between 1947 and 1952, used as part of a talk given by him at the ICA in 1952. They were first exhibited in 1972. These print collages bear the date 1947/1972, or 1972. The title of the earlier version of this article, as it appeared in *Organised Sound*, was *Just What Is It That Makes Today's Noise Music So Different, So Appealing?* Which is a marginal transposition of pioneering Pop artist Richard Hamilton's collage *Just What Is It That Makes Today's Homes So Different, So Appealing?* (1956).

the first time, always not that, let's just say that noise is not a this or a that, it does not belong like an attribute to a thing, and neither is it a thing. Instead, it is both product (of some sort of judgement, good or bad) and process (interaction of meaningfulness, recognition with their opposites). That this is not transparent is not a problem, it is the problem of noise, and to think otherwise is to give in, to duck under what is most challenging, absurd, creative, destructive in the imagining of noise.

There are genres of noise, there are histories, there are claims and discussions which fix in place central figures whether we like them or not, but the fixing in place, in time is not noise. The recognition of originality, of avant-gardeness, is not the end of the story of noise but the place around which noise *circulates*. For there to be, or for there to have been, a noise sequence, we have to acknowledge that rupture, disturbance and refusal are what link those moments, rather than there-being a smooth developmental curve. Even within this simple and teleological tale lies a curiosity, which is that the many moments along it all comprise a rejection of standard forms of music, in favour of an at least implied musicality outside of what is or was at one point considered music. Because of this, many of the reference points are outside of music. The Fluxus movement, in its 1960s heyday, produced much that could be considered noise music (noise occurring in place of music), within wider art events (hence Michael Nyman's positing of Fluxus and also minimalism as genuine experimental music, as opposed to direct inheritors of 'classical music' in programme music, however adventurous).[1] When considering 'noise music', some regard swathes of music as being outside consideration entirely. Nonetheless, the playing out of noise as disruptive othering of expectation or of formal practice is (the) noise of music that is acting, at a given moment, as noise music. In other words, many types or instances of music can become noise, through processes of assessment, rejection or acceptance, disruption or assimilation. This is not a subjective way of seeing noise as a thing that is personally found to be good because noise, or bad because noise. It is instead based on statistical or normative listening that deems something to be outside. More radical still is the avant-gardeness that is out from outside, as Moten says, and therefore liable to disrupt time as measure, measure as rightness (*In The Break*, 33).

The question of origins, precedents and influences is a vexed one for 'noise musicians', listeners and critics alike, but the key is that if what is going on is something like noise, then it must raise the question of influence even as it plays it out in the production of works. In the artists I am looking at in this chapter, we can see that influence and canon play out literally and obliquely, and I will claim that this type of playing out might be one way of identifying something as noise music (without saying these artists 'are' noise or 'belong' to noise music).

Specifically, I will be looking at two artists who have been active for around forty years: Nurse With Wound and The New Blockaders, and I will use them to identify questions of precedence, stated origins and reference points and how these concepts are essential to the functioning of their work. The question of influence, of influence made into question, occurs differently in the two cases, but the connection is the time they started recording (1979 and 1982 respectively) – shortly after punk, and in the midst of industrial music (a term contested with regard to the industrial referent in the music), and the connections to both *musique concrète* and looser music and art from a similar period (but more concentrated in the 1960s). As well as what they do with influence, I will also think about influence as something that issues from their work.

Nurse With Wound was, for their first album, Steven Stapleton, Heman Pathak and John Fothergill. Over the years, the personnel have altered, expanded, bulged and contracted, with Stapleton the constant, and Colin Potter and Andrew Liles regular contributors. As their early music is often harsh and peculiar, combined with erotic or violent imagery, they were assimilated into the category of 'industrial music', and despite what Stapleton says, and despite the range of references that crop up in Nurse With Wound, I imagine that this is how the early audience saw their material. Over the course of time, the music has become subtler, stranger, more variegated and always hovering on the margins of musicality. Stapleton has been consistently explicit about the sources and location of his project, which is, broadly, in the lineage of experimental art music, whether rock-based (like 'kosmische' music or 'krautrock') or more in the 'high art' tradition (like *musique concrète*). He also emphasizes his connection to visual arts movements of the early twentieth century: Futurism, Dada and Surrealism. It is this last, above all, that permeates Stapleton's oeuvre:

> 'Nurse music is surrealist music', Stapleton asserts. 'Today surrealism has been swamped by advertising and has lost all of its purity. That's why it's down to me to carry the banner for what's genuinely odd, giving a completely different angle to the way instruments and compositions are looked at'. His notion of 'surrealism in sound' involves channelling the murky subconscious into music that provokes unpredictable reactions and tests particular mental states.
>
> (Keenan, *England's Hidden Reverse*, 52)[2]

This faith in a movement that is more popular than critically rated (due to its de-emphasis on formalism) is striking, and whilst I would not say Nurse With Wound achieve the communicative dream of Surrealism – the transfer of mental states through art – they manage to be faithful to that movement and work as an avant-garde entity (which arguably Surrealism never was, being more of call to order, compared to Dada, than the freeing up it presented itself as). Other than at some points on the early albums, Stapleton avoids cheap quirkiness, and the model of Surrealism we should have in mind is the darker side – of Max Ernst and Georges Bataille, rather than the vacuous Dalí – in line with J.G. Ballard's work (despite this latter's strange championing of Dalí), and with the playfulness of Frank Zappa.

Nurse With Wound's first album is *Chance Meeting on a Dissecting Table of a Sewing Machine and Umbrella* (1979), a clatter of toys, tools, instruments played 'unmusically' (except for some misplaced guitar 'work', which I suppose adds to the oddness by contrasting with the rest). There are howls, scrapes, drones, rattly and bumpy percussions, arrhythmic rhythms (complex but not necessarily worked out in advance as structuring devices), croaky vocals. The longest track, 'Blank Capsules of Embroidered Cellophane', is the most satisfying part, mildly structured by the return of bursts of skittering percussion, often, I would think, one-handed, which is an important strategy for undermining the temptation to uniform rhythm. There is plenty of scraping and scratching and two bursts of electric saw, once about halfway though, the next after 23.30 minutes.

The title comes from Lautréamont's *Les Chants de Maldoror* (The Songs of Maldoror), a book that was a great inspiration to Surrealism, as it combined eroticism, violence, arbitrariness and a sense of absurdity as a potential for creativity, and ties in with the practice at work in the production of the album, which essentially consists of live improvisations, free of rehearsal, plan or pretty much any other sort of musical convention.[3] Instead, sounds would encounter each other randomly, without the skills usually associated with jazz or jazz-based improvised music. The blank materiality of the music (free of meaning, explicit purpose etc.) is counterposed with the accompanying materials. The title's provenance also contrasts with the origin of the cover image, a detailed drawing of a leather-clad dominatrix, breasts exposed and whip in hand, from a porn magazine cover. Beyond this, we have a photographic collage (in the inside on the first CD issue) including bits of the members' faces. Then comes the key element: the famous list of influences, a simple and lengthy list (numbering in the hundreds) of influences, and stuff from Stapleton's record collection. Fanatics have long sought to chase down the more obscure parts of the list, and it is not entirely trustworthy for this purpose.[4]

The list itself is introduced with the title 'Categories strain, crack and sometimes break, under their burden – step out of the space provided' (*Chance Meeting* liner notes). Few albums can have come with such an extensive framing. The sounds within it are to be imagined as a crystallization of those influences – a crystallization through *listening*, rather than through musical training in the standard sense. We have to remember that in 1979 there was no established discourse of a history of experimental music, or noise, or noise music: the explicit and implicit workings of the reference points were far less obvious then, more bizarre. At a factual level, many of the artists listed have since been made available on CD or record, or achieved a higher profile as experimental or avant-garde rock music built up an audience. At another level, the list should not be seen as a manual but as a properly arcane document, which does not contain the music but matches it. The listener is encouraged to follow up the names in the list, but the initial effect is to show the immensity of potential strangeness that is 'out there'. Even the reference to Russolo on the back cover's collage might well be a given today, but not so then, and presumably not so now, to people new to peculiar music. The overall form of *Chance Meeting* is not to encourage knowledge as possession, but knowledge as process, involving mystery and loss of control. The notion of arcane knowledge is faithful to Surrealism, but not restricted to it: it can often mean replacing understanding with fascination. The initiates will gradually acquire understanding, but at every stage in arcane knowledge, mystery is the key – there is always to be something left out, something kept from meaning. As well as the use of noises to make a noisy deconstruction of music in the material of *Chance Meeting*, the noise of this album is in its dissemination of a new subversive canon, but the way that this new canon is constructed creates difficulty, not a shortcut. In short, to track down the sources, or congratulate yourself on how many you already know is to miss the point.

The sheer range of reference also mitigates against the idea of a simply linear story of the progress of 'noise music', where the cognoscenti can bask in having processed all preceding forms, and where the next move can be the only best move. The proliferation of reference here substitutes a contemporary evolutionary model of branching, bottlenecks and hidden continuities for a sub-Darwinian belief in progress toward greater, better, harsher experimentation. Across, within and above the list is a vaginal cut, with Nurse With Wound written in it: from these NWW was born, perhaps, but also a cut, a break, a point of separation, a giving over of agency. The masculine linearity of the list is disrupted but also permitted by the feminine intervention.

This process is exaggerated, taken to excess, on the 2001 reissue of *Chance Meeting*, subtitled 'special edition'. In addition to the original tracks is a replaying of the list in all its proliferating potential. Long-term collaborator (and leader of Current 93) David Tibet intones the names on the list, manipulated by Colin Potter. Further sounds are produced by Stapleton. The track 'Strain, crack, break' takes off from the heading of the list, and is made to repeat many times at the opening part of the track, emphasizing, for those who had not eyes to see it, but maybe can hear, that the list is not about authority but immersion. Tibet's voice comes over in many layers, forming a choral round. The list is worked through, in the order it was written, by one of those 'voices', but this 'voice' continues to change after every few names. Other 'voices' start at different points or come to be only to halt, stammer and stutter one name (e.g. 'Guru Guru'). Gradually, what are now trademark Stapleton sounds – drones, screeching metals, clatters and so on – come in, while the voice is further slowed down, sped up, twisted, echoed and cut. The 'messiness' of the track fights any suggestion of the idea of canon as a rigid set of materials to master, but it comes at a point where Nurse With Wound have themselves become canonical, hence the importance of turning on their material, making it turn in on itself: through the list's dispersal, and with Tibet's voice itself continually altered. Arriving into the canon has further revealed the fragility of 'the' canon, and the randomness of influence.[5]

This process of working through the canon by disrupting it is also in evidence in the move to a more manipulated sound, redolent of *musique concrète*, but also apart from it. Like Pierre Schaeffer, who sought to remove the 'dramatic context' of sounds in order to make new narratives (Schaeffer, *Pour une musique concrète*, 32), the albums that follow *Chance Meeting* are atmospheric collages, with cuts and harsh intrusions never allowing an easy ambience to settle. Unlike Schaeffer, Nurse With Wound allowed a musicality that did not rely on this alienation of sound from origin. Instead, as on 'I Am Blind' on *Homotopy to Marie* (1981), music is approached to be withheld. On this track, moans combine with metallic, reverbed clicking and clattering, and gradually these give way to creaking and stranger vocalizing. Just as with Schaeffer's idea of *musique concrète*, music is allowed in, but its purpose is not to be one sound among many, rather it is something to punctuate the possible portentousness that builds up (like the 'comedy brass finale' of 'The Schmürz' on the same album). The context of Nurse

With Wound is significantly different to that of Schaeffer's State-sponsored and laboratory-style approach, coming after a huge amount of experimental and often untutored 'rock' versions of what *musique concrète* was up to, and arriving at a point where punk and 'industrial' music had altered audience expectations and demands. Whilst Stapleton's macabre visual aesthetic perhaps leads to a too-easy identification with early industrial music, there is always an unlaboured and authentically Surrealist humour going on (even if there are slightly too many 'mysterious' French vocals on the early albums) – at its height in the *Sylvie and Babs Hi-Fi Companion* (1985), which is an extended run at classic roll 'n' roll and easy listening tunes, with a 'cast of thousands'. As well as being a very early musical mobilization of experimental as opposed to ironic kitsch, it also provides a way into the notion of a noise 'cover'.

It might be tenuous to say that certain musical approaches offer a different way of doing covers, but it seems to me that, if an experimental artist does a cover, it raises curious questions: how does the artist who wishes to break with musical convention engage with respect? Is an homage by Nurse With Wound any different to a pop 'diva' doing the same? Possibly not, and this risk is part of what is *not* at stake for the pop performer. Is the artist attacking the 'original', making it kitsch, where once it at least tried not to be? Such 'irony' would be simply a statement about the superiority of the covering artist, self-reflection heightening the rationalist, controlling force that already structures music (and that noise tries to undermine or avoid). Nurse With Wound fall into neither trap, even on *Sylvie and Babs*, which announces itself as kitsch, its cover mimicking the conductor-led easy listening albums of the 1950s and 1960s, claiming it to be completed 'with titillating orchestrations by Murray Fontana'. Among the pop titles is Nurse With Wound's 'Astral Dustbin Dirge'.

Visually, this album is in the genre of Bert Kaempfert, James Last et al., whose easy listening world is (slightly) defamiliarized by the slightly dubious and seedy collage on the inside cover. Musically, 'You Walrus Hurt the One You Love' promises something wry, even quirky. Luckily, the collaging of easy listening, soundtrack material, mid-twentieth-century pop songs with bursts of sawing, shouting, random vocal interjections, sound effects and so on, raises the album, or more accurately lowers it from the podium of smug appreciation of the awful. Instead, the album has to be seen as a multilayered 'homage', as it recalls the work of early studio experimenters like Les Baxter and Joe Meek. It is worth noting that the vast bulk of 'easy listening' orchestral collections were already covers – were being brought into the easy soundworld – just as here those songs and snippets are brought into that of Nurse With Wound. The album is also like a variety show, starting off with cocktail piano and gradually introducing a cast of dozens of Stapleton's associates (as the Murray Fontana Orchestra). Particularly now, and since the advent of easy sampling through computers, Stapleton is far from the only person to have surmounted kitsch in reappropriating music deemed worthless, dated or too pleasant, but what made this album interesting was the contrast between sample and something like 'noise music', which is where a noise relation is set up. 'Great Balls of Fur', the other half of the album, is much more performed, a combination of uncongealing cosmic rock and karaoke by the lost and bewildered.

Stapleton would return to this vein of music, but with a different approach, on *Who Can I Turn to Stereo?*, a Lynchean and near-melodious reworking of the music of Perez Prado, and it is in the even more direct cover of Jacques (sometimes Jac) Berrocal's 'Rock 'n' Roll Station' that we can see the cover incorporating the original, not as part of a repertoire, or even of an accumulation of cultural capital through reference points, but in making the originality of the original tangential. Nurse With Wound issued *Rock 'n' Roll Station* in 1994, revisiting it as *Second Pirate Session* in 1998. 'Second pirate session' is a line from within the song 'Rock 'n' Roll Station'. In this, the vocalist (Vince Taylor for Berrocal, Stapleton in the cover version) recites a story that may be about an observatory, or a recording session ('this is a session where we can do what we want to do'), or may be the telling of one of those stories within another. It continually refers to itself, and to the possibility of coming into existence, of music as potential ('Jacques's bicycle is music. Everything is possible. Possible.'). Berrocal is indeed playing his bicycle, while an unchanging bass riff supplies rhythm. The track 'itself' fades away, and is replaced by clinking cups and laughter, as people listen to a recording of 'rock 'n' roll station' in the background. Nurse With Wound's version replaces the bass with a digitally created rhythm, paced exactly the same as Berrocal's version.

Jacques's bicycle as music grows another layer as it becomes an influence on Stapleton, and the potential continues to multiply – because of the play (of music, of potential, of self-reference) always already launched in the 'rock 'n' station', nothing needs to be added. The performing is the adding, not just through another reading of a text, but because this song is recursive and viral in the first place. Nurse With Wound conclude by replicating the 'coda' of the 'original' (an original many heard after hearing Nurse With Wound's noisily faithful rendering) through a very particular substitution. As the 'cover' ends, Stapleton intones a few lines about Russolo, over a different backing, and in the (aural) distance. The detail of the operation to heighten the proliferation of the 'original' can be heard further, if we return to Berrocal's album *Parallèles* (originally 1977, reissue 2001). The track 'Bric-à-Brac', which constituted side two of the LP, ends with a French-accented voice (uncredited, but feasibly Berrocal) intoning a few lines about Russolo, and returning to some of the lines of the track 'Rock 'n' Roll Station'. Through Nurse With Wound's bookending, Stapleton is able to incorporate the rest of 'Bric-à-Brac' as influence – with its banging, scraping, odd instruments and atmosphere, where improvisation creates what in hindsight was always already an acoustic version of Nurse With Wound.

Through a range of opposing strategies, Nurse With Wound have managed to summon influence without either letting it go, becoming slavish to it or even adapting it. The original influences become incorporated into a world of an 'other musicality' apart from a musical reference system which would think of a lineage, of greats and timeless classics. With Stapleton, music or art become timely, even if that time is now complex, one of a sequence of returns and reversals in precedence. This is not absolutely different from all covers, nor is it separate from plunderphonic use of samples, like, for example, Ground Zero's 'cover' of Heiner Goebbels and Alfred 23 Harth's sampling cover of the Revolutionary Peking Opera (*Revolutionary Pekinese Opera ver 1.28* [1996]) but what Nurse With Wound's approach to influence indicates is something of the complex existence (only ever fleeting, only ever gone or to come) of the avant-garde, and also of how influence, when not treated as a simple, ranked list, is uncontrollable.

Like Nurse With Wound, The New Blockaders combine use of non-musical instruments, art inspiration and a critique of musicality that is designed to renew. The New Blockaders, who are R. Rupenus and P.D. Rupenus, released their first album *Changez Les Blockeurs!* in 1982 (also on *Gesamtnichstwerk*, CD 1). The 'instrumentation' is made up of objects and bits of rooms being scraped, dragged, thumped, scratched etc. The soundworld that emerges is something that continues throughout their work, albeit sometimes featuring more processed elements, especially if in collaboration with others. What marks out this first album is its refusal to go beyond what is actually a very limited set of sound possibilities – whilst there is continual clatter, it does not aspire to variety. Unlike other of their releases, there is a dynamic, with changes in emphasis, mainly in the percussive elements – 'part one', for example calms down toward the end, dissipating any momentum it might have acquired and in place of what could have been construed as rhythms are staccato metallic scrapes. Throughout, the percussiveness is jerky, but also insistent, as if trying to create an object that is both resistant, mass-ive and also something that exists only to be pummelled away. 'Part two' ends with quiet creaks (having taken in a dog yapping and something like elephantine trumpeting). Clatters give way to bumps and finally, a hiss like dust.

On the face of it, this is very similar to the near-contemporary recordings and performances of early phase Einstürzende Neubauten, who use electrical tools, metals, bits of buildings and so on at about the same time. But the German group are *using* destruction, where The New Blockaders are destructive of instrumentation. The New Blockaders refuse the *evocations* that characterize 'industrial music', and collapse signification into material. Initially, unlike Schaeffer or Nurse With Wound, the sound seems to maintain its 'dramatic context' – i.e. we know, and are encouraged to notice, what is being played, however unusual it is in the context of music (recording, performance, artwork). But The New Blockaders refuse a virtuosity of the newly musicalized object. If a chair or wall is to be used 'as percussion' it will not be salvaged as a musical instrument, but will retain its flatness, its essential unmusicality. Later recordings and performances even lose the residual possibility of 'properly playing' objects in an indistinction of sound.

Refusal is a key part of their strategy. Also in 1982 came 'The New Blockaders Manifesto', which lays out a strong rejection of all art, the past and meaning. In being 'anti-music, anti-art, anti-magazines, anti-books, anti-films, anti-clubs, anti-communications', they aim for new thoughts, new actions etc. (The New Blockaders, *Gesamtnichtswerk* sleeve notes). Their rejection is purposeful, but also contains the same seeds of contradiction propagated by the multiple Dada manifestos: 'we will make a point of being pointless'. Their philosophical nihilism (as opposed to the use of that word as an accusation of hypocrisy, cynicism or violence) is complete: everything is to be refused, even the meaning of the refusal. In this, The New Blockaders set themselves apart from Nurse With Wound: the former are genuinely rehearsing and re-presenting the purpose of Dada – a continual questioning and destruction being in its own right creative, and not just a way of clearing a path or effecting a cleansing (as some parts of Futurist manifestos suggest). The manifesto does announce 'we must destroy in order to go forward!', but the important thing is how this is achieved – the going forward of The New Blockaders music is always a dwelling in the destruction of musicality. Nurse With Wound's reclamation of Surrealism is different, even if the sound strategies can seem similar: for Surrealism is about revealing more creation, finding more references and allusions.

Beyond the connections to specific movements, both groups recall the era of high modernism as a refusal of all that came before or at the same time. The New Blockaders manifesto summons a moment where the artistic avant-garde imagined they could change society through art and exclamation marks. This manifesto becomes like the Nurse With Wound list: it doesn't quite work in the way it seems to at first – it is much more of a commentary on writing manifestos, a meta-manifesto, which, because it takes 'the manifesto' idea seriously, ends up being less than a manifesto (and this in a good way). It both means what it says and realizes the impossibility of this working, replaying Nietzsche's dictum 'Everything is false! Everything is permitted!' (*The Will to Power*, section 602). The sounds that we get are in place of music, and this writing is in place of a real programme for change. Above all, what characterizes the attitude and the sound is refusal – hence the 'blockade', but how to keep this fresh without changing is a dilemma.

One of the ways out has been collaboration, and ultimately the outward contagion that bears fruit on *Viva Negativa!*, two four-album sets of 'versions' of The New Blockaders's works. But before we get there, it is worth tracking The New Blockaders a bit further in their own right. The 'Live Offensives' of *Gesamtnichtswerk*, CD 2, continue the harsh, often jerky percussiveness, with pipe rolling and bashing to the fore on 'Morden Tower <10/83>'. All four performances establish a mass of sound that avoids light and shade in favour of a randomly phased strobing of sounds. There is no attempt to make high-quality recordings, so tape hiss and loss of sharpness also become part of the block of sound that is set up. Noise music is always an attempt to reassert the material over the musical, and this means not hiding the process of production as digital sound attempts/claims to do. Loss of quality is not inherently something to do with noise music, as MP3 sound compression and selective heightening of vocals over other elements demonstrate, but the boundary between means of reproduction and material to be reproduced in The New Blockaders material blur, as does the line between what is acceptable and unacceptable on a recording, as does the distinction between music and non-music (where, in this case, music would just mean the sounds purposely created or replayed by 'musicians').

Everything about The New Blockaders entails refusal, and yet this refusal to even be anti-art is potentially problematic, because, firstly, it is a common gesture, and secondly, it had in this case produced a large body of 'not-even-anti-art'.

The title of their collection, *Gesamtnichtswerk*, is important here. It reminds us of Wagner's dream of the 'total art work' – the *Gesamtkunstwerk*, but the art is replaced by nothing, a nothing that is emphasized in the sleeve notes, as being outside of everything, an emptiness that becomes total rather than being a contained space of nothingness, or some sort of nothing reserve. In place of art, then, is nothing – no renewal, no radicality to inspire. As it is a collection, it is not about a total single moment of nothing, but the sprawl of nothing where there should be something, which means the 'total' part refers to the entirety of music and art (scraps of which litter the booklets). Although creation has occurred in this nothingness, creation based on refusal is not the same as affirmative art, art that believes itself, and this because, not despite, of the 'manifesto'. The gesture is backed up by a material working-through of 'nothing' where art/music is supposed to be, and where a space has been cleared, there will be no building, only more clearing.

The third CD of *Gesamtnichtswerk* offers two 'symphonies': 'Simphonie in X Major' and 'Simphonie in O Minor', neither of which are recognized keys for composition. 'Simphonie in X Major' begins with huge industrial blasts, and moves through phases of machinery destroying itself – there are rhythms, made up of booming and howling. After 7.10 in the 'First Movement', the noisier part stops and gives way to scraping and thumping, building back up to more overwhelming blasts. The 'Second Movement' is crashier. 'Simphonie in O Minor' is mostly quiet tape hiss, fizzing, and, gradually rising in volume from virtual inaudibility, a background throbs within it (see Chapter 6 above for more on this piece). The symphony is, of course, the privileged mode of 'classical' music at its height as an elitist art (culturally as well as in terms of class reception and production). Like the realist novel, its steady narrative and teleology reassures the higher classes of European society. Its structure makes it easy to construct a linear history of aesthetic beauty around it, suggesting a sense of order at all levels. Modernist experiments moved away from the symphony and/or sonata form, and in the case of noise music, attempted to leave form behind (somewhat optimistically and didactically). The New Blockaders take the symphony into the woods and pound it until it stops speaking its language of reconciliation and resolution. Narrative is specifically undone through the non-linear trudge through 'non-music' in the first 'simphonie', and through absence in the second (without being the smug silence of John Cage's 4'33"). This rejection of narrative is crucial in returning us to the question of influence – which can no longer be heard in terms of inheritance but must be seen as agonistic and retrospective.

Not only this, but it is undone – not refused, the spurious belief in individual genius unconnected to history stripped back.

This rejection of the notion of the creative genius (as seen in Dada) extends to The New Blockaders's collaborations, which range from Organum through the Haters to Merzbow, to the 'versions' or 'tributes' on *Viva Negativa!* and on to the three-CD set *Changez Retravaillé* (2019) comprising remangled versions (by thirty different artists) of *Changez Les Blockeurs* The working methods are kept obscure, but it mostly seems as if material is being shared and altered, rather than the jazz model of the individual player finding a like-minded spirit and realizing some sort of meeting of musical minds through presence. Similarly, The New Blockaders's collaboration is not like remixing, where one self-present individual brings their style to another, in a mutual reinforcement of supposed greatness. Instead, individuality is swamped as the material gets more isolated from any controlling 'artistic' force, and aims for the self-generation and self-maintenance of living organisms. From the descriptions here, it might seem this is a very dry 'music', but it breathes, albeit slightly toxically. Its self-containedness, its removal from individual fingerprints being the key to its uncontrollability for listener and performer alike. This is not to say there is no recognizable style, or that a The New Blockaders/Organum recording (such as *Pulp*) doesn't suggest elements of individual styles combining. But once the 'music' is essentially made of noises, structured noisily and disruptively, without offering a welcoming form, any recombination takes it further from artistically recognizable modes of talent, skill etc. even if a certain audience would 'appreciate' this music *as if* it had those attributes.

The manifesto, too, exists *as if* it were a manifesto, as if it returned us to Dada, but without being merely a knowing reference or something in a 'retro' style. It is there again at the opening of the *Viva Negativa!*. Underneath it lies several hours of material, where The New Blockaders's material has been ingested by others and 'tributes' made: the manifesto's seriousness (it is *not* ironic, in the sense of smugly deriding those early twentieth-century manifestos, but it is a humorous take on the idea, I think) is essential for its own failure, and therefore its capacity to set up a tortuous, 'aporetic' path through the material. Its contradiction through eight albums of 'covers', four of them literally coming after the manifesto, in box 1, is part of the noise not being simply within The New Blockaders's 'music', as it establishes an effect that stretches out of the record itself, between records, between The New Blockaders and others, between The New Blockaders and listeners, and so on. Like Dada, the manifesto cannot but does succeed. It becomes impossible to fail, but to succeed as 'not-even-anti-art' is failure. This 'failure' is what defines noise in its encounter with music, for noise must fail to be noise if it is accepted, and of course it fails if not heard as well. This failure is where noise resides, the fate it selects for itself, or has selected for it. Noise must be only as if it were music, not a new musicality, and all this is signalled in the relations set up in The New Blockaders's manifesto and their actual musical practice, something akin to Bataille's 'formless', which travels between and undermines both form and formlessness, 'a term that serves to bring things down in the world' (Bataille, 'Formless', 5).[6]

No assessment of influence and the way it plays out in art should ignore Harold Bloom's influential *The Anxiety of Influence*, originally published in 1973 (or maybe it should – is ignoring references more noisy than using them? Is it better to twist them, get them wrong, gently deviate them?). Bloom argues that a later poet is in a continual struggle with precursors, and realizes their work as if free of influence, but all the while making that influence come to be, in the new poem. Many have misunderstood the 'anxiety' of the title, as Bloom is not shy of pointing out in his preface to the second edition. The anxiety is not separate or prior to new creation: 'what writers may experience as anxiety and what their works are compelled to manifest, are the *consequence* of poetic misprision, rather than the *cause* of it. The strong misreading comes first' (*The Anxiety of Influence*, xxiii).[7] The later poet develops as artist through six stages or 'ratios', beginning with a misreading that is never excised ('clinamen') and continuing through various reworkings until, ultimately, the later poet becomes the precursor, thereby belatedly making the earlier poet into precursor ('apophrades'). Influence becomes unavoidable, and something that 'cannot be reduced to source-study, to the history of ideas, to the patterning of images' (7).

Anxiety and influence come late, not early, such that 'a poem is not an overcoming of anxiety, but is that anxiety' (94).[8] Bearing in mind the seeming absence of worry in Nurse With Wound and The New Blockaders with regard to their artistic precursors, they offer good examples of Bloom's idea of 'anxiety': the presence of Dada or Surrealism, for example, represent a creative misinterpretation rather than a happy wallowing in older, better forms. That those movements are thought to belong to the past (chased away by a succession of other avant-garde movements) heightens the possibility of 'misreading', without becoming cosy irony or nostalgia, but an awareness of the influence as an inevitable connector. Paradoxically, Nurse With Wound's cover of Berrocal's 'Rock 'n' Roll Station' is not a case of relaxed recognition, but a highlighting of the peculiarity of the presence of music within a 'non-musical' approach.[9] Nurse With Wound have also recorded with Berrocal, and, as with The New Blockaders's collaborations, this represents a way of incorporating influence, of annulling it respectfully. The collaboration is a way of realizing equality, but what is produced heightens Bloom's idea of anxiety in that influence cannot be surmounted and all attempts to do so only emphasize its lurking (creative) force.

Influence is no longer linear, in this view, and nor is it capable of being clearly delineated: 'misreading does not simply occur between two texts, but spans and in fact constitutes the *history* of the poetic tradition' (Graham Allen, *Harold Bloom*, 19).[10] Again, it is worth noting that 'misreading' is not the implication of an error by Bloom, but the process of reading itself, which is always removed from the source (and we could extend this to the author). The field of poetry, of creative writing in general, even art in general, is composed of misreadings. So when the influence of influence is raised, as it is by Nurse With Wound and The New Blockaders, to become something problematic, rather than hidden, this is a playing out of Bloom's theory. In fact, they can tell us something about its reach, can display its functioning. This is in large part because the actual precursor, for Nurse With Wound or The New Blockaders (seen from a Bloomian perspective) is not a movement, or an artist, but music. It is music that must be re-read (misread), re-appropriated, denied, destroyed and so on, and finally music is brought back to an origin through its denial (i.e. the beginning of all music is its emergence from other sounds, which then become thought of as noise).

The New Blockaders's *Gesamtnichtswerk* even undoes the idea of a historical compilation, not just through conceptual framing, but also through closing on the twenty-minute silence of 'Null bei Ohr' [Nil by Ear]. This is not a reference to, or repetition of, Cage (but, in being silent, it makes itself the anxiety of such a repetition). At the end is nothing, in place of noise music. As it occupies time, the listener awaits, attentive – is it going to burst into sound? Is it made of frequencies beyond hearing? Is it about the machinery of recordings? All of this was never about listening, it almost says. But not long after this non-explosion, the *Viva Negativa!* collection appears, offering a validation of The New Blockaders's influence – one way of stemming the original anxiety of coming late (in the history of art experimentation). As the many artists rework The New Blockaders's material, and despite the subtitle of being a 'tribute', it comes across as being very much a collaboration (or even more a The New Blockaders's creation than their 'own' stuff). On the other hand, whilst it is often louder or harsher than the original materials, it is almost never noisier, so what we hear is an extinction of noise, just as there is an *extinction* of influence, a playing out of the fullness and permeability of influence. With Nurse With Wound we get an *exhaustion* of influence. Both artists are playing out the terminal condition of influence, glimpsed by Bloom as something inevitable, but perhaps not something that could be accelerated by noise. Noise music, then, is not just an example of a rethinking of influence, but where that rethinking is occurring, then there is something like noise. Or, better, if the thinking is undone, or replaced, or lost, or repeated.

In 2018, Nurse With Wound took on The New Blockaders directly, with Stapleton remixing, undoing, thickening the latter's first album, *Changez Les Blockeurs!* Like the versions and variants of the *Viva Negativa!* collections, this is much more or less than a reconstruction, and more, or less, like an unearthing of a field recording. Or the replacing of the first album with a new one. Like Pierre Menard's work with regard to Cervantes, this album is by the 'new' author, but in terms of the title it remains the same book (also like Marcel Broodthaers's version of Stéphane Mallarmé's *Un Coup de dés jamais n'abolira le hasard*, where the text was removed).[11] A further complication is the appearance of a section of this very chapter (in its 2008 version) as the text on the inner sleeve. This chapter, then, now, has to function as part of a loop that it did not expect to occur, a noisy loop within which it has acquired the possibility of extending the loop in order to comment on it. But, thankfully, we move on.

Nurse With Wound have managed to make a harsher yet smoother *Changez Les Blockeurs*. Trudging repetitiveness replaces uncontrollable spikes, and the overall experience is of a morass where there is no change, constantly. The review on Boomkat describes the effect as a 'mechanically reclaimed reflux'.[12] The burden of influence and creativity with and against the influence is all made solid, particularly on side two of the LP, with 'T.N.B. Amen' (possibly referring to long-term New Blockaders's collaborator Organum's relentless chimed drones of the *Amen/Sanctus/Omega* albums), that, despite the title, shows no prospect of ending until it eventually slopes off. The CD adds 'And', a more accelerated, crisp and echoey pursuit of absented music. All the tracks represent non-event music, where the eventfulness of The New Blockaders's scrapes, scratches and groans are strained, cracked and sometimes broken, resulting in a purposefully mushy slew, cutting slowly on 'And'. This 'And' is an addition, a cover, an homage that turns in on itself, on the Nurse With Wound list and The New Blockaders's manifesto alike (as well as its commentators, even) and on musical performance.

Vile Heretical Misprision: Dante's *Commedia* as Metal Theory

Three beasts circle the intrepid poet (Dante on the way to begin his journey through hell and on to Paradise) in the dark wood: the leopard, the lion and the she-wolf. What threats await him there, midway through his life and looking for answers? Traditionally, and following the book of Jeremiah (in the Christian Bible), these animals are seen as sins – false pleasure, pride and avarice, with the last also burdened with the leash of political subtext. What if Dante's fear is that these beasts are capable not of being read, but of reading him? What if we recast this encounter as three modes of threatening to devour the poet's burgeoning humility? Then I should propose that the leopard is Dantology, made from centuries of lithe and hungry fans of the writer, the lion is the powerful voice of theology and the she-wolf is, of course, black metal theory, 'gaunt yet gorged on every kind of craving' (Dante, *Inferno*, I, 50).[1] Really, my allegory needed four animals, even five, for the she-wolf is three in one: she is theory, she is metal music and she is the spirit of these in strange collusion, this: black metal theory, a trinitarian she-wolf, equipped as Lucifer or Cerberus with three heads. Instead of fleeing into the arms of the doubly subjugated Roman poet Virgil (by his sin and by his pathetic craving to be rid of it), let the she-wolf take us down, up and all around the three zones of the *Commedia*. Thinking through the lessons of gnostic, atheistic and sometimes Satanist music can shed more dark on Dante's work. This chapter will not analyse metal music in depth, but instead place it in what Moten might accept as a type of apposition – an entrapped yet radicalized way out through 'outness' which may, of course, look a lot like being further in. In the dim, unwanted, inappropriate light of metal, Dante's book is recursively *heard* as itself metal, an unwitting attack on all that is holy.

Earlier version presented as part of the Dante lectures at University College Cork, curated by Daragh O'Connell, in 2016.

Dante brings us on a journey through an extremely detailed set of netherworlds where humans and other creatures receive their 'reward' for their actions and thoughts or, indeed, their nature as beings. *Inferno* is full of gleeful descriptions of aptly apportioned sufferings, *Purgatory* is a relentless bureaucracy with little prospect of escape and *Paradise* is a song-filled beatific realm, where Dante is led, finally, by his childhood beloved, Beatrice. Each realm is carefully delineated geologically and geographically. Denizens are always in the right place, and the most powerful creatures – Satan and, ultimately, the Christian God – are uncannily abstract and part of an overall system, rather than above it. This bio-necropolitical set of realms is completely about control, power, violence that religion justifies to itself, and the need to bow down and accept your lot.

I thought that it would be *Inferno* that had a relevant tale to tell when thinking of metal (music), but of course, as we all know, and as the celestial power has it, the three modes of being that are hell, purgatory and heaven depend on each other, and so whilst *Inferno* is the most radical of Dante's spaces, it only becomes so against the backdrop of the bureaucratic oppression of the two other realms. But we cannot enter under the famous gates just yet, without pausing on the passage to black metal that led to 'black metal theory'.

From the late 1960s, heavy metal bands played with imagery of Satanism and hell. Hell became a representational synonym, and undeveloped as a concept, it was just a term for bad behaviour recast as good. Hellraising was not about anything demonic but about having a good time. Mostly this good time consisted of a circular argument, where rock 'n' roll was looking for freedom, and freedom meant being able to rock 'n' roll. This included, but was not restricted to, acts of blues-based music, but also drinking, drug-taking and fornicating. If the devil had the best tunes, he was also having the best time, free of mundane moralities. Rock stars such as Brian Jones and Jimmy Page, even Mick Jagger, took an interest in doctrines that were broadly black magickal, or Satanist, as ways of justifying the total freedom they actually felt was already theirs. Perhaps it was a way of understanding their position as semi-sacrificial idols. Black Widow and Black Sabbath made the connection more overt, and in the 1980s hell was everywhere, and as AC/DC had it, it wasn't a bad place to be. In other words, its charge had been entirely lost. New generations of heavy metal were spawned – thrash, death metal, doom and black metal all sought to make metal more extreme. So what? Even as it sought ever-more hyperbolic rebellion, and lost ground to much more experimental, much darker musics, it became more serious about hell, about its attack on God and its views of a barren universe shorn of hope. For the most part, hell was part of a set of stock imagery that did not get beyond the thematic, the shorthand, the easy cipher. But with black metal (following the social critique matched in the hyperactive cut and chop of thrash metal and grindcore) the thematic gives way to form (and this is the way in which we can read-hear the formal sonic choices made by Dante, underneath, *below* his desired religious vision encompassing social and political critique).

Although it is Brazilian band Sarcófago who really brought black metal into being, Venom had a bloody dream of its rising, with their song 'Black Metal', with 'In League With Satan' and the endless epic 'At War With Satan'. Satan and hell are seen as the resistance, a new side to actively choose – which in the context of Christian legal complaints about blasphemy and endangerment in metal music, made total sense. Venom's sound was muddy, low resolution, deskilled, the sounds of the songs mirroring the lyrical descent. They took legendary names: Cronos, Abaddon, Mantas, and raged in what now seems quite a polite way about the oppressive nature of religion, whilst praising violent mythical or historical characters (such as blood-bathing sixteenth-century mass murderer Erszébet Báthory, whose surname was taken by a late 1980s Norwegian band, while Iron Maiden took theirs from the nailed casket she used to extract blood from tortured victims). In Scandinavia, black metal became a phenomenon in the early 1990s, a musical, lyrical, behavioural rejection of historically imposed religious morality and its avatars (what they saw as the lies and hypocrisy of liberalism).[2] Its thoroughgoing rejectionism then ultimately became (in the 2010s) a paradigm for a heretical take on critical theory. What if, the writers of this style thought, the form of the music was thought, not just subject to theory, but capable of functioning as theory? Black metal theory is inspired primarily by the music, but also thinkers such as Georges Bataille and radical ecologists, more dark than the deep ecology pioneered by Arne Naess, or the darkish ecology of Timothy Morton. They try to work towards a post-human understanding of cosmological forces that impinge on the managerialist rhythms of digitalized consumer culture.

Black metal completed a journey of heightening authenticity within metal – as the rebellious element moved to an individualism that was formally lost in the blurred speed of recordings that sounded like they had been found in the woods. What initially may well have come from necessity was quickly adopted as a desirable sound, a morass of human loss, an almost abiotic sludge, a return to the ooze. Although I am not going to plunge my hands into the sounds of Burzum, Mayhem et al., I would like to pause on one release by Abruptum –

In Umbra Malitae Ambulabo – in Aeternum in Triumpho Tenebraum.[3] The one sixty-minute track that comprises this album is one of the oddest black metal releases, I think: clanking, groaning, some percussion, some guitars and a claustrophobic sense of no escape and timeless trudging unpredictability. An anti-ambience. That the 'darkness' of this album is also absurd does not go against it, rather it confirms the need to step outside of norms of achievement, beyond making tunes that are a bit distorted, or talking a lot about Satan with your face coloured a mix of black and white (corpsepaint). In fact, it is Dante we need to hear, in the aural light or dark of Abruptum's early work, in that of others like Trepaneringsritualen, Pissgrave or MZ412. So much noise:

> sighing, sobbing, moans and plaintive wailing
> all echoed here through air where no star shone,
> and I, as this began, began to weep
> Discordant tongues, harsh accents of horror,
> Tormented words, the twang of rage, strident voices, the sound, as well, of
>   smacking hands
>
> (Inferno, III, 22–27)

So much like the grisly gristly thumping of metal once the joy of whisky and screwing were ditched for, well, rolling around in the ditch of misery and railing into the thankless night. It seemed to the she-wolf that this was a lot like the music or 'amusica' of black metal (as Scott Wilson calls it).[4] Was *Inferno* perhaps a place where suffering was so great it undermined the edifice of divine reward and retribution? As black metal theory uses listening as a way of analysing, could it be that sound in the *Commedia* told us much more than we expected? More than the sound of the damned, perhaps metal musicians would be the punished whistleblowers, the ultimate sowers of dissonance and disruption, of whom the inhabitants of Malebolge 9 (*Inferno* XXVIII) who 'sowed schism, scandal and discord' (XXVIII, 35) were merely one tame example?

So let's listen to hell. What for Dante, or at least his readers, are the sounds of eternal nightmare, are for black metal the sound of eternal injustice, the sound of might making right and the sonic, vocal and physical made to bear witness to the cruelty of the divine. Black metal embraces Canto III's uproar, the sound of a panic physicality, of nature unbound, of punishment to the point of mindless brutality, and, more than embracing, it harnesses them: in Abruptum, Mayhem, Darkthrone, but also the more technical Deathspell Omega. Where heavy metal banged on about hell, sin and 'Satan' in a loud syncretism of Sudoku and Boggle, and death metal dragged around a putrid corpse, or took a single idea and pummelled it into unconsecrated ground (the properly monomaniacal Deicide), black metal looked for something more alchemical – less thematic and more visceral, more physically expressive. Building from clichés, and never fully spurning them, they found unexpected depths in relentless repetitions and stripping away of clarity, such that the sound would be all, a sound at once relentless and also impossible to fully grasp.

Dante's hell is full of noise, the screams of the damned, their many ways of sonically expressing their fate only one component in the soundscape of *Inferno*. Hell is really fucking loud: as well as the shades bellowing, grunting, shrieking, we get the roar of animals (*Inferno*, V Minos, VI Cerberus, XIII hogs), and many variations on the sounds of nature. From the people, we hear raging (IV), hum and gurgle (VII), spitting and hissing (VIII), screaming and slapping, lamenting and cries (IX). In XII, 'souls well-boiled, gave vent to high-pitched yells'; in XXI, a devil 'makes a trumpet of his arse'; in XXII, 'in damned unison, the chorus shrieked'. In XXVIII, our sowers of discord are rent in two, slit open in punishment for their speech; in XXVII, Dante gleefully uses Phalaris of Sicily's invention, the brazen bull (which amplified the screams of a person inside it as the bull was heated with flames, as a way of imagining the sound of one oppressed soul, materializing as fire in front of him). The voice that is most obviously distorted, as opposed to merely pushed to the limits, is in XXIV, where 'issuing from the ditch beyond, there came a voice – though one unfit for human words' (XXIV, 65–66). The deathgrowl vocal is perhaps the most obvious version of this but it applies to all metal vocalist attempts to physically create the sound of the inhuman, alinguistic voice, often outside of expected tonal and pitch range for voices. Such voices are not restricted to metal, as evidenced most harshly in Diamanda Galás. Demons, for the most part, although seemingly complicit with the damned, as after all they are stuck there for all eternity too, are barely to be heard – as functionaries, they have tasks to commit to. In fact, they are heard as part of the overall effect of hell, as in the battle of Canto XXXI.

Nature in hell is a source of unrelenting noise – it is 'a place that moans' (V), full of 'all that din' (XIII), replete with the thundering rivers of XVI, and 'resounding there, a blackened stream – the din of which would soon have stunned our ears' (XVI, 104–05) and 'the roar of some appalling cataract' (XVII, 119). In Canto XIII, this dark ecology is made even stranger by the ironic ecological dream of a fusion between human and nature in the form of souls made into trees. Sound confirms the edges of hell – just as Canto III opened Dante's ears and scrubbed them dirty, and as the city of Dis is heavy with its enclosed yet mobile cacophony, so the end is marked by sound. After the amazing sight of mindless Lucifer, in Canto 34, lobotomized in all three heads by his mirror trinity superior, eating the great traitors Judas Iscariot, Brutus and Cassius, gore running down his chins as the treacherous are renewed just enough to be rent forever, Dante and his companion find the way out through hearing, a place 'known not by sight but rather by the sound/of waters falling in a rivulet' (XXXIV, 129–30). The resulting erosion has created a secret path up and out of hell.

Hell is loud because Dante tried to create a sensory overload, a sense of not being able to process what was coming in – a strategy of volume, of harshness and of perversely sounding the physicality (and therefore unelevated) nature of the realm of punishment. But noise is also troubling because it represents a threat. More than representing or symbolizing, it is a threat – the danger of proximity, of excess and of mobility. Noise cannot be spatially limited, even here where punishments are allocated to designated areas, and lost souls toil at their own doom and decay in subdivisions of misery – noise is the very face of that which cannot be controlled.

If it sounds like hell is driven by the bureaucratic concerns of infernal biopower, then Purgatory is the locus of managerialism. Here, the souls are not only trained into correct behaviours, but lap it up, willingly accepting an endless diet of dogmatic mantras supposed to let them out of their rut on the mountain. Only one person of many millions is on the way out and up, showing that the purgatorial phase of existence will continue indefinitely for most, while highlighting the utter ineffectiveness of prayer and penitence except if judged on an exploitative level (the purgatorial souls work ceaselessly and eternally in order to possibly achieve freedom). If those in hell are the most exploited, it is those in purgatory who are most alienated, least aware of how much their data-mining serves an officious economy of scant reward. Just as in *Inferno*, it is sound that tells us this: each tranche of unlucky timeservers begins their round of a layer of mountainous Purgatory (in Dante's hearing at least) with a specific hymn, signalling their proximity to the vindication of their self-improvement. The sounds of Purgatory are human, achieving an imitation of holiness through harmonizing, but it is only when Beatrice appears in Canto XXX that either 'the poet' or the reader finally gets to hear properly celestial music. Dante/the poet is not subject to the most literally visualized/auralized pyramid scheme across all the realms. He finds ways of clambering out of each step and moves upward as millennia of the dead create holy energy in a perfectly sustainable and virtuously exercising way, through walking and singing.

Paradise is the locus of all power, and, far from the denizens of black metal's blasted lands, the saved bask in light more than sound. For human souls, this may be the endpoint (or an endpoint) but, for God, it is just as much the beginning. Power emanates from here, and brings the other realms into being in a moment of simultaneous creation, such that the three parts play off one another like sub-atomic forces, always already in relation to each other, spatially, dynamically and, in this case, morally. Heaven, as you might imagine, is full of song, an endless harmonizing of joy and worship. We would expect that – the rapturous music's unity is the only possible response to God's proximity. But both sound and singing in Paradise are more interesting than that. Firstly, there is indeed the harmony of mass singing: 1,000 voices together in Canto V, a 'votive cry' and voice sounding clear in VIII, 'and voice with voice harmonious change and chime/sweetness unknown, there only knowable' (*Paradise*, X, 146–47). Dante stills his own song in recognition of its properly pathetic character in this company (I, XXIII), but the 'court of heaven rings with the *Te Deum*' (XXIV), choirs sing sweetly in XXV and XXVI, all heaven together sings in XXVII. Proximity heightens both scale, unity and sweetness. The harmony of the spheres is not a Pythagorean regularity but an exponential and ecstatic scale.

Harmony is not just a response to God's glory, it is an internally reflected part of it, as the Law is total and cannot but be obeyed. Choice and deviation have been removed from this realm, which after all is the emanating point of total power. For as singing increases, and we near the glimpses of God, Mary and Christ, Dante asserts the potency of the architect of all these rigidly delineated spaces, and also of what is plainly identified as the 'threshing floor' that is Earth (XXII). 'God's patternings cannot be moved' once initiated (VII, 68–69), it is 'God's ordering touch' that is to be admired, not the recovery of a sinner (IX). Paradise is where God's perfection is manifest – it exists everywhere, but here it is also the inherent and sole nature. Here, there is 'no contingency' (XXXII), everything is subject to control so absolute, that control no longer has anything to control, to paraphrase William Burroughs, in 'The Limit of Control'.[5]

Instead of being a place of rest for the lucky/virtuous/previously repentant/ holy, Paradise is the location of the display of brute power. Just as black metal suspects and atheism forgets there is, or was, a God, and his key creation is his own dominion. Within this, everything is subject, and the God is sovereign. This tyrant has made a set of rules that must be obeyed and give his creatures the illusion of freedom. Many will perish for ever in hell, suffering for eternity for misbehaving in a tiny sliver of time that is one human life. Dante is instructed not to question God's justice:

That heavenly justice should to human vision
Appear unjust arises from belief,
And not from vile heretical misprision

(*Paradise*, IV, 67–69)

This danger is reiterated to Dante in XIX and XX, and in the numerous statements of the totality of justice and power throughout the book. Cantos XVIII to XX witness the astonishing display of power that is the Eagle, and which help us introduce a further sonic element that distinguishes the tyrannical alienated misery of Paradise from the rebellious clamour of hell. The souls of the sphere (of Jupiter), as lights, form themselves into the pattern of the phrase *Diligete iustitiam qui indicates terram* ('Love justice ye that judge the Earth' [*Paradise* XVIII, 91–93], in the translation by Sayers and Reynolds). This noble statement about equity and equitable treatment is soon belied by the further megalomania of the process. A thousand souls congregate on the final M marked out in lights, which M can itself suggest 1,000 (in Roman numerals), the (apocalyptic) millennium and monarchy. The souls form a nodule within the crest of the two arches, perhaps summoning the installation *Fucking Hell* (2008) by Jake and Dinos Chapman, which introduces numerous Ronald McDonalds into a hypergothic Nazism of tortured and torturing figures. The clump of light-souls slowly moves around so that the M gradually becomes an eagle, the Eagle. This creature speaks not just with a united voice, but as The United Voice, 'blended of many loves, a single sound' (*Paradise*, XIX, 17), brushing off Lucifer's fall. The Eagle roars (XVIII), 'bade silence' to all (XX), causing the 'angelic chimes' to become 'mute' (XX). Such disruption in Paradise is only possible as a function of God's intervention, no other dissonance is possible. Dante responds by imagining the truth of the Eagle's statements about total justice and power entwined in terms of a lark, gradually becoming silent:

Like to the lark which soars into the sky
Singing at first, and then, with utter bliss
Filled to the full, falls silent by and by

(*Paradise*, XX, 73–75)

Total power brings silence out of harmony, as harmony is only a sufficiency, not apotheosis. The souls in heaven, racked in rows so they cannot move (XXXI) have no choice but to harmonize, sing as part of a monochordal choir. Their song, their notes, their voice – all are taken up in the total sound. The idea is that souls would want this, that we seek annihilation in heavenly bliss, losing identity for the greater being, as one with the reflections of the Deity (God is not present, even in Heaven, other than in manifestation as effect). But souls are merely automata, singing vessels ventriloquized by the self-praising absent structure of God. Maybe God is here, part of the structure, a tragic God who set all the machines running and has no choice but to move his own parts within the machinic realm, but mostly, for Dante's eyes and ears, he is not at all in the room. Equally, much is being withheld from Dante/the poet, sometimes as it would be too much for him, at other times because it is not worth the choir producing its beautiful sound as he won't be able to hear it (XXI).

All harmony here is about the Law, and is the vibration of a justice that cannot be questioned. So there can be no diversion, no invention, no abstention, no individuality. Of course, to take these ideas as ideals of artistic creation is profoundly anachronistic, but why allocate individual souls to beings in the first place and punish the acts of individuals if infinity minus three score and ten is going to be lived free of any characteristic being? The individuals Dante meets seem to have been temporarily awarded a shape, and any part of the amorphous light mass could have supplied the energy. In short, perhaps the concern with the individual should be thought of as untimely, uchronic, as happening outside of divine time. In any case, where early black and death metal railed against the vicissitudes of God and religion in the name of individual freedom from tyranny, black metal loses sight of this individual, in favour of an ever-emptying universe where the individual is a temporal or temporary blight within an unfolding emptiness.

The harmony is the least of it – for all Paradise's singing, it is dominated by silence. In XIII, there is the 'hush of the harmonious hallows' (32), in XV, music is silenced and 'reduced to stillness all its strings' (4–5). The Eagle is all about silencing as part of his assertion of power, in XXI, the sound of Paradise's singing is withheld from Dante (58–63); the Court of Heaven's song is beyond the reach of mortals, Dante himself is silenced (both XXIV). St John, of Revelations fame, makes silent the harmony of heaven (XV). Sound in Paradise is either being reduced to silence, so harmonious it is as if there is no music, and on other occasions its immensity takes it out of auditive range. All of these phenomena communicate the potency of God's power as manifest in the shapes of Paradise (as when his apostles 'His word their lips escapes' [XXIX, 113]). The nearer we rise to the ultimate hierarchy of thrones, arrayed for the refracted and involuntary pleasure of the herds of saved, the more we encounter something writers have begun to think of as 'the unsound', 'the possibility of sound becoming something other than acoustic or sonic (Thacker, 'Sound of the Abyss', 191).

The unsound not only hovers at the fringes of audibility, it defines the realm of the audible as a subset of sounds that can be heard/made/imagined/dreamt/perceived by other organs/other hearers/sounds that can never be made or heard. The unsound is the complete realm within which the sonic rests, anthropomorphically imagined as something essential in the universe.[6] Dante shows us that the sonic and hearing have limits, and in the ultimate places of the world/universe, sound gives way to its other, its unsound – as maybe every sound carries within it the prospect of unsound, just as each soul carries in it the prospect of its eternal fate.

Black metal eats away at sound, not only harsh-sounding and distorted, but also feeble, straining, failing, not representing, flailing pointlessly at arbitrary laws, events and processes. The only process that can resist is death, and its associated decay, the true sign of the meaning of death as nothing. The sympathetic connection to hell is clear, but black metal can also tell us about the endpoint of all things, for just as it searches for total collapse and the end of individuals, the end of nature, and its sound is the playing out of those processes, of what Maurice Blanchot called 'le mourir', the experience of conscious dying, so Dante's vision of Paradise is a permanent premonition of its own end. One day, all the souls who are to be saved will be there, and all will produce a harmony so unified there is no space from which to hear it, or even hear it as a note. This will be the unsound as totalization of the sonic. In the real universe, entropy will one day become total, as heat exchange is no longer possible. Galaxies, planets, stars, all will dissipate until every single particle is evenly spaced from the other. Either way, this will be the unheard non-moment of complete harmony where Law will be realized and where total dominion is over nothing, as every thing, actually every thing, has become unified into an absent or zombie existence. The total power to be heard, if only just, in Paradise, informs the eternal woe of those below, in the 'doom inflicted by the cross' (*Paradise* VII, 40). In that realm, 'man must pay with all that's his. The debt of sin in its entirety' (VII, 92–93). As we have *heard*, God's justice cannot be questioned, it is THE force of nature. And the place of God's justice is the virtually silent harmony of those who also have no choice but to sing. So the damned make their racket as protest, as a claim to a microcosm of sovereignty within the dead weight of torment. In this, they are, of course, making metal music. But an even better, because worse, refusal could be possible. The lesson of black metal lies not in the vindication of some Satan, but in the emptying of your own punished existence. Black metal resistance fades in front of the onslaught, loudly, but with the mission to become dust, to withhold collusion.

Dante's heretical black metal furrow is not a conscious one, but the economy, or distribution, of sound across the realms makes his text dissonant with regard to his properly devout message. In fact, the two messages co-exist, no doubt with many others, all locked in their own firepit, trundle-circle or numberless singing booth in heaven, and this, this is the reading of metal: instead of certainty of redemption, or the confirmation of the value of faith, the justice, power and glory of the triplicate world are exposed to a critical undermining, even as they are expressed as righteous. Black metal is the theoretical corrosion that Dante has always already heard and slowly released as his own perverse, unsound treachery.

Noise Hunger Noise Consumption:
The Question of How Much Is Enough

enough

Noise is not what it used to be. Or so we hear. Have we had enough? Too much? Can you have too much, can you have enough? Can you be sated, satisfied, or must you keep gorging? How much do YOU need to be full of it? How much do you want to take it all for yourself and consume so you can feel you have taken it from others?

THE ARTWORLD ALLOWS FOR SUCH SAFE POSTMODERN DISTANCING. JUST LIKE TREADMILL FETISHISTS NEED. JUST AS REDUCED LAZY PERVERTS SPOUT WHEN THEY'RE FRANTICALLY TRYING TO DEFEND THEMSELVES AGAINST CRIMINAL PROSE-CUTION. GRUBBING JOB-HUNTING ARTISTS AND ART AFICIONADOS WHO PREFER ART THAT 'RAISES QUESTIONS' ARE CERTAINLY AS DISGUSTING AS THOSE RUBBERED DILETTANTES WHO RECOGNISE THAT THE ANSWERS ARE WHAT YOU MASTURBATE OVER. ONCE YOU'RE OUT OF ELEMENTARY SCHOOL, YOU CAN'T APPRECIATE MERE QUESTIONS. UNLESS, OF COURSE, YOU'D PREFER TO NOT ACKNOWLEDGE THE RESPONSES THAT THOSE QUESTIONS PRODUCE IN PUBLIC.
SO BETTER TO JUST SHUT YOUR FUCKING MOUTH
(Whitehouse, *Cruise*, 2001)[1]

Is there a moment, for an individual, a subject, a society, or a part of the mass, where and when fullness of noise was achieved? Maybe it was too bitter, too rich, too spicy, too dry, too earnest, too much fun, and you got worried as you shovelled it in. Maybe you want a detox, a colonic. It's time to clean up, thank god that's

Earlier version given as a talk at *Noisexistänce*, Bremen, 2016.

over, I feel slightly queasy, and shamed. Did I really think that noise was cool, revolutionary, outside, inside, dangerous, excessive, subversive, transgressive and even paradigmatically tasty? Did you think it was a panacea, a purgative, a dose of illness to keep the consumer society away? Well, if you ever had a thought of what noise was and why you liked it, valued it, searched for it, then someone will tell you it's wrong, get over it, get over all that juvenile nonsense. We are all full now and we must retire to the smoking room as we pull our pants back on. The room will be hosed down with corrective and a new discipline of fear.

Noise comes charged: on the one side, negative – loss of meaning, pain, confusion, doubt, uncertainty; then, there is the turning of this wrongness into positivity, making the world safe for clean noise: noise can go from wrongness to rebellion, from wrongness to normality, from strange to familiar. Over time, it has signalled to many the possibility of joyous loss of self (exemplaries here: Eugene Thacker, Simon Reynolds, Salomé Voegelin). Even more positively, noise can become a thing in its own right – not an object, not a true thing that lies beneath appearances/audiences, but a non-relational joyous sprouting of the new – I'm thinking of when noise becomes the source of creativity, a new foundation: Michel Serres wants us to imagine a primordial noise; Deleuze, in *Difference and Repetition*, has offered difference as inherently positive, a complex grounding yet still an essential one; others, such as Malaspina, reach for information theory, eliding its historical boundedness, or, as Sterne says, in his insightful relativizing of Shannon and Weaver, noise becomes part of 'the communicative order' (Sterne, *MP3*, 122). Outside of people thinking about noise or wondering if such a thing is possible, noise begins to acquire value too, and between its valorization and devaluing it becomes a contested commodity: up for grabs, up for auction. So many people want something from it, and in taking what they want, seek to devalue the noise someone else has foraged …

Some of these ideas – the transgression of noise, the denial of it – feel like historic questions whose time has gone, reliant on a listenership with a different experience of the new, the unexpected, the offensive (in music or art) as something that represented a now separate from the past. But nobody is in that listenership any more – everything exists horizontally, and at that point noise seems like novelty or, worse, all novelty comes across to someone as noise. The post-Dada affect of diagnostic noise suffers in times where transgression is either all too real – based on abuse, right-wing extremism or contempt for minorities – or subject to apathy. Ultimately, apathy could be the perfect noise listener response – and inside noise, if you will, in the rarefied gentrified tussle for definition and models of hope, the relentless positivizing and accepting of noise has further dampened the impetus for any kind of noise. But we should never be mistaken, your triumph as a knowledgeable Hegelian, overcoming your fear of noise by making it knowable, is part of an entirely predictable failure of noise, that will happen again and again. The demonetized genrification (*sic*) of noise is of noise music, the hybrid, multiple, genre-defying music with a focus on industrial music and noise music from Japan. Noise will not emerge as a true thing but as an unexpected movement *against*. This is why noise remains in a logic of negativity that means react, respond, transgress, exceed. No autonomous existence for noise.

This is why I remind 'us' again of the lowering, debasing power of negativity. Negativity is not badness, it is a declaration of nihilist relational connectedness. It never attributes thingness to noise, outside of an instant that will inevitably be subsumed, so that noise is always happening as potential, but almost never there. The commodification of noise as symbolic or cultural capital, or as financially and fetishistically object material to be acquired has left noise music behind, as if ashamed that its noble aspirations for social dissidence are limited by the eruption of dissonance. We must somehow worry about it, or go against it. There is a broad misunderstanding that a gentrified noise is to be overcome, and it is this pathetic desire to overcome noise music that we must think about today. It is now other music that needs the imprint of noise gentrification – a misunderstanding based in a presumed equivalence between noise and noise music, between novelty and noise.

Even if noise is going nowhere, it is a nowhere, or a not-going, that is properly *diagnostic*. So how did we get so full we can only glance longingly at the empty record shops, inactive music distributors, shuffle obediently to the last venues with our arms crossed and chat to our global friends, in the post-economies of internet-based music that paved the way for the end of paid labour, while imagining a glorious time in saturated colour when the future was noise? Because noise didn't stop. Noise music did not ruin either the idea of noise, or the practice of avant-garde shock. Noise did not become a sad refuge for the solo sex man. Well .... Maybe it did, but what we can observe is the sense of relief that noise is in some way over, as the rush to think away from music, away from noise in the place of music, creates a stampede into the safe space of sound studies on the one hand, back to real music that is somehow containing of noise on a middle hand, and the tragic fate of the expert who has 'heard it all' on the other, third, post-Stelarcian, hand. So, to begin, one way we became full, or overfull, with noise is through a sense of abjection that creates a 'need' to attack, as Kristeva argues when addressing the anti-Semitism of pioneering cut-up writer Louis Ferdinand Céline, in *The Powers of Horror*.[2] For all the talk of ears not being able to close, or how there is never silence, it is the ingestion of noise that troubles – consumption without processing.

Writers on noise have been keen to distance themselves from ideas of noise that are too connected to the realm of music production, too beholden to something called 'noise music'. Steve Goodman asserts that avant-gardist noise has failed (*Sonic Warfare*, 7) and we should abandon what he calls the 'exhausted uses and practices that result from the paradoxical "genrification" [*sic*] of noise' (8); Marie Thompson notes that we should look beyond the narrowly transgressive variants of noise music as these 'reduce' it (*Beyond Unwanted Sound*, 6); Voegelin wants to cover the range from rave to classical drone (*Listening to Noise and Silence*, 46–51).[3] Hegarty spent a large time of *Noise/Music* talking about everything from jazz to prog rock to near-silence. So I agree that noise and music are not connected in the forms sanctioned by 'noise music' of a particular set of genres in the 1980s and 1990s, but what is going on in the use of noise in the plain, thankful and relieved rejection of the actual material that led to the conceptualizations? Rather than praise ourselves for getting beyond any kind of noise, writers should acknowledge that other than Jacques Attali (first edition only of *Noise*) we have been slow to decentre the idea of noise as a creation of thought, where music that was or would be caught up in tangled sets of judgements about what would or should not count as music, or as music of a particular genre, or of appropriateness. I think that the rush away from noise music as thought experiment or experience is because many are afraid to dwell in the space of last musics, and want to kickstart the endlessly rejuvenating and liberating dream of a sublimated noise 'both good *and* bad, generative *and* destructive, serendipitous *and* detrimental', as Thompson has it, in a not entirely positive, yet still utopian-recuperative mode (*Beyond Unwanted Sound*, 3), as it is a site of 'reinvigoration and revitalisation' (5) – exactly the error Bataille pinpointed in Surrealist appropriations of de Sade.[4]

There is, then, the idea that sound or noise need to be thought of more broadly than in the context of a very specific set of experimental music-ish performance (Frances Dyson wishes there was no noise other than the noise of rebellion, i.e. rebellion, any rebellion as noise).[5] Others have the idea that maybe sound art and sound theory can explore sound where there is no sound – a place certainly safe from noise (Thacker, Eleni Ikoniadiou, Seth Kim-Cohen), in a parodic and therefore lovingly perverse counter-rendering of acoustic ecology's hippy dream. And all this, ALL THIS insider rejection of noise as event in the place of music happens while fans may well think it is hypocritical to reflect on noise at all. Does the unsound map an imposition of silence (after all, can everyone equitably enter the realm of the unsound, or have some been unsounded, or oversounded already?) onto a wish to move on from avant-gardist disturbance? Not necessarily, and not in the writers mentioned above, but the space for avant-garde noise is shrinking.

distemper

The walls are closing in and, instead of super-saturation, we are experiencing a refusal of noise that is often very interesting, but also reveals a deeper malaise, in the maintenance of auto-reinforcing elites that like a steady diet of new stuff they can discover first, write about first, make as sound first. Noise is caught in a circuit of hope and disappointment, of hunger and regurgitation. Critics and indeed proponents of something like noise music have mostly ended up in the same narrative Simon Reynolds produces in *Blissed Out* in 1990 when he said that 'the rhetoricians of noise actually destroy the power they strive to celebrate' (*Blissed Out*, 58) – it is vital to be aware that this dismissal is itself historic, and as accurate as the near-contemporaneous *End of History* by Francis Fukuyama.[6] This is the model: here is some newly noisy music; here is why it is only a pretend version of what you're looking for, and now, behold, here is some real noise, in a form that is praised for being truly more noisy than the literal noise antics of power electronics, noise or industrial (but you can insert the 'real noise that happens not to be noise music' of your choice here). What Reynolds does in this essay migrates across time as a territorializing template, identifying the quest for ecstatic consumption, feeling saddened by its loss in either commercialism or over-literalism, then overcome these worries by closing off the disturbance. That never happened, so I can't miss it. Or – in a slight variation, that was great, I'll never have it again, so I will impose my fan superiority to make sure nobody else can have it.

A more serious point lies within this melancholic rigour, which is the maintenance of a subjective reaction to noise (in whatever form) as transferable: what *I* now think or decide is what everyone must think, as *I* have achieved dialectical progression. The soulful and tasteful noisy lover wants to bring it all inside him. I consume so you cannot, *I* have consumed and now mourn *my* lost ingestion. Rejection of noise music is a tragic necessity that this heroic figure has accomplished, and in this slowly congealing skin of repression, all that went in is now trapped there.

Some of this fullness as abject rejection, or ab-jection, would be worth considering in more detail, but first we should identify the fullness that maybe many feel has justified the feeling of there being enough noise. I refer, of course, to harsh noise wall, a particularly dense form of noise that some might choose as their expression of 'real noise' now that all else is 'gone'. While harsh noise wall makers are no doubt all fans of Japanese noise, what is new and even radically different about wall noise is the rejection of constant contingency in favour of a permanent state of exception. Where noise music (now often described as harsh noise) sought to be constantly on the move, shifting, collapsing, blocks of sound fighting one another, tailing off, exploding, in an aural restiveness that stimulates to no *end*, harsh noise wall is a solid, unchanging and dense soup of sounds – often multilayered, where nothing arises, it all congeals, it starts and stops, but without logic, without the comfort of the sanctioned unexpectedness of electronic noise. It, too, does not *end*, even if it finishes.

When I first wrote about noise and fullness (in *ctheory* in 2001), it was to try and capture the infiltrating capacity of noise, the solidity that built despite possible critical barriers a listener, a public, a society might have. I thought of noise as something that could overwhelm, but that this would soon pass, in a nihilist reconception of Kant's sublime, that also referred to Bataille. This is as true now as ever … Or, alternatively, there is nothing to do with truth in the making and experiencing of noise. But there is theorizing, there is world modelling, there is a categorical operativity that fills those present in noise performance with their own absence.

Since the beginning of the twenty-first century, there has been a steady commodification of noise, in all respects – symbolic capital of extremes, collector capital, thought capital – as consumption regularized so that noise music did become a genre, whether we like it or not. Like all anti-art, success is failure, and I don't mean in any deconstructive way – the spread of noise as an idea into the mainstream, of awareness of noise music, of easy access to recordings, obviously means that any radical charge is normalized. This should not surprise us, even if noise is in any way a different type of genre to others, then its normalization is exemplary of how all 'authentic' new styles receive the imprint of acceptance. If it's any comfort to those worried about the genrification of noise, at least this 'selling out' comes at no monetary gain to the performers, record labels or even specialist sellers (more on this in Chapter 8 above).

The normalization of one type of noise – 'noise music' – is far from being the end of noise – and maybe the normalization of noise music has been overstated by an elite listenership and professionalized writership. Whatever happens to one expression of noise in a given moment, disturbance does not go away – but it might be harder in a realm without a belief in a succession of either avant-garde progress, avant-garde failure or avant-garde temporal succession, at least. Disturbance might be the only ontological necessity – and, in a domesticated way, there might always be new experimental surprising art things, but to be 'after noise', if out of noise we are supposed to come, is more interesting than to be done with it.

So harsh noise wall brings us to the moment of being 'after noise'. In one way, it is the end of noise, the end of music – the final sound. This is too boring a view to treat seriously, but it is a passage for the listener to traverse – it is a rhetoric based on overcoming and also on exhaustion, and it is this part that is more interesting, as it includes the prospect that harsh noise wall is an ending that implies the living on in the end. For Vomir, the crucial element of harsh noise wall is the removal of stimulus, of narrative, meaning, politics, and the creation of an obscure reaction that you can only blame yourself for. It is about ending, not completion – a way out of satiety – when it stops you will not be satisfied, whatever else you have told yourself to feel or hear. That this is a political or politically charged act and approach should go without saying, but nihilist politics is hard to read as having a clear mission, and people like clear missions in an age witnessing a sharp increase in parallel truths and para-fascisms. Difficulty is part of harsh noise wall, and this lurks within a superficially very basic sonic reality.

Harsh noise wall is a sign of completion, of being sated with noise, and is one of the last sounds, even if it does not happen at the final moment of history. In this, it is like all avant-gardes – none of these imagined they were a way station to the next movement. All operated as endpoints, auto-manifestos of the superseding of all that had gone before such that nothing need come after. And, of course, the thing we would call noise music, of the 1980s and 1990s, had to be like all avant-gardes. You will not be the last sound, there is always one more, a last sound +1, which, if noisy, will also respect Deleuze and Guattari's hope for the n-1, echoing Moten's take on the soloist in Anthony Braxton's work: 'not (all) one. 1-n, having been rendered less than one, but not simply because of that, she is and instantiates a power of n+1' (*The Universal Machine*, 128).[7] The sound beyond all sound, beyond all noise, is where you can find the crypto-modernism of Deleuze and Guattari, as they wish that experimental writing could shed the last dream of conveying the truth of fragmentation, or loss, or alienation (see *Thousand Plateaus*, 17, 21).

The term, or notion, of harsh noise (referring to noise in the style of Japanese noise, or American para-punk noise, or post-compositional electronica, or post-digital junk, or DIY handmade electrical-electronic noise making), arose out of a disgust for the colonization of the idea of noise by anyone making new music in an independent context; in particular, it represented a reaction to the land grab of the 'experimental' by outsider music, by quirk-fusions, jazz-metal, soundtracks, the slow creep of stoner drones, and indie music that was unfamiliar to the ghettoized noise listener. Harsh noise wall, with its seemingly monolithic sonic presence, claims to be a deeper, misanthropic rejection of social as well as aesthetic values. It taps into now-traditional imagery and titling of industrial and power electronics, and is sometimes properly, significantly tragic, at other times, just sad (I recommend a scour of Bandcamp, or other content-housers, to see the tired, exploitative imagery of much Harsh Noise Wall; of course, this is not the full story – but it is a genre marker). I do not wish to say that harsh noise is the culmination of noise music, neither, thankfully, will I say that we're over it, and now we can listen to some nice folk music, or electronic sounds, horror soundtracks, new fusions, someone else's cratedigging. What's interesting is that harsh noise has to imagine itself as the end, to the point where it is not even the end. As it fills, it empties, a purgative circular breathing.

bound and unbound

Harsh noise wall is not the culmination of noise, but it is a type of ending that is aware that it does not triumphantly conclude a dialectical history of either ever-greater noise, or ever-more domesticated, familiarized noise. Instead, it tells us about noise as fullness, taking us back to the remusicalization of the world that Douglas Kahn found in *Noise Water Meat* when writing about John Cage. Fullness is extension in all directions, and the historical arrival of ever more challenging noise, with the necessary de-noising of a noise in itself being only one dimension. Another dimension is, for convenience, horizontal, a spatial recognition of the noise of a now that surrounds us – the now of 4′33″ that seeks to iconically exemplify all 'nows' and the total sound of accumulated, past current and potential nows in the belief of an attentive human presence, knowingly wrapped in a welcoming soundworld that, while amniotic, is also ever-expanding. Like space-time, Cagean soundspace grows in the events that bring it into being. We can extend Kahn's respectful critique of Cage as someone who refuses noise through the rendering of the world as music, and consider that Cage had established an empire of potential which would expand through the initial inflation of the one precise piece. It is a mistake to consider all the other Cage silent pieces as further evidence – it is the framing of 'silence' in the place of music, as designated by the time of the title, that opens up music to musicality, to sound instead of rigidly organized sound, and therefore not to the simple existence of sound, noise or music, but the ultimate medium of the human ear.

The soundworld has no limit, and as Kahn has observed, sound energies have structured the universe before the existence of the ears, which evolved as part of the contingent form of the human. The sounds of the universe captured through telephony, and other electrical, then electronic media, come into being for us, close to hand, in the period since the mid-nineteenth century, he argues in *Earth Sound Earth Signal*, and this accelerates from the mid-twentieth century on. Its development through artistic practice coincided with the vital notion of 'sonic plenitude' opened (and closed as fullness) by Cage. Kahn outlines the idea:

> Sonic plenitude was constructed in relation to constrained and expanded notions of what qualified as musical sound, it was either all the sounds in the world, including the musical sounds, or all the other sounds in the world. A plenitude could be rhetorically summoned in implicit or explicit ways, be invoked through techniques of listening and directing of attention, be alluded to formally in practice (the glissando was understood as scanning the plenitude of pitches actually existing in the world), or be reproduced through allusion, imitation, or most notably, technological means, [including] the generation of hitherto nonexistent sounds ... which promised to bolster sonic plenitude, seemingly preventing it from being exhausted.
>
> (*Earth Sound Earth Signal*, 126)

Once you add in the potentially sonic phenomena that criss-cross the material universe without touching human hearing, or that may one day be transduced so that they do, the plenitude becomes all-encompassing: rather than being a description of a state of fullness, Kahn's model suggests a permanent filling, and a permanent capacity to ingest. Outside of consumption, sound will still be produced, travel, generate local sonic bubbles – but, as far as humans are concerned, much of this will be happening in the mode of waste, expenditure without gain. If Cage musicalizes everything, then the plenitude implied in his thought and extended by Kahn implies the positivization of all possible sound within the plenitude. All sound, all places and time capable of sound, all sounds open to being heard. It becomes increasingly hard to imagine anything that could at least point to an outside, or perhaps not come into existence. Well, I wonder if some noise might still residually offer itself as outside, even if as outside open to subsumption, as it orbits, unknown and unheard, unconsumed, like Seth Kim-Cohen's 'non-cochlear' sound art explored in *In the Blink of an Ear*. Perhaps, noise, or harsh noise is in that mode: a noise that has become not-noise, that comes into being as the wiping out of noise, of its non-aural, proximate absence. For noise to not happen in a way that is noise requires something direct, not an abstraction, nor a literalized materialization of an easily identified object bedrock of all other sound. Only the noise that approaches plenitude can hope to not be noise, to get out of genre, to become something that stops the consumption of noise.

Once again, we see the trap of the Reynolds's dialectic that ends in 'the real noise', but it is precisely the vacuity *and* the reconfiguration as cheap DIY genre that makes it a good example of thinking about the limit of noise, as well as noise as limit, in completely material, non-abstract, located terms. Where a writer like David Novak (in his comprehensive ethnogaphical work, *Japanoise*) tries to bring us back to the basics of harsh noise as a physically located music made by specific performers in particular scenes and heard by publics in ways they testify as being ecstatic but not appropriate for reflection, I think if noise does not pretend to be something more or other than music then we are not talking about noise, but punk, or metal or sound art.[8] And – if it has no claim beyond the power of the live experience – then neither is it any more interesting than rock music. Noise music, of course, has no real basis in imagining itself to be a hyper-genre, and neither can it escape the circuits and monetizations of being liked.

Just as it is interesting when hippy or punk music 'sells out', it is very interesting when something sets out to not be musical, to explicitly escape not one previous avant-garde, but all existing sound, and seeks to live in the richly textured end of all sound, and when this thing collapses into what it is not. This transitioning is the point noise happens, whether leaving or entering music. Wall noise tells us that the fascinating complexity of much 1990s Japanese noise music has crossed into the readable. Wall noise is not more extreme, it is about a diminishing of extremity, a condensation into one point, a point that then extends out with no logic to why it ends or indeed begins, or whether it has even done either, as maybe it was always there and we just tuned in to a part that drifted our way.

Wall noise is parodic plenitude, an intervention in the dream of perfect listening in accommodating environments, opening their sonic blooms for us to inhale in doses we decide upon. This does not mean it is high definition – mostly it is not. Vomir's releases range from very crisp to very murky. The presence of the medium/format is vital for the recordings that are released. Bridging harsh noise and harsh noise wall, precisely through the quality of the tape's presence, is Puce Mary's *Piss Flowers* from 2010. Since then, Puce Mary has developed a more delineated and complex aesthetic, but this recording stands up as a perfect expression of something we might imagine as late noise. Opening track 'Oval Court' pushes the recording equipment to the point of failure where audiophiles might opine that this really is just noise. Extremes of frequency are almost buried in thick clumps of wind pressure type sounds and muted squalls of electronics, and even as it tries to rise to an apocalyptic ending the sound cuts out, acoustically glitching, and this staccato breakdown continues in the title track. These two tracks map a fullness that is too much to consume, while not being quite flat either. The remaining track, 'Repulsion/Puce Moment', has Hoffmeier's voice, samples and a significantly higher level of fidelity, but still playing out over a bed of 'flat' feebly surging noise. The second half of the track offers more of a usual power electronics vista, but so much is lost in the failing recording, the low-grade format, it seems to withhold what could be construed as 'noise music'. Like harsh noise wall's reductiveness, *Piss Flowers* is noise about noise.

Sonic plenitude is always charged, just as noise is. It acquires the value of positive existence, a universe for us to hear in, or, for us not to hear all that can be sounded, but where it will happen anyway, a cosmic or divine (tone) generator. Sonic plenitude is part of the dream of acoustic ecology, where harmonious nature intersects with composed listening. Beneath the value of making us better listening citizens lies the value of sound as presence, or that through which presence comes to know itself. So the prospect of plenitude is also one of immersion and completeness of being (from a sound studies or humanist perspective) or acknowledgement of the overwhelming objecthood of the sonic that is its completeness (from an object-oriented metaphysical point of view). All observations of plenitude are not just observations of what is or could be, 'out there', but also of accomplishment, completion and therefore goodness. Wall noise replaces all this with a flat fullness of frequency, layers and so on, a fullness that is not about everything in its place (as Bernie Krause proposed and explores across his career but perhaps best expressed in *The Great Animal Orchestra*). Instead of locational certainty or even drift, it is about the removal of locatedness (in a way that parodies, exceeds, smothers Reynolds's ecstatic listener-ownership model). Wall noise does not trump plenitude with its own last trump of the apocalypse, it does not win. Neither does it fail, in any sense. Instead it structures itself differently to music and to most noise in that it does not seek expansion or discovery, but involution, emptying, solidification, through a parodic condensation of the plenitude of all sound, an absurd rendering of McLuhan's 'allatonceness'.

pleroma

Before harsh noise wall stakes its claim as a radical variant on fullness, and offers itself as a diminishing, a privation of sound (see Agamben, *The Time That Remains*, 101–02), sonic plenitude is posed as a good – it has positive value, it positively exists, and it acquires tradeable commodity status as potential for social and individual improvement.[9] I have already asked about what happens when we are too full – do we reject, eject, de-assimilate, ab-ject and excrete it? Or do we seek out ever-richer variants to satisfy our hunger for noise? What if fullness itself needs further thought? Fullness is mostly thought of in good terms – having enough to eat, matching need with input, desire with object, in adequation. Fullness in the context of noise can also suggest the full-spectrum frequency or massive volume that fills air and bodily passages and tissue with a new ambient density. But fullness also carries a superior value in itself, in the shape of the idea of the pleroma, as addressed by the Christian Bible, by early Gnostic thinkers and in passing by Carl Jung, Gregory Bateson and Giorgio Agamben, and it is the last that offers the most incisive understanding in a way that helps clarify what noise can be when it is not part of consumable commodity, or the thing that consumes.

Sonic plenitude, in all directions – in time, space, historically, in nature – partakes of this 'pleroma' in that higher reality is conceived as being the wholeness of perfection – as seen either in the figure of God, or how he imbues everything else, or how it comes into being as that which imbues or fills. So, even in the Christian New Testament, the pleroma of divine fullness is a messy category. The version taken up by Jung and then by Bateson is one where the pleroma is basically the noumenal world – the true world, beyond human reductionism in the encounter of subject and object. Pleroma, says Jung in his 'Seven Sermons to the Dead', is both 'everything and nothing', while Bateson draws a functional parallel between pleroma and creatura, where the latter consists of our attempts to process, symbolize, understand and delimit that which lies outside us ('Form, Substance and Difference', in *Steps to an Ecology of Mind*).[10] So, as we navigate from godhead mystics through negative theological mysticism into whatever it is that Jung was doing and into the techno-mysticism of Bateson, we see the concept of pleroma, the possibility of fullness, moving toward materiality, a brute materiality that we engage in matching, rather than ignoring or understanding.

So we can see how harsh noise wall might be something like this, or how it might work something like this – as a parallel to how the world is that which is understood but held as absent by human minds, but we are only part of the way there, because this has only transferred the positive value of noise from attribute or object to process. Agamben offers something much more challenging, and, weirdly, he uses the first theorist of Christianity, St Paul, to do this. For Agamben, the fullness, the plenitude of pleroma and/or of being saved has been radically misunderstood as representing a culmination in completion. In *The Time That Remains*, Agamben rethinks the idea of the messianic as something that occurs in a now that is not quite present, and as something that is necessarily and meaningfully incomplete.

Let's remember the example of sonic plenitude again: the world is or can be musical. Or, the whole world seems like noise, but becomes music after its acceptance in the obliteration of the avant-gardism of a particular moment. But how does this plenitude work? As I mentioned before, it needs a virtuous listener, and a world to listen to. Both of these are based on presumptions of subjective unity and objective solidity: me here, the world there, *as* there. But if each needs each other (no sonic plenitude without listening, no listener without the fullness of the acoustic world), then clearly each is incomplete. Listener and world need each other as supplements to complete their supposedly already complete sufficiency.

But, says Agamben, that which will be saved, or offers hope for salvation through a range of liberatory methods, is actually a remnant – the part that survives, and that forms a new whole: this is 'neither the all nor a part of the all, but the impossibility for the part and the all to coincide with themselves or each other' (*The Time That Remains*, 55). So 'the remnant is therefore an excess of the all [it is that which survives the passing of the all] with regard to the part, and of the part with regard to the all [it is that which survives the passing of what was only a part]' (56). The relevance of this semi-theological thinking is that sonic plenitude carries its own remnant in the shape of noise: noise is bigger than the whole, while it is of course also only a part of sound, and in overcoming the whole (or any part of sound), it becomes not more but less: less than noise, less than plenitude. When noise happens, it undoes itself, and is 'unredeemable', so therefore removes rather than adds value. Harsh noise theorizes the world the same way: it offers a fullness that blocks the sonic plenitude beloved of the sensitive listener, and it offers a purposeful limitation: it becomes a remnant as it progresses. If we think of it this way, we can finally imagine a noise that tries to overcome everything, that overturns the platitude of the 'world of all sound' in favour of a rigorous emptying of the place of listening. The world of sound and listener both become remnants of the harsh noise wall that is itself a remnant. To paraphrase Ian Gillan and Lemmy Kilmister, everything less than everything else.

So that could work with one experience of harsh noise wall, but surely it is just empty after that? Just more of the same, so we are too full and seek to reject it. In fact, many do, many say that it is a fine joke but can we stop now. When Werewolf Jerusalem, Vomir and The Rita assembled like wall avengers, for *Threesome Slitting* (2018), the expectation would be for an ultra-noise event, particularly as it refers back to the five-way wall tag of *Total Slitting of Throats* – instead, the album fizzles through an unchanging overloaded buzz, the harshness dissipating as it 'progresses'.[11] You can discern how the chopped up sounds of The Rita might play against the walls of the other two artists, but the album has such disastrously 'bad' production that it does not even fail. Instead, it opens up another vista of emptied noise, where noise turns sonically inward, curves, waves, peaks, troughs all merge in something without even the monolithic stasis of Vomir. This is another type of cosmic fullness, a staging of the end of what order there is in noise as the disorder of noise. An ending to noise music. Only one.

But this is noise that cannot stop, as it is not the end, neither is it on the way anywhere. This, finally, is where noise can strip the commodity of all sense. Like Yves Klein offering the same size blue paintings for different prices, an artist like Vomir is offering pieces with different titles and covers, that seem to be basically the same, precisely because of the massive condensation of sound in his work. So collecting as an activity, and the accumulation of cultural wisdom through expertise, become devalued, and harsh noise sweeps through the last residues of fetish collectable items. As the only thing that distinguishes many of them is the sound quality of the tape or CD, and more importantly the duration, all notions of framing a named sequence of time, as Cage did, and letting the world occur to be heard, are stripped out, swallowed and lost in the folds of harsh noise fat.

Both sonic plenitude and the hope of eternal noise are like the belief in endless economic growth – much more difficult is the prospect that noise is a lessening. With harsh noise, we do not encounter noise filling up and enriching or nourishing its listeners with political, moral or aesthetic hope. Wall noise is an asphyxiating sludge, viscous passage-filling that deadens capacity for other sound. It is, on a more cosmic model, a properly late-entropic system (leaving aside the definition offered by Shannon and Weaver as the mass of possible information that in fact also resembles a pleroma, with more information representing a higher degree of entropy [Weaver, 'Some Recent Contributions', 16]). In this system, identified by Boltzmann as the fundamental state of the universe, increasing sameness is the norm, as the heat/information transfers decline and all we are left with is equally spaced particles, in infinite extension: 'the whole universe is, and rests forever, in thermal equilibrium' ('Certain Questions of the Theory of Gases', 209).[12] A never-ending decline, where the ordered world, even of 'noise music', is a tiny and almost impossible zone of order in a massive non-communicating fullness that is empty of dynamism, and 'our world would return more and more to thermal equilibrium' (209). Ultimately, harsh noise wall stills the hunger for ever more noise, ever more tradable expertise/experience and rare records. Which, of course, means that there will still never be too much.

Notes

Nothing is Not the End

1 For a reading of the (over-)use of stories in launching theorizations, models and concepts, see Nicholas Mathew and Mary Ann Smart, 'Elephants in the Music Room: The Future of Quirk Historicism', *Representations* 132 (1) (Fall 2015), 61–78.

2 The 'etc.' returns at several points in this book, a soft excess that hints at the undefinable prospect of noise.

3 For the rest of it, see Perrot's website http://www.reclusoir.com/. Accessed 2 October 2019.

4 Clive Henry, 'Listening to the Void: Harsh Noise Walls', in Jennifer Wallis (ed.), *Fight Your Own War: Power Electronics and Noise Culture* (Truro: Headpress, 2016), 137–54. Henry also covers the 'spectrum' of harsh noise wall, in terms of sound, themes, approaches and history, noting how the genre is often associated with particular violent themes, illustrating how this is a far from accurate stereotyping and also questions the presumption of the presence of a fixated obsession on the part of the wall maker. Wallis's volume is at its most powerful when Wallis herself and her contributors use their in-depth practitioner knowledge to open up areas that are currently dominated by the views of hostile critics or by people who last heard some power electronics or noise twenty years ago or saw an album cover they did not care for.

Chapter 1

1 Georges Bataille, *Theory of Religion* (New York: Zone, 1992 [*c*. 1948]), 20–21. Translated by Robert Hurley.

2 Numerous phenomena have been recorded in the 2010s, and it would seem that an anthropocentric view of the universe(s) has insisted on the absence of medium for sound to occur in is really about an absence of a medium through which sound can transmit to humans for them to hear. Hear NASA's experiments at listening and translating sounds into the human audio range, such as this one: https://www.nasa.gov/feature/goddard/2017/nasa-listens-in-as-electrons-whistle-while-they-work. Accessed 3 September 2019.

3   Giorgio Agamben, *Language and Death: The Place of Negativity* (Minneapolis: University of Minnesota Press, 1991 [1982]). Translated by Karen E. Pinkus with Michael Hardt. See 44–45 in particular. I leave aside Agamben's anthropocentric grab-bag idea of 'the animal' he expresses here.

4   On radio as a defining negotiation of human hearing and the universe, see Douglas Kahn, *Earth Sound Earth Signal: Energies and Earth Magnitudes in the Arts* (Berkeley: University of California Press, 2013), and also Kahn, 'Preface', in Douglas Kahn and Gregory Whitehead (eds), *Wireless Imagination: Sound, Radio and the Avant-garde* (Cambridge, MA: MIT Press, 1992), 1–29 (19–26).

5   Ludwig Boltzmann, 'Certain Questions of the Theory of Gases', in Ludwig Boltzmann, *Theoretical Physics and Philosophical Problems* (Dordrecht and Boston MA: D. Reidel, 1974), edited by Brian McGuinness, 201–09 (208). Translated by Paul Foulkes.

6   On the absence of incoming alien-identified sound, see Paul Davies, of SETI (Search for Extraterrestrial Intelligence), in his *Eerie Silence: Searching for Ourselves in the Universe* (London: Penguin, 2010).

7   This usage of sound has been questioned for some time: see Michele Hilmes, 'Is There a Field Called Sound Culture Studies? And Does it Matter?', *American Quarterly* 57 (1) (March 2005), 249–59.

8   Steve Goodman, *Sonic Warfare: Sound, Affect and the Ecology of Fear* (Cambridge, MA: MIT Press, 2009).

9   On this problem, see Brian Kane, 'Musicophobia, or Sound Art and the Demands of Art Theory', *Non-site* #8 (2013), https://nonsite.org/article/musicophobia-or-sound-art-and-the-demands-of-art-theory. Accessed 29 July 2019.

10 Consult http://www.howmanypeopleareinspacerightnow.com/for the latest number.

11 Often Kahn notes an example of a real sound that has been masked, diverted, misheard or unheard by humans: 'since the nineteenth century, naturally occurring electromagnetism-as-nature has been overridden by purely anthropic notions of technological transformation' (*Earth Sound Earth Signal*, 12–13). Like Baudrillard, Kahn identifies a whole world of human processing and re-imaging, and always a true nature lurks as that which falls into representation. It should go without saying that my model, based on Bataille, also views the world as having some sort of minimal, negative, yet actual, quality of nothingness that has been traduced by human society.

12 Jacob Smith, *Eco-Sonic Media* (Berkeley: University of California Press, 2015).

13 See Arne Naess, 'The Shallow and the Deep, Long-Range Ecology Movement', in *Inquiry* 16 (1973), 95–100.

14 Jean-Yves Bosseur, *Musique et environnement* (Paris: Minerve, 2016).

15 See R. Murray Schafer (ed.), *Five Village Soundscapes* (Vancouver, BC: ARC, 1977) for a practical demonstration of what is good to record, hear and experience.

Further documents from that excursion into acoustics of an ideal ecology are at https://blogs.bl.uk/sound-and-vision/2013/07/five-european-villages.html. Accessed 1 September 2019.

16 See Karen Barad, *Meeting the Universe Halfway: Quantum Physics and the Entanglement of Matter and Meaning* (Durham, NC: Duke University Press, 2007), 135 and throughout.

17 Dominic Pettman, *Sonic Intimacy, Voice, Species, Technics [Or, How to Listen to the World]* (Stanford: Stanford University Press, 2017).

18 Seth Kim-Cohen, *In The Blink of an Ear: Towards a Non-Cochlear Sonic Art* (New York: Bloomsbury, 2009).

19 David Rothenberg, *Sudden Music: Improvisation, Sound, Nature* (Athens, GA: University of Georgia Press, 2016).

20 David Rothenberg, 'Whale Music: Anatomy of an Interspecies Duet', *Leonardo* 18 (2008), 47–53.

21 Marie Thompson, *Beyond Unwanted Sound: Noise, Affect and Aesthetic Moralism* (New York: Bloomsbury, 2017). Thompson continues to dissect the moralism of soundscapers and acoustic ecologists, and R. Murray Schafer in particular (90–104).

22 The leading guardian organization is the World Forum for Acoustic Ecology https://www.wfae.net/. Accessed 3 August 2019.

23 Mark McLaren, 'Interview with Chris Watson', *Binaural* (Winter 2006), http://www.binauralmedia.org/images/texts/theory_survey/watson_web.pdf. Accessed 23 July 2019. Watson too is annoyed by urban noise (1) and strongly favours the sounds of nature, but he accepts that nature is not only about the pleasure of sounding, the joy of listening securely.

24 For a varied portfolio of Watson's recordings of animals and environments, see his album *Outside the Circle of Fire* (1998).

25 Bernie Krause, *The Great Animal Orchestra: Finding the Origins of Music in the World's Wild Places* (New York: Little, Brown, 2012).

26 Thompson cites this piece as a counter to acoustic ecology's limitations (*Beyond Unwanted Sound*, 87–88), but I am about to argue, in this and the next chapter, that it still relies on a core presumption of realness inherent to a true listening experience, and so it *improves* on the problems of acoustic ecology as opposed to solving them.

27 Pierre-Yves Macé, *Musique et document sonore: Enquête sur la phonographie documentaire dans les pratiques musicales contemporaines* (Dijon: Presses du réel, 2012).

28 Jean-Luc Nancy, *Listening* (New York: Fordham University Press, 2007 [2003]). Translated by Charlotte Mandell.

29 Immanuel Kant, *Critique of Judgment* (Indianapolis, IN: Hackett, 1987 [1790]). Translated by Werner S. Pluhar.

30 See Scott Wilson, 'Introduction to Melancology', in Scott Wilson et al., *Melancology: Black Metal Theory and Ecology* (Winchester: Zero Books, 2014), 5–24, and Eugene Thacker, 'Sound of the Abyss', in Wilson et al., *Melancology*, 182–94.

31 Chris Beckett's trilogy (*Dark Eden* [London: Corvus, 2012], *Mother of Eden* [London: Corvus, 2015] and *Daughter of Eden* [London: Corvus, 2016]) takes place on a planet with no sunlight; *Pitch Black* (dir. David Twohy, 2000) likewise. These are good examples of Bataillean over-literalizing of 'dark' to take us further into what would be dark about a dark ecology that eschews the terracentric imaginary of a sun that gives life. Bataille's sun only ever gives life through excretion and self-immolation. As it spurs evolution, it also relies on death.

32 Georges Bataille, 'Rotten Sun', in Bataille, *Visions of Excess: Selected Writings, 1927–1939* (Minneapolis: University of Minnesota Press, 1985), edited by Allan Stoekl, 57–58. Translated by Allan Stoekl, Carl R. Lovitt and Donald M. Leslie Jr.

33 Georges Bataille, 'Mouth', in Bataille, *Visions of Excess*, 59–60.

34 You can see 'Cruel Nature: Lions Eating their Prey While it is Still Alive!' at https://www.youtube.com/watch?v=VECtHHQjCqg or the de-facing of a warthog with mostly wind sounds at https://www.youtube.com/watch?v=XmOFCntOIPo. Accessed 15 August 2019.

35 Georges Bataille, *The Accursed Share* (New York: Zone, 1988 [1949]). Translated by Robert Hurley.

Chapter 2

1 To read accounts from sound artists about their practice, ways of listening and thinking about hearing the world, see Cathy Lane and Angus Carlyle (eds), *In The Field: The Art of Field Recording* (Axminster: Uniformbooks, 2011).

2 Lawrence English, 'A Beginner's Guide to Field Recording', *Fact*, 18 November 2014, https://www.factmag.com/2014/11/18/a-beginners-guide-to-field-recording/. Accessed 7 August 2019. François J. Bonnet, *The Order of Sounds: A Sonorous Archipelago* (Falmouth: Urbanomic, 2016 [2012]), 58–59. Translated by Robin Mackay.

3 Stephen Benson and Will Montgomery (eds), *Writing the Field Recording: Sound, Word, Environment* (Edinburgh: Edinburgh University Press, 2018).

4 See R. Murray Schafer, *The Soundscape: Our Sonic Environment and the Tuning of the World* (Rochester, VT: Destiny Books, 1993 [1977]).

5 Jonathan Sterne, *The Audible Past: Cultural Origins of Sound Reproduction* (Durham and London: Duke University Press, 2003), particularly 311–33.

6 I have used field recordings (since 1999) in multiple layers as part of noise performances and recordings, but I think that while altering field recording is common, complexity is mostly presented as an internal part of any one field recording.

7   These are Skruv (southern Sweden), Nissingen (southern Germany), Cembra (northern Italy), Lesconil (western France) and 'Dollar in the Lowlands of Scotland' (*Five Village Soundscapes*, 1).

8   Steven Feld, 'From Schizophonia to Schismogenesis: On the Discourses and Commodification Practices of "World Music" and "World Beat"', in Charles Keil and Steven Feld, *Music Grooves* (Chicago: University of Chicago Press, 1994), 257–89.

9   For a reading of how the field is processed in field recording of birdsong in the twentieth century, see Joeri Bruynincks, *Listening in the Field: Recording and the Science of Birdsong* (Cambridge, MA: MIT Press, 2018). This book does not quite empty 'the field', but it does dismantle the idea of the field as something that can be objectively captured.

10 Jessica O'Reilly, *The Technocratic Antarctic: An Ethnography of Scientific Expertise and Environmental Governance* (Ithaca: Cornell University Press, 2017).

11 For more detail, see http://soundingmuseum.com/wordpress/?page_id=93 and for the transcript of the printed material, see http://www.transcript-verlag. de/978-3-8376-2856-2/the-sounding-museum-box-of-treasures/. Accessed 6 August 2019.

Chapter 3

1   Claude E. Shannon, 'Communication Theory – Exposition of Fundamentals', in Shannon, *Collected Papers*, edited by N.J.A. Sloane and Aaron D. Wyner (New York: IEEE Press, 1993), 173–76.

2   Douglas Kahn, *Noise Water Meat: A History of Sound in the Arts* (Cambridge, MA: MIT Press, 1999).

3   Hillel Schwartz, *Making Noise: From Babel to the Big Bang and Beyond* (New York: Zone Books, 2011).

4   Ludwig Boltzmann, 'The Second Law of Thermodynamics', in Boltzmann, *Theoretical Physics and Philosophical Problems*, 13–32.

5   Alain Corbin, *Village Bells: The Culture of the Senses in the Nineteenth Century French Countryside* (New York: Columbia University Press, 1998 [1994]). Translated by Martin Thom.

6   Friedrich Nietzsche, *The Will to Power* (New York: Vintage, 1968 [1901]). Translated by Walter Kaufmann and R.J. Hollingdale.

7   Jonathan Sterne, *MP3: The Meaning of a Format* (Durham and London: Duke University Press, 2012).

8   Warren Weaver, 'Recent Contributions to the Mathematical Theory of Communication', in Claude E. Shannon and Warren Weaver, *The Mathematical*

Theory of Communication (Urbana, IL: University of Illinois Press, 1969 [1949]), 3–28. Hereafter 'Recent Contributions' and *Mathematical Theory* respectively.

9   R. Haven Wiley, *Noise Matters: The Evolution of Communication* (Cambridge, MA: Harvard University Press, 2015).

10   Shannon, 'General Treatment of the Problem of Coding', in Shannon, *Collected Papers*, 177–79.

11   Rosalind Krauss, 'Sculpture in the Expanded Field', in *October* 8 (Spring 1978), 30–44 (37–38).

12   Benjamin H. Bratton, *The Stack: On Software and Sovereignty* (Cambridge, MA: MIT Press, 2015).

13   Cécile Malaspina, *An Epistemology of Noise* (London: Bloomsbury, 2018), 28–29 in particular, where Malaspina introduces the similarity between Boltzmann's entropy equation and the understanding Shannon has of it. Beyond the equations for entropy, Boltzmann has a broader entropy which is about absence as well as (potential) loss. For Shannon, entropy is a rich, too rich *source*, whereas for Boltzmann, entropy is a state of removal.

14   See Ludwig Boltzmann, 'Certain Questions of the Theory of Gases', 208–09.

15   Ludwig Boltzmann, 'The Second Law of Thermodynamics', in Boltzmann, *Theoretical Physics and Philosophical Problems*, 13–32.

16   Rendering at least partially obsolete Ray Brassier's idea (hope?) that noise would fail to avoid becoming generic ('Noise is Obsolete', in *Multitudes* 28 (Winter/Spring 2007), http://www.multitudes.net/Genre-is-Obsolete/) as opposed to scraping away parodically at genre as a category of categories.

17   Caleb Kelly, *Cracked Media* (Cambridge, MA: MIT Press, 2009); Greg Hainge, *Noise Matters: Towards an Ontology of Noise* (New York: Bloomsbury, 2013), 128–38.

18   Hito Steyerl, 'Too Much World: Is the Internet Dead?', in *Too Much World: The Films of Hito Steyerl*, edited by Nick Aikens (Berlin: Sternberg, 2014), 29–40.

19   Maria Eriksson, Rasmus Fleischer, Anna Johansson, Pelle Snickars and Patrick Vonderau, *Spotify Teardown: Inside the Black Box of Music Streaming* (Cambridge, MA: MIT Press, 2019).

Chapter 4

1   See also Philippe Decrauzat and Mathieu Copeland (eds), *A Personal Sonic Geology* (Milan: Mousse, 2017), in which the earlier version of this article appeared, 370–80 (French), 430–38 (English).

2   Gilles Deleuze and Félix Guattari, *A Thousand Plateaus* (Minneapolis: University of Minnesota Press, 1987 [1980]), 150. Translated by Brian Massumi.

3   Michel Serres, *The Parasite* (Baltimore, MD: Johns Hopkins Press, 1982 [1980]). Translated by Lawrence R. Scher. See 51–55 for his parable of rats, parasites, hosts and intermittent yet always-present noise as oscillatory potential. Noise becomes benign intervention.

4   See the as-yet-untranslated second edition, Jacques Attali, *Bruits: Essai sur l'économie politique de la musique* (Paris: Fayard, 2001).

5   Alex Ross, *The Rest is Noise: Listening to the Twentieth Century* (London: Harper Perennial, 2009).

6   Pascal Quignard, *La Haine de la musique* (Paris: Calmann-Lévy, 1996).

7   Fred Moten, *In The Break: The Aesthetics of the Black Radical Tradition* (Minneapolis: University of Minnesota Press, 2003).

8   Note that intermedia is not just about things that cross media, or are in effect multimedia in nature. Intermedia, as Fluxus artist Dick Higgins conceived it, represents a new, unstable form or 'medium' that cannot be categorized as one particular thing and cannot be made to settle into established categories. See Dick Higgins and Hannah Higgins, 'Intermedia', in *Leonardo* 34 (1) (2001), 49–54. The original idea was posited in 1965, and that original text forms the first part of the 2001 version.

9   His thoughts are gathered in Luigi Russolo, *The Art of Noises* (New York: Pendragon, 1986 [1913]). Translated by Barclay Brown.

10 Alfred Wegener, *The Origin of Continents and Oceans* (Mineola, NY: Courier 1966 [1915]).

11 The premiere of this ballet took place at the Théâtre des Champs-Elysées on 29 May 1913, and led to an actual riot.

12 Gustav Metzger, *Writings (1953–2016)*, edited by Mathieu Copeland (Zurich: JRP Publications, 2019).

Chapter 5

1   Lloyd Whitesell, 'White Noise: Race and Erasure in the Cultural Avant-Garde', *American Music* 19 (2) (Summer 2001), 168–89.

2   Jennifer Lynn Stoever, *The Sonic Color Line: Race and the Cultural Politics of Listening* (New York: NYU Press, 2016).

3   Fred Moten, *In The Break: The Aesthetics of the Black Radical Tradition*, and *Black and Blur: consent not to be a single being 1* (Durham and London: Duke University Press, 2017).

4   Theodor Adorno, 'On Jazz', in Adorno, *Essays on Music* (Berkeley: University of California Press, 2002), edited by Richard Leppert, 470–95. Multiple new translations by Susan H. Gillespie. This essay translated by Jamie Owen Daniel.

5 Tricia Rose, *Black Noise: Rap Music and Black Culture in Contemporary America* (Hanover, NH: Wesleyan University Press, 1994), 1.

6 Moten, *Black and Blur*, 260.

7 Tricia Rose, "'Fear of a Black Planet": Rap Music and Black Cultural Politics in the 1990s', *The Journal of Negro Education* 60 (3) (Summer 1991), 276–90 (279).

8 Malaspina asserts, in order to make a strong case that noise is basically about information theory, that noise is nothing to do with being against 'established norms' (*An Epistemology of Noise*, 9).

9 'What the Data Say about Police Shootings', *Nature* (4 September 2019), https://www.nature.com/articles/d41586-019-02601-9. Accessed 15 September 2019.

10 Imani Perry both notes and corrects Rose's critique of Attali – taking both beyond their ostensible positions to where their writings make similar points about history and cultures deemed threatening (*Prophets of the Hood: Politics and Poetics in Hip Hop* [Durham, NC: Duke University Press, 2004], 200).

11 Julian Jonker, 'Black Secret Technology (The Whitey on the Moon Dub)', *ctheory* (2002), http://www.ctheory.net/articles.aspx?id=358. Accessed 15 September 2019.

12 Room had been made for the virtuoso black performer in rock and pop, and musicians such as Jimi Hendrix (or Prince, later on) function as exceptions, precisely indicating that only massively original non-white performers will be allocated a place in the rock pantheon.

13 George Lewis, *A Power Stronger than Itself: The AACM and American Experimental Music* (Chicago: University of Chicago Press, 2008).

14 Marie Thompson, 'Whiteness and the Ontological Turn in Sound Studies', *Parallax* 23 (3) (2017), 266–82 (273).

15 The 'modesty' of sound art lies in post-Cagean valorization of sounds themselves and of the artist letting those sounds just occur, floating free of anything but a supposedly objective sonics.

16 In an exciting parody of collecting, Chang now has 2,000 copies of the album, https://www.pri.org/stories/2018-11-15/we-buy-white-albums. Accessed 20 August 2019.

17 For the relevant US Federal Standard (1037c), see https://www.its.bldrdoc.gov/fs-1037/fs-1037c.htm. Accessed 13 July 2019.

18 Arguably, there is a hybridity in Body Count's music as it bridges metal and rap, but I would argue that this identification can overstate the 'rap' element through a race-essentialist reading of genres.

19 See http://www.metalsucks.net/2016/07/11/slipknots-corey-taylor-shares-thoughts-blacklivesmatter/. Accessed 9 January 2019. Taylor's explanation is clear and well expressed, designed to win over fans of his music, yet still caught up in a logic of universalism.

20 YouTube has a video feature on Demogoroth Satanum from Soweto, who formed in 2009, https://www.youtube.com/watch?v=9hMPFVpKh0E. Accessed 9 January 2019.

21   For Gagneux's statement about how the idea of Zeal and Ardor came about, see https://noisey.vice.com/en_us/article/6wqvnb/zeal-and-ardor-interview. Accessed 9 January 2019.

Chapter 6

1   Martha Mockus, *Sounding Out: Pauline Oliveros and Lesbian Musicality* (London and New York: Routledge, 2008).

2   See Judy Chicago, *Through the Rose: My Struggle as a Woman Artist* (London: Women's Press, 1982), 41–44.

3   The text is from her film *Kitch's Last Meal* (released 1976). The piece was performed in 1975 and 1977, then recreated for seven performers reading as each extracts their scroll, and extended in form into a film in 1995. The reworked piece's title is *Interior Scroll – The Cave*, made with Maria Beatty, and is available on YouTube, https://www.youtube.com/watch?v=XHvXs6f02Ls (age restricted). Accessed 6 September 2019.

4   See Carrie Leigh-Page and Dana Reason, 'Playing Like a Girl: The Problems with Reception of Women in Music', *New Music Box*, https://nmbx.newmusicusa.org/playing-like-a-girl-the-problems-with-reception-of-women-in-music/. Accessed 6 September 2019. Worse still is that the authors find that 'only 10% of works by living composers were by women'. In other words, whilst the headline figure is atrocious, the persistence of misogyny not as idea about past 'neutral' greatness, but as exclusionary and active practice of actual women composers continues.

5   https://www.audiblewomen.com/, https://feminatronic.com/http://hernoise.org/, http://www.metalladies.com/all-female-metal-bands/, http://www.kapralova.org/LIST.htm (women composers list). All accessed 6 September 2019.

6   Cosey Fanni Tutti, *Art Sex Music* (London: Faber and Faber, 2017).

7   See D. Ferret, *Dark Sound: Feminine Voices in Sonic Shadow* (New York: Bloomsbury, 2020) for a detailed and theoretically complex reading of female experimental musicians of the last four decades.

8   Tara Rodgers, 'Introduction', in Tara Rodgers (ed.), *Pink Noises: Women on Electronic Music and Sound* (Durham, NC: Duke University Press, 2010), 1–23.

9   Jessica Rylan interview in Rodgers, *Pink Noises*, 139–55.

10   David Novak, *Japanoise: Music at the Edge of Circulation* (Durham, NC: Duke University Press, 2013).

11   Rylan, interview in Rodgers, *Pink Noises*, 155. We could add to this the greater visibility in recent years of a range of more complex gender identities.

12 Rodgers refers to this as one of a range of understandable positions taken by musicians (*Pink Noises*, 17).

13 Jacques Derrida, 'Plato's Pharmacy', in Derrida, *Dissemination* (Chicago: University of Chicago Press, 1981 [1972]), 63–171. Translated by Barbara Johnson. For more on Derrida's distinction between voice and speech, see Derrida, *Artaud the Moma* (New York: Columbia University Press, 2017 [2002]). Translated by Peggy Kamuf.

14 Jean-François Lyotard, *Libidinal Economy* (Bloomington and Indianapolis: Indiana University Press, 1983 [1974]). Translated by Iain Hamilton Grant.

Chapter 7

1 "'Music is the cup which holds the wine of silence. Sound is that cup, but empty. Noise is that cup, but broken". This aphorism dates from the spring of 1980 when [Robert] Fripp was playing in Paris with The League of Gentlemen', https://www.dgmlive.com/news/winesilence-cups-music. Accessed 15 August 2019.

2 Christof Migone, *Sonic Somatic: Performances of the Unsound Body* (Berlin: Errant Bodies, 2012).

3 Kahn, *Noise Water Music*.

4 George Michelsen Foy, *Zero Decibels: The Quest for Absolute Silence* (Scribner: New York, 2010); Thich Nhat Hanh, *Silence: The Power of Quiet in a World of Noise* (London: Ebury, 2015); Erling Kagge, *Silence in the Age of Noise* (London: Penguin, 2017).

5 Pauline Oliveros, *Deep Listening: A Composer's Sound Practice* (New York: iUniverse, 2005), 77.

6 Craig Dworkin, *No Medium* (Cambridge, MA: MIT Press, 2015). *4′33″* is the first work cited by Dworkin in a substantial and wry 28-page review of silent works (145–73).

7 See it at https://www.youtube.com/watch?v=yoAbXwr3qkg. Accessed 6 September 2019.

8 Martin Heidegger, 'The Origin of the Work of Art', in *Basic Writings* (London: Routledge and Kegan Paul, 1978), edited by David Farrell Krell, 143–203. Translated by Albert Hofstadter. Frances Dyson notes that 'Heidegger's philosophy is grounded in the metaphor of silence', in *Sounding New Media: Immersion and Embodiment in the Arts and Culture* (Berkeley and Los Angeles: University of California Press, 2009), 11.

9 Tara Rodgers, 'Toward a Feminist Historiography of Electronic Music', in Jonathan Sterne (ed.), *The Sound Studies Reader* (London and New York: Routledge, 2012), 475–89.

10 This 'we' is assumed to be one of middle class urban dwellers who can choose which part of a city to live in (see *Zero Decibels*, 50).

11 Very much like The Silence, an alien hive entity and religious sect that hovers mostly unnoticed, and impossible to keep in memory, in *Doctor Who*, notably in the 2011 story *The Impossible Astronaut*.

12 For more on the genealogy of the symphony, see the Yves Klein website, http://www.yvesklein.com/en/articles/view/3/monotone-silence-symphony. Accessed 8 September 2019.

13 By median ear, I do not mean to judge, approve or disapprove of listening or hearing capacity, but instead invoke the use of statistical averaging for human ears as well as for 'effective' sound transcription.

14 For a technical comparative list, see this discussion on Stack Overflow, https://stackoverflow.com/questions/39891683/audio-format-where-silence-would-not-affect-file-size. Accessed 8 September 2019.

15 In fact, even the presence of silence at commemorative events is far from silent, as demonstrated on Jonty Semper's compilation of over eighty commemorative silences as recorded on media since the 1929 (*Kenotaphion*, from 2001). The silences are mostly framed by bells, and/or cannon fire, some weather, presenter announcements – heightening the sense of the artificiality of the silence (precisely what works well in these settings). In addition, the listener can hear the media themselves as the archive recordings change format, delivery method and 'fidelity' levels.

16 Observations on the 'transfer' of this piece into digital format are based on email conversations with Richard Rupenus, conducted in May 2019. Any errors are mine, a bonus noise track.

17 Slightly further from silence, but fully dwelling in the near-silence that demands extra attention is López's *Presque Tout (Quiet Pieces 1993–2013)*. The duration of seven hours is what pushes this into a noisy difficult mode of perception as opposed to just replicating sound art's tendency to make us improve our listening, https://lineimprint.bandcamp.com/album/presque-tout-quiet-pieces-1993-2013. Accessed 8 September 2019.

Chapter 8

1 N. Adriana Knouf, *How Noise Matters to Finance* (Minneapolis, MN: University of Minnesota Press, 2016).

2 On the foundational role of Chicago's AACM, see Lewis, *A Power Stronger Than Itself*.

3 Ben Watson, *Derek Bailey and the Story of Free Improvisation* (London and New York: Verso, 2004).

4   Gillian Siddall and Ellen Waterman, 'Introduction', in Siddall and Waterman (eds), *Negotiated Moments: Improvisation, Sound and Subjectivity* (Durham, NC: Duke University Press, 2016). Kindle edition, loc 120. That negotiation is one in which 'agency is understood to be hard won, highly contingent and relational' (loc 178).

5   Adam Smith, *The Wealth of Nations, I–III* (London: Penguin, 1982).

6   Nick Smith, 'The Splinter in Your Ear', *Culture Theory Critique* 46 (1) (April 2005), 43–59.

7   This is a point well made by Bill Bruford in *The Autobiography: Yes, King Crimson, Earthworks and More* (London: Jawbone, 2009), 181.

8   GegenSichKollectiv, 'Anti-self: Experience-less Noise', in Michael Goddard, Benjamin Halligan and Paul Hegarty (eds), *Reverberations: The Philosophy, Aesthetics and Politics of Noise* (New York: Continuum, 2012), 193–206.

Chapter 9

1   Marshall McLuhan and Quentin Fiore, *The Medium is the Massage: An Inventory of Effects* (London: Penguin, 1967).

2   See Richard Leppert, *The Sight of Sound: Music, Representation and the History of the Body* (Berkeley: University of California Press, 1995) and also Leppert, 'The Social Discipline of Listening', in Jim Drobnick (ed.), *Aural Cultures* (Toronto and Banff: YYZ Books and Walter Philips Gallery, 2004), 19–35.

3   Walter Benjamin, 'A Berlin Chronicle', in *Reflections: Essays, Aphorisms and Autobiographical Writings* (New York; Schocken, 1978), 3–60 [written 1932], Translated by Edmund Jephcott.

4   These are the privatized and exterior-privatory versions of the moving and transitory audio devices explored by Brandon LaBelle in *Acoustic Territories: Sound, Culture and Everyday Life* (New York: Bloomsbury, 2010).

5   The 2010s have even helped the spectacle of viewing come along, with the proliferation of gameplay watching and video blog commentaries spawning the valorization of the viewing of these viewings.

6   Chris Ruen, *Freeloading: How Our Insatiable Hunger for Free Music Starves Creativity* (London: Scribe, 2012).

7   For the details about how Spotify built up value and assets and how it uses these to empty the market of competitors, paid musicians and record labels, see Eriksson et al., *Spotify Teardown.*

8   See Goldacre's 2009 blog piece (https://www.badscience.net/2009/06/home-taping-didnt-kill-music/), accessed 18 August 2019, which refers to a *Guardian* article (https://www.theguardian.com/music/2009/apr/21/study-finds-pirates-

buy-more-music) making the astonishing claim that free downloaders are ten times more likely to buy 'legitimate' streamed music. The meaning and quantifiable nature of being 'more likely' to buy or even buying an amount commensurate with the amount acquired for free is not discussed in either of the admittedly brief articles. The context of that buying has, of course, moved on since then with so-called pirates having won and emptied out the music industry to better profit from it. I agree that people are willing to pay someone something, but that someone is not the content provider, as I'm sure Goldacre would acknowledge eleven years on.

Chapter 10

1   In mid-2019, we could consider this report, on the massive success of Record Store Day, which happens in spring, in many countries in independent record stores, https://www.digitalmusicnews.com/2019/04/24/record-store-day-vinyl-sales-record/; or this, purportedly on the ecological cost of records, but more about their success, https://www.theguardian.com/music/2019/may/11/vinyl-revival-is-there-an-environmental-cost-to-record-sales; or this one, with an infographic showing the vinyl tide on the rise, after 2018's record record sales, https://www.statista.com/chart/7699/lp-sales-in-the-united-states/. But if you miss one, another will be along soon. All accessed 19 August 2019.
2   Dominik Bartmanski and Ian Woodward, *Vinyl: The Analogue Record in the Digital Age* (New York: Bloomsbury, 2015).
3   The vinyl revival, https://en.wikipedia.org/wiki/Vinyl_revival. Accessed 19 August 2019.
4   In July 2016, there was this one, https://www.forbes.com/sites/millystilinovic/2016/07/21/back-in-the-groove-why-vinyl-is-experiencing-a-revival/#52c606e07b99, in January 2017, there was https://www.forbes.com/sites/jordanpassman/2017/01/12/vinyl-is-officially-booming-the-new-billion-dollar-music-business/#2c550aa54054. In September 2018, Forbes found out yet again that vinyl was 'big', in https://www.forbes.com/sites/millystilinovic/2016/07/21/back-in-the-groove-why-vinyl-is-experiencing-a-revival/#52c606e07b99 and in January 2019, one of two articles on the vinyl resurgence saw Forbes cheerleading once more, in https://www.forbes.com/sites/jamos/2019/01/22/the-nostalgia-infused-resurgence-of-vinyl-and-how-high-definition-may-propel-it-even-higher/#204786e847ac. All accessed 19 August 2019.
5   See https://www.theguardian.com/music/2019/feb/23/cassette-tape-music-revival-retro-chic-rewind. Accessed 19 August 2019.
6   For the 2018 market assessment, see https://www.theverge.com/2018/3/22/17152120/digital-downloads-cd-vinyl-riaa-2017-report. Accessed 19 August 2019.

7   A largely ignored issue with streaming is that the pay-per-play model will always benefit music that is easier to listen to, more forgiving in different contexts, less worrying when shuffled to your ear. This is not a judgement about the 'masses' or, on this occasion, Spotify, but about how many times an experimental or noise record needs hearing for it to still work, or resonate. The same could be said of any twenty-minute track, any 12-inch mix, as opposed to a clean industry standard three- to four-minute tune.

8   Attali, when re-editing his *Bruits* book in 2001, and like many in the early 2000s, saw great utopian potential in the growth of home recording capacity and the sharing of listening. The dying market is the last gasp of believing or conveying this belief to those who want objects as media.

Chapter 11

1   See Greg Hainge, 'Of Glitch and Men: The Place of the Human in the Successful Integration of Failure and Noise in the Digital Realm', *Communication Theory* 17 (2007), 26–42.

2   Úna Clancy and Liam Miller, 'CALL Technology for Listening and Speaking', in Fiona Farr and Liam Miller (eds), *The Routledge Handbook of Language Learning and Technology* (Abingdon and New York: Routledge, 2016), 491–508.

3   For a fuller account of the role of tape in music experimentation at this time, see Joel Chadabe, *Electric Sound: The Past and Promise of Electronic Music* (Upper Saddle River, NJ: Prentice Hall, 1997), 63–80.

4   Paul D. Miller, 'Algorithms: Erasures and the Art of Memory', in Christoph Cox and Daniel Warner (eds), *Audio Culture: Readings in Modern Music* (New York and London: Continuum, 2004), 348–54.

5   Thurston Moore (ed.), *Mix Tape: The Art of Cassette Culture* (New York: Universe, 2004).

6   Mixtapes are also produced by DJs and MCs as a showcase for their skills, and therefore target a wider audience.

7   Nick Hornby, *High Fidelity* (London: Indigo, 1996).

8   Rob Sheffield, *Love is a Mix Tape: A Memoir* (London: Portrait, 2007).

9   Part of the imagined progress of recording media involves progressive disappearance of the medium itself, culminating in the digital format. At the same time, sound itself becomes more visible, indexed as a visual waveform that offers itself for direct manipulation. However, digital sound has only moved the location of technology, such that there are now parallel digital supports, rather than one reproductive machine (record, tape, cartridge, etc.) and one processor (the player of the object). In order to achieve the invisibility of a medium, much more complex mediating machinery is necessary.

10 Theodor Adorno, 'The Curves of the Needle', in Adorno, *Essays on Music*, 271–76.

11 Theodor Adorno, 'The Form of the Phonograph Record', in Adorno, *Essays on Music*, 277–82.

12 Samuel Beckett, *Krapp's Last Tape*, in Samuel Beckett, *The Complete Dramatic Works* (London: Faber and Faber, 1990), 213–23.

13 Christian Marclay has realized a variant of this in his *Moebius Loop* (1994) where hundreds of cassette tapes are netted together to form a fence-like structure with a kink to make it that infinite non-dimensional figure. This parody of intensities creates a failed synthesis (the tapes are kept discrete) through the failure of the functionality of the tapes. This giant tape shows the necessity of limiting, of factoring in failure instead of the ironic closure of the infinite 'libidinal' band.

14 Jean-François Lyotard, *Economie libidinale* (Paris: Minuit, 1974). Translation mine.

15 Gilles Deleuze and Félix Guattari, *Anti-Oedipus* (Minneapolis: University of Minnesota Press, 1983). Translated by Helen R. Lane, Robert Hurley and Mark Seem.

16 Robin Lydenberg, 'Sound Identity Fading Out: William Burroughs' Tape Experiments', in Kahn and Whitehead (eds), *Wireless Imagination*, 409–37.

17 Deleuze and Guattari write that 'breaking down is part of the very function of desiring machines' (*Anti-Oedipus*, 32), where a 'desiring machine' is opposed to and supersedes ordinary machines, as it sets up open-ended processes and relations, rather than being fixed into an object. They underestimate the capacity for machines to have always, from the start, been part of a more interesting and relational machinicity.

18 William S. Burroughs, 'Electronic Revolution', in William S. Burroughs, *Ah Pook is Here* (London: John Calder, 1979), 123–57.

19 Eugene Thacker identifies the intersection of biology and human as 'biomedia', such that 'the biological and the digital domains are no longer rendered ontologically distinct, but instead are seen to inhere in each other; the biological "informs" the digital, just as the digital "corporealizes" the biological' (Eugene Thacker, *Biomedia* [Minneapolis: University of Minnesota Press, 2004]).

20 Genetics and recording share a history as part of a technology of 'coding' as identified by Baudrillard in 1976 (see *Symbolic Exchange and Death* (London: Sage, 1993 [1976]). Translated by Iain Hamilton Grant). Baudrillard is primarily interested in a binary code, which comes to supplant other forms of reality, and finds its apotheosis in computer code, digitality and, ultimately, virtual reality. Nonetheless, computing history is of course utterly caught up not just with code, but code as carried by tape. Tape had found a new habitat inside various hardwares. We might also note that DNA is caught up within a history of recording, with X-ray photography one of the key tools in the 'revealing' of DNA's structure.

21 Lynn Margulis, *Symbiosis in Cell Evolution: Microbial Communities in the Archean and Proterozoic Eons* (New York: Freeman, 2003).

22 All information on Voyager's tape system is courtesy of the Voyager team at Nasa's Jet Propulsion Laboratory (JPL), who offered considerable time, assistance and information (in 2008 when this article first appeared). Any errors in presentation of their data are mine.

23 These tapes are long: 12697.5 inches on Voyager 1, and 12873.75 inches on Voyager 2. There are nine tracks, with the ninth being a tachometer track indicating the portion for transmission.

24 A similar process is suggested in Marclay's *Tape Fall* (1989), where an open reel tape recorder plays the sound of falling water as the tape (not connected to a second spindle) falls slowly to the ground from the raised tape player, forming an outcrop of unwound tape.

Chapter 12

1 Michael Veal, *Dub: Soundscapes and Shattered Songs in Jamaican Reggae* (Middletown, CT: Wesleyan University Press, 2007).

2 Peter Hook, *Unknown Pleasures: Inside Joy Division* (London: Simon and Schuster, 2012).

3 Bernard Sumner, *Chapter and Verse: New Order, Joy Division and Me* (London: Corgi, 2015). Kindle edition, loc 1516. See also Chris Ott, *Unknown Pleasures* (New York: Continuum, 2003), 75–76 and innumerable interviews from the early part of summer 2019, in honour of forty years since the original release of the album.

4 Sumner, *Chapter and Verse*, Kindle edition, loc 1498.

5 Stephen Morris, in Jake Kennedy, *The Making of Unknown Pleasures* (London: Unanimous, 2006), 55; Morris, in Simon Reynolds, *Totally Wired: Post-punk Interviews and Overviews* (London: Faber and Faber, 2009), 229–43 (232).

6 Stewart Home, *Cranked Up Really High: Genre Theory and Punk Rock* (Hove: Codex, 1995) and online at https://www.stewarthomesociety.org/cranked/content. htm. Accessed 26 August 2019.

7 See Jacques Derrida, 'Force of Law: The "Mystical Foundation of Authority"', in Drucilla Cornell, Michel Rosenfeld and David Gray Carlson (eds), *Deconstruction and the Possibility of Justice* (New York and London: Routledge, 1992), 3–67. Translated by Mary Quaintance. Montaigne's teeth example is on 12.

8 As argued by Pierre-Yves Macé, in *Musique et document sonore* (as discussed elsewhere in this volume).

9 See Bataille, 'Base Materialism and Gnosticism', in Bataille, *Visions of Excess*, 45–52.

10 Jon Savage, '"good evening, we're joy division"', on Joy Division, *Heart and Soul* liner notes, n.p. Sumner writes that 'Joy Division sounded like Manchester: cold, sparse, and at times, bleak' (*Chapter and Verse*, Kindle edition, loc 91).

Chapter 13

1 Otto Rank, *The Double: A Psychoanalytic Study* (Chapel Hill, NC, University of North Carolina Press, 1971). Translated by Harry Tucker Jr.

2 Sigmund Freud, 'The Uncanny', in Freud, *Standard Edition of the Complete Psychological Works* 17 (London: Hogarth, 1955), 219–52. Translated by Alix Strachey.

3 Jackman has said that he wanted to make something totally new, but 'instead, Organum music came out sounding really ancient, like something from the very beginning of music-making' (interview with Paul Lemos, originally in *Unsound* 24–25 [1988]). This is available, along with other articles and a very detailed discography at http://www.chronoglide.com/organum.html. Accessed 3 September 2019.

4 Some of his 1990s releases based on recordings from Britain's Imperial War Museum have covers that refer to their source materials: the neo-classical machine-gun operator on 'Machine Gun', or the details of bomber flights on 'Flak', but Jackman had used war imagery on other releases, so these can also be seen as continuations of a pictorial narrative that mostly parallels his music as a whole, and here comes briefly into phase with musical content.

5 See Jean-Jacques Rousseau, *Discourse on the Origin of Languages* (London: Penguin, 1985 [1755]), translated by Maurice Cranston; Kant, *Critique of Judgment*, 169, 173, 200.

6 John Cage, *Silence: Lectures and Writings* (London: Marion Boyars, 1978).

7 See Martin Heidegger, 'Building Dwelling Thinking', in Heidegger, *Basic Writings* (London: Routledge and Kegan Paul, 1978), 347–63.

8 Mark Wigley picks up on this, writing that 'the alienating space of the home veils a more fundamental and primordial homelessness' and that 'it is because the house conceals the unhomeliness that constitutes it that the "mere" occupation of a house, which is to say the acceptance of its representation of interior, can never be authentic dwelling' (*The Architecture of Deconstruction* [Cambridge, MA and London: MIT Press, 1995], 98 and 113 respectively).

9 When 'Pulp' and other Organum/The New Blockaders's collaborations are added together on the *Pulp* CD (2002), the twelve short tracks taken together do not add up to a greater picture, but just happen to be in sequence. It is as if too many minimalist sculptures have been put on display in the same room.

10 In the era of 78 rpm records, all records could only store small amounts of information, so an 'album' would be spread across many sides. The 1950s saw the development of the 33 rpm album, with the possibility of having several tracks on each side, and this in turn contributed to the single as being something other, something more immediate. This moment is being re-played in the twenty-first century as the return of the 7-inch single follows the spread of individual downloads

and streams that literally marginalize the pop or mainstream rock album – the 7-inch pop record today is both part of that phenomenon and resistance to it.

11 Pierre Schaeffer talked of this need, for genuine *musique concrète* to lose its 'dramatic context' (*À la recherche d'une musique concrète* [Paris: Le Seuil, 1952], 46).

12 Deleuze and Guattari deal with this when writing of Hitchcock that 'when [he] does birds, he does not reproduce bird calls, he produces an electronic sound like a field of intensities or a wave of vibrations, a continuous variation, like a terrible threat welling up inside us' (*A Thousand Plateaus*, 305). Deleuze and Guattari do not seem to want to confront the strong possibility that any such intensity or 'becoming' that transcends music and listener alike will become a style, a signifier. That this is highly likely is not the issue, the question is whether something already has become a representation of 'intensity' or the uncanny (or many other things), and never, even fleetingly, becomes a 'terrible threat'.

13 The single 'Crusade' is a different take on power through asymmetry, where this time the second side does use the same material as side one, but collapses it into a shorter and denser location.

14 There are exceptions, for example in the singles based on sound recordings from the British Imperial War Museum, notably on 'Flak'. Even with this material, Jackman (and these are releases by David Jackman, rather than Organum) can defamiliarize the idea of material as source (i.e. to be manipulated, processed etc.), so 'Machine Guns' is just that, the sounds are left completely 'as they are', and looped.

15 Recent times have seen a further estranging of self from itself, and other from its other, in the use of very similar material (piano chords, bell sounds, small rustling sounds) across different track divisions on three separate CD albums: Organum, *Raven* (2018), David Jackman, *Herbstsonne* (2019) and David Jackman, *Silence in That Time* (2020).

16 Ronald Bogue, *Deleuze's Wake: Tributes and Tributaries* (Albany, NY: SUNY Press, 2004).

Chapter 14

1 Michael Nyman, *Experimental Music: Cage and Beyond* (Cambridge: Cambridge University Press, 1999 [1974]).

2 David Keenan, *England's Hidden Reverse: A Secret History of the Esoteric Underground* (London: SAF, 2003).

3 Lautréamont [Isidore Ducasse], *Les Chants de Maldoror* (Paris: Garnier-Flammarion, 1999 [1874]).

4   The record label Finders Keepers is starting to release a series of compilations of
    the artists on the list, with its first volume released in September 2019. *The Quietus*
    previewed it in July of that year, https://thequietus.com/articles/26823-nurse-with-
    wound-list-finders-keepers. Accessed 7 January 2020.

5   Concerned for his own mortality at the time, Tibet did not produce a box set or a
    best of, but played all of Current 93's output in layers on/as the album *The Great in
    the Small* (2001).

6   Bataille's short text appears in full in both French and English in Yve-Alain Bois
    and Rosalind Krauss, *Formless: A User's Guide* (New York: Zone, 1997), 5.

7   Harold Bloom, *The Anxiety of Influence: A Theory of Poetry* (New York: Oxford
    University Press, 1997).

8   It is worth noting that for all his intentions to make anxiety a textual product
    of a creative writer, the standard version of anxiety as a worry about replicating
    someone else's work does appear often in Bloom's text, and even in his new preface.

9   A writer is not allowed the luxury of the cover version, without rewriting a text to
    a very large extent. One exception to this is the great and 'fictional' Pierre Menard,
    who aims to write Cervantes' book out in full (Jorge-Luis Borges, 'Pierre Menard,
    Author of the *Quixote*', in Borges, *Labyrinths: Selected Stories and Other Writings*
    (New York: New Directions, 1964 [1939]), 36–44. Translated by Anthony Bonner.

10 Graham Allen, *Harold Bloom: A Poetics of Conflict* (New York: Harvester
    Wheatsheaf, 1994).

11 Broodthaers took Mallarmé's famous modernist poem *Un Coup de dés jamais
    n'abolira le hasard*, first published in 1887, and replaced the text with block shapes
    of print, on transparent paper.

12 Unnnamed reviewer of *Changez Les Blockeurs And*, https://boomkat.com/products/
    nww-play-changez-les-blockeurs. Accessed 3 October 2019.

Chapter 15

1   Dante's *Commedia*, a.k.a. *The Divine Comedy*, consists of three books, *Inferno*,
    Purgatorio and *Paradiso*, written in the early 1300s. Each is structured in
    thirty-three Cantos, with one further introductory Canto in *Inferno*. So the Cantos
    go up to thirty-four in the first volume. The editions are as follows: *Inferno* (London:
    Penguin, 2012), translated by Robin Kirkpatrick; *Purgatory* (London: Penguin,
    1985), translated by Mark Musa; *Paradise* (London: Penguin, 1962), translated by
    Dorothy L. Sayers and Barbara Reynolds. Quotations will refer to Canto and line.

2   See Michael Moynihan and Didrik Søderlind, *Lords of Chaos: The Bloody Rise of
    the Satanic Metal Underground* (Port Townsend, WA: Feral House, 1998), the first
    detailed account of the 'true black metal' scene.

3   According to the Wikipedia page on the band, the title translates as 'Walk in the shadow of evil, in the triumph of darkness forever'. https://en.wikipedia.org/wiki/Abruptum. Accessed 2 September 2019. Latin is very metal.

4   Scott Wilson, '*musica amusica*', in Wilson et al., *Melancology*, 213–39.

5   William S. Burroughs, 'The Limit of Control', in Burroughs, *The Adding Machine* (London: John Calder, 1985), 116–20.

6   Michel Chion has extended his defining of all sounds in films to include things or people not making sound that they could have, or that they could be imagined to have made. He names this *athorybos* in *Words on Screen* (New York: Columbia University Press, 2017 [2013]), 60 and throughout. Translated by Claudia Gorbman.

Chapter 16

1   Text by William Bennett and Peter Sotos.

2   Julia Kristeva, *Powers of Horror* (New York: Columbia University Press, 1982 [1980]). Translated by Leon S. Roudiez.

3   Salomé Voegelin, *Listening to Noise and Silence* (New York: Bloomsbury, 2010).

4   Georges Bataille, 'The Use-Value of D.A.F. de Sade', in *Visions of Excess*, 91–102.

5   Frances Dyson, *The Tone of our Times: Sound, Sense, Economy, Ecology* (Cambridge, MA: MIT Press, 2014).

6   Simon Reynolds, *Blissed Out: The Raptures of Rock* (London: Serpent's Tail, 1990); Francis Fukuyama, *The End of History and the Last Man* (New York: Free Press, 1992).

7   Fred Moten, *The Universal Machine* (Durham NC and London, Duke University Press, 2018) – the third volume of *consent not to be a single being*.

8   Novak, *Japanoise*.

9   Giorgio Agamben, *The Time That Remains: A Commentary on the Letter to the Romans* (Stanford, CA: Stanford University Press, 2005). Translated by Patricia Daley.

10 Carl Gustav Jung, 'Seven Sermons to the Dead', in Stephan A. Hoeller, *The Gnostic Jung and the Seven Sermons to the Dead* (Wheaton, IL: Quest, 1982), 44–58 (45); Gregory Bateson, *Steps to an Ecology of Mind* (Chicago: University of Chicago Press, 1972).

11 *Total Slitting of Throats* is a harsh noise wall collaboration between Mania, Sewer Election, The Cherry Point, The Rita and Theriksroset, originally released in 2005, re-released in 2017.

12 See Chapter 3 above for Boltzmann's cosmic-scale entropic model, and Boltzmann, 'On Statistical Mechanics', in Boltzmann, *Theoretical Physics and Philosophical Problems*, 159–72 (172).

Bibliography

Adorno, Theodor, *Essays on Music* (Berkeley: University of California Press, 2002), edited by Richard Leppert, including multiple new translations by Susan H. Gillespie.

Agamben, Giorgio, *Language and Death: The Place of Negativity* (Minneapolis: University of Minnesota Press, 1991 [1982]). Translated by Karen E. Pinkus with Michael Hardt.

Agamben, Giorgio, *The Time That Remains: A Commentary on the Letter to the Romans* (Stanford, CA: Stanford University Press, 2005). Translated by Patricia Daley.

Aligheri, Dante, *Paradise* (London: Penguin, 1962). Translated by Dorothy L. Sayers and Barbara Reynolds.

Aligheri, Dante, *Purgatory* (London: Penguin, 1985). Translated by Mark Musa.

Aligheri, Dante, *Inferno* (London: Penguin, 2012). Translated by Robin Kirkpatrick.

Allen, Graham, *Harold Bloom: A Poetics of Conflict* (New York: Harvester Wheatsheaf, 1994).

Attali, Jacques, *Noise: The Political Economy of Music* (Minneapolis: University of Minnesota Press, 1985 [1977]).

Attali, Jacques, *Bruits: Essai sur l'économie politique de la musique*, second edition (Paris: Fayard, 2001).

Barad, Karen, *Meeting the Universe Halfway: Quantum Physics and the Entanglement of Matter and Meaning* (Durham, NC: Duke University Press, 2007).

Bartmanski, Dominik and Ian Woodward, *Vinyl: The Analogue Record in the Digital Age* (New York: Bloomsbury, 2015).

Bataille, Georges, *Visions of Excess: Selected Writings, 1927–1939* (Minneapolis: University of Minnesota Press, 1985), edited by Allan Stoekl. Translated by Allan Stoekl, Carl R. Lovitt and Donald M. Leslie Jr.

Bataille, Georges, *The Accursed Share* (New York: Zone, 1988 [1949]). Translated by Robert Hurley.

Bataille, Georges, *Theory of Religion* (New York: Zone, 1992 [c. 1948]). Translated by Robert Hurley.

Bateson, Gregory, *Steps to an Ecology of Mind* (Chicago: University of Chicago Press, 1972).

Baudrillard, Jean, *Symbolic Exchange and Death* (London: Sage, 1993 [1976]). Translated by Iain Hamilton Grant.

Beckett, Chris, *Dark Eden* (London: Corvus, 2012).

Beckett, Chris, *Mother of Eden* (London: Corvus, 2015).

Beckett, Chris, *Daughter of Eden* (London: Corvus, 2016).

Beckett, Samuel, *The Complete Dramatic Works* (London: Faber and Faber, 1990).

Benjamin, Walter, 'A Berlin Chronicle', in *Reflections: Essays, Aphorisms and Autobiographical Writings* (New York: Schocken, 1978 [1932]), 3–60. Translated by Edmund Jephcott.

Benson, Stephen and Will Montgomery (eds), *Writing the Field Recording: Sound, Word, Environment* (Edinburgh: Edinburgh University Press, 2018).

Bloom, Harold, *The Anxiety of Influence: A Theory of Poetry* (New York: Oxford University Press, 1997).

Bogue, Ronald, *Deleuze's Wake: Tributes and Tributaries* (Albany, NY: SUNY Press, 2004).

Bois, Yve-Alain and Rosalind Krauss, *Formless: A User's Guide* (New York: Zone, 1997).

Boltzmann, Ludwig, *Theoretical Physics and Philosophical Problems* (Dordrecht and Boston, MA: D. Reidel, 1974), edited by Brian McGuinness. Translated by Paul Foulkes.

Bonnet, François J., *The Order of Sounds: A Sonorous Archipelago* (Falmouth: Urbanomic, 2016 [2012]). Translated by Robin Mackay.

Borges, Jorge-Luis, *Labyrinths: Selected Stories and Other Writings* (New York: New Directions, 1964 [1939]). Translated by Anthony Bonner.

Bosseur, Jean-Yves, *Musique et environnement* (Paris: Minerve, 2016).

Brassier, Ray, 'Noise is Obsolete', in *Multitudes* 28 (Winter/Spring 2007), http://www.multitudes.net/Genre-is-Obsolete/.

Bratton, Benjamin H., *The Stack: On Software and Sovereignty* (Cambridge, MA: MIT Press, 2015).

Bruford, Bill, *The Autobiography: Yes, King Crimson, Earthworks and More* (London: Jawbone, 2009).

Bruynincks, Joeri, *Listening in the Field: Recording and the Science of Birdsong* (Cambridge, MA: MIT Press, 2018).

Burroughs, William S., *Ah Pook is Here* (London: John Calder, 1979).

Burroughs, William S., *The Adding Machine* (London: John Calder, 1985).

Cage, John, *Silence: Lectures and Writings* (London: Marion Boyars, 1978).

Chadabe, Joel, *Electric Sound: The Past and Promise of Electronic Music* (Upper Saddle River, NJ: Prentice Hall, 1997).

Chicago, Judy, *Through the Rose: My Struggle as a Woman Artist* (London: Women's Press, 1982).

Chion, Michel, *Words on Screen* (New York: Columbia University Press, 2017 [2013]). Translated by Claudia Gorbman.

Clancy, Úna and Liam Miller, 'CALL Technology for Listening and Speaking', in Fiona Farr and Liam Miller (eds), *The Routledge Handbook of Language Learning and Technology* (Abingdon and New York: Routledge, 2016), 491–508.

Corbin, Alain, *Village Bells: The Culture of the Senses in the Nineteenth Century French Countryside* (New York: Columbia University Press, 1998 [1994]). Translated by Martin Thom.

Davies, Paul, *Eerie Silence: Searching for Ourselves in the Universe* (London: Penguin, 2010).

Decrauzat, Philippe, and Mathieu Copeland (eds), *A Personal Sonic Geology* (Milan: Mousse, 2017).

Deleuze, Gilles and Félix Guattari, *Anti-Oedipus* (Minneapolis: University of Minnesota Press, 1983). Translated by Helen R. Lane, Robert Hurley and Mark Seem.

Deleuze, Gilles and Félix Guattari, *A Thousand Plateaus* (Minneapolis: University of Minnesota Press, 1987 [1980]). Translated by Brian Massumi.

Derrida, Jacques, 'Plato's Pharmacy', in Derrida, *Dissemination* (Chicago: University of Chicago Press, 1981 [1972]), 63–171. Translated by Barbara Johnson.

Derrida, Jacques, 'Force of Law: The "Mystical Foundation of Authority"', in Drucilla Cornell, Michel Rosenfeld and David Gray Carlson (eds), *Deconstruction and the Possibility of Justice* (New York and London: Routledge, 1992). Translated by Mary Quaintance.

Derrida, Jacques, *Artaud the Moma* (New York: Columbia University Press, 2017 [2002]). Translated by Peggy Kamuf.

Dworkin, Craig, *No Medium* (Cambridge, MA: MIT Press, 2015).

Dyson, Frances, *Sounding New Media: Immersion and Embodiment in the Arts and Culture* (Berkeley and Los Angeles: University of California Press, 2009).

Dyson, Frances, *The Tone of our Times: Sound, Sense, Economy, Ecology* (Cambridge, MA: MIT Press, 2014).

English, Lawrence, 'A Beginner's Guide to Field Recording', *Fact*, 18 November 2014, https://www.factmag.com/2014/11/18/a-beginners-guide-to-field-recording/.

Eriksson, Maria, Rasmus Fleischer, Anna Johansson, Pelle Snickars and Patrick Vonderau, *Spotify Teardown: Inside the Black Box of Music Streaming* (Cambridge, MA: MIT Press, 2019).

Feld, Steven, 'From Schizophonia to Schismogenesis: On the Discourses and Commodification Practices of "World Music" and "World Beat"', in Charles Keil and Steven Feld, *Music Grooves* (Chicago: University of Chicago Press, 1994), 257–89.

Ferret, D., *Dark Sound: Feminine Voices in Sonic Shadow* (New York: Bloomsbury, 2020).

Foy, George Michelsen, *Zero Decibels: The Quest for Absolute Silence* (Scribner: New York, 2010).

Freeman, Alan and Steve Freeman, 'Chance Meeting at the Rock 'n' Roll Station: The Nurse With Wound Interview', *Audion* 28 (Spring 1994), 7–14.

Freud, Sigmund, 'The Uncanny', in Freud, *Standard Edition of the Complete Psychological Works* 17 (London: Hogarth, 1955), 219–52. Translated by Alix Strachey.

Fukuyama, Francis, *The End of History and the Last Man* (New York: Free Press, 1992).

GegenSichKollectiv, 'Anti-self: Experience-less Noise', in Michael Goddard, Benjamin Halligan and Paul Hegarty (eds), *Reverberations: The Philosophy, Aesthetics and Politics of Noise* (New York: Continuum, 2012), 193–206.

Goodman, Steve, *Sonic Warfare: Sound, Affect and the Ecology of Fear* (Cambridge, MA: MIT Press, 2009).

Hainge, Greg, 'Of Glitch and Men: The Place of the Human in the Successful Integration of Failure and Noise in the Digital Realm', *Communication Theory* 17 (2007), 26–42.

Hainge, Greg, *Noise Matters: Towards an Ontology of Noise* (New York: Bloomsbury, 2013).

Hanh, Thich Nhat, *Silence: The Power of Quiet in a World of Noise* (London: Ebury, 2015).

Heidegger, Martin, 'The Origin of the Work of Art', in *Basic Writings* (London: Routledge and Kegan Paul, 1978), edited by David Farrell Krell, 143–203. Translated by Albert Hofstadter.

Heidegger, Martin, 'Building Dwelling Thinking', in Heidegger, *Basic Writings*, 347–63. Translated by Albert Hofstadter.

Henry, Clive, 'Listening to the Void: Harsh Noise Walls', in Jennifer Wallis (ed.), *Fight Your Own War: Power Electronics and Noise Culture*, 137–54.

Higgins, Dick and Hannah Higgins, 'Intermedia', in *Leonardo* 34 (1) (2001), 49–54.

Hilmes, Michele, 'Is There a Field Called Sound Culture Studies? And Does it Matter?', *American Quarterly* 57 (1) (March 2005), 249–59.

Home, Stewart, *Cranked Up Really High: Genre Theory and Punk Rock* (Hove: Codex, 1995).

Hook, Peter, *Unknown Pleasures: Inside Joy Division* (London: Simon and Schuster, 2012).

Hornby, Nick, *High Fidelity* (London: Indigo, 1996).

Jonker, Julian, 'Black Secret Technology (The Whitey on the Moon Dub)', *ctheory* (2002), http://www.ctheory.net/articles.aspx?id=358.

Jung, Carl Gustav, 'Seven Sermons to the Dead', in Stephan A. Hoeller, *The Gnostic Jung and the Seven Sermons to the Dead* (Wheaton, IL: Quest, 1982), 44–58.

Kagge, Erling, *Silence in the Age of Noise* (London: Penguin, 2017).

Kahn, Douglas, *Noise Water Meat: A History of Sound in the Arts* (Cambridge, MA: MIT Press, 1999).

Kahn, Douglas, *Earth Sound Earth Signal: Energies and Earth Magnitude in the Arts* (Oakland, CA: University of California Press, 2013).

Kahn, Douglas and Gregory Whitehead (eds), *Wireless Imagination: Sound, Radio and the Avant-garde* (Cambridge, MA: MIT Press, 1992).

Kane, Brian, 'Musicophobia, or Sound Art and the Demands of Art Theory', *Non-site #8* (2013), https://nonsite.org/article/musicophobia-or-sound-art-and-the-demands-of-art-theory.

Kant, Immanuel, *Critique of Judgment* (Indianapolis, IN: Hackett, 1987 [1790]). Translated by Werner S. Pluhar.

Keenan, David, *England's Hidden Reverse: A Secret History of the Esoteric Underground* (London: SAF, 2003).

Kelly, Caleb, *Cracked Media* (Cambridge, MA: MIT Press, 2009).

Kennedy, Jake, *The Making of Unknown Pleasures* (London: Unanimous, 2006).

Kim-Cohen, Seth, *In The Blink of an Ear: Towards a Non-Cochlear Sonic Art* (New York: Bloomsbury, 2009).

Knouf, N. Adriana, *How Noise Matters to Finance* (Minneapolis, MN: University of Minnesota Press, 2016).

Krause, Bernie, *The Great Animal Orchestra: Finding the Origins of Music in the World's Wild Places* (New York: Little, Brown, 2012).

Krauss, Rosalind, 'Sculpture in the Expanded Field', *October* 8 (Spring 1978), 30–44.

Kristeva, Julia, *Powers of Horror* (New York: Columbia University Press, 1982 [1980]). Translated by Leon S. Roudiez.

LaBelle, Brandon, *Acoustic Territories: Sound, Culture and Everyday Life* (New York: Bloomsbury, 2010).

Lane, Cathy, and Angus Carlyle (eds), *In The Field: The Art of Field Recording* (Axminster: Uniformbooks, 2011).

Lautréamont [Isidore Ducasse], *Les Chants de Maldoror* (Paris: Garnier-Flammarion, 1999 [1874]).

Leigh-Page, Carrie and Dana Reason, 'Playing Like a Girl: The Problems with Reception of Women in Music', *New Music Box* (2008), https://nmbx.newmusicusa.org/playing-like-a-girl-the-problems-with-reception-of-women-in-music/.

Lemos, Paul, 'Interview with David Jackman', http://www.chronoglide.com/organum.html.

Leppert, Richard, *The Sight of Sound: Music, Representation and the History of the Body* (Berkeley: University of California Press, 1995).

Leppert, Richard, 'The Social Discipline of Listening', in Jim Drobnick (ed.), *Aural Cultures* (Toronto and Banff: YYZ Books and Walter Philips Gallery, 2004), 19–35.

Lewis, George, *A Power Stronger than Itself: The AACM and American Experimental Music* (Chicago: University of Chicago Press, 2008).

Lydenberg, Robin, 'Sound Identity Fading Out: William Burroughs' Tape Experiments', in Kahn and Whitehead (eds), *Wireless Imagination: Sound, Radio and the Avant-Garde*, 409–37.

Lyotard, Jean-François, *Economie libidinale* (Paris: Minuit, 1974).

Lyotard, Jean-François, *Libidinal Economy* (Bloomington and Indianapolis: Indiana University Press, 1983 [1974]). Translated by Iain Hamilton Grant.

Macé, Pierre-Yves, *Musique et document sonore: Enquête sur la phonographie documentaire dans les pratiques musicales contemporaines* (Dijon: Presses du réel, 2012).

Malaspina, Cécile, *An Epistemology of Noise* (London: Bloomsbury, 2018).

Margulis, Lynn, *Symbiosis in Cell Evolution: Microbial Communities in the Archean and Proterozoic Eons* (New York: Freeman, 2003).

Mathew, Nicholas and Mary Ann Smart, 'Elephants in the Music Room: The Future of Quirk Historicism', *Representations* 132 (1) (Fall 2015), 61–78.

McLaren, Mark, 'Interview with Chris Watson', *Binaural* (Winter 2006), http://www.binauralmedia.org/images/texts/theory_survey/watson_web.pdf.

McLuhan, Marshall and Quentin Fiore, *The Medium is the Massage: An Inventory of Effects* (London: Penguin, 1967).

Metzger, Gustav, *Writings (1953–2016)* (Zurich: JRP Publications, 2019), edited by Mathieu Copeland.

Migone, Christof, *Sonic Somatic: Performances of the Unsound Body* (Berlin: Errant Bodies, 2012).

Miller, Paul D., 'Algorithms: Erasures and the Art of Memory', in Christoph Cox and Daniel Warner (eds), *Audio Culture: Readings in Modern Music* (New York and London: Continuum, 2004), 348–54.

Mockus, Martha, *Sounding Out: Pauline Oliveros and Lesbian Musicality* (London and New York: Routledge, 2008).

Moore, Thurston (ed.), *Mix Tape: The Art of Cassette Culture* (New York: Universe, 2004).

Morton, Timothy, *Hyperobjects: Philosophy and Ecology After the End of the World* (Minneapolis: University of Minnesota Press, 2013).

Moten, Fred, *In The Break: The Aesthetics of the Black Radical Tradition* (Minneapolis: University of Minnesota Press, 2003).

Moten, Fred, *Black and Blur: consent not to be a single being 1* (Durham, NC and London: Duke University Press, 2017).

Moten, Fred, *The Universal Machine: consent not to be a single being 3* (Durham, NC and London: Duke University Press, 2018).

Moynihan, Michael and Didrik Søderlind, *Lords of Chaos: The Bloody Rise of the Satanic Metal Underground* (Port Townsend, WA: Feral House, 1998).

Naess, Arne, 'The Shallow and the Deep, Long-Range Ecology Movement', *Inquiry* 16 (1973), 95–100.

Nancy, Jean-Luc, *Listening* (New York: Fordham University Press, 2007 [2003]). Translated by Charlotte Mandell.

Nietzsche, Friedrich, *The Will to Power* (New York: Vintage, 1968 [1901]). Translated by Walter Kaufmann and R.J. Hollingdale.

Novak, David, *Japanoise: Music at the Edge of Circulation* (Durham, NC: Duke University Press, 2013).

Nyman, Michael, *Experimental Music: Cage and Beyond* (Cambridge: Cambridge University Press, 1999 [1974]).

Oliveros, Pauline, *Deep Listening: A Composer's Sound Practice* (New York: iUniverse, 2005).

O'Reilly, Jessica, *The Technocratic Antarctic: An Ethnography of Scientific Expertise and Environmental Governance* (Ithaca: Cornell University Press, 2017).

Ott, Chris, *Unknown Pleasures* (New York: Continuum, 2003).

Perry, Imani, *Prophets of the Hood: Politics and Poetics in Hip Hop* (Durham, NC: Duke University Press, 2004).

Pettman, Dominic, *Sonic Intimacy, Voice, Species, Technics [Or, How to Listen to the World]* (Stanford: Stanford University Press, 2017).

Quignard, Pascal, *La Haine de la musique* (Paris: Calmann-Lévy, 1996).

Rank, Otto, *The Double: A Psychoanalytic Study* (Chapel Hill, NC: University of North Carolina Press, 1971). Translated by Harry Tucker Jr.

Reynolds, Simon, *Blissed Out: The Raptures of Rock* (London: Serpent's Tail, 1990).

Reynolds, Simon, *Totally Wired: Post-punk Interviews and Overviews* (London: Faber and Faber, 2009).

Rodgers, Tara (ed.), *Pink Noises: Women on Electronic Music and Sound* (Durham, NC: Duke University Press, 2010).

Rodgers, Tara, 'Toward a Feminist Historiography of Electronic Music', in Jonathan Sterne (ed.), *The Sound Studies Reader* (London and New York: Routledge, 2012), 475–89.

Rose, Tricia, '"Fear of a Black Planet": Rap Music and Black Cultural Politics in the 1990s', *The Journal of Negro Education* 60 (3) (Summer 1991), 276–90.

Rose, Tricia, *Black Noise: Rap Music and Black Culture in Contemporary America* (Hanover, NH: Wesleyan University Press, 1994).

Ross, Alex, *The Rest is Noise: Listening to the Twentieth Century* (London: Harper Perennial, 2009).

Rothenberg, David, 'Whale Music: Anatomy of an Interspecies Duet', *Leonardo* 18 (2008), 47–53.

Rothenberg, David, *Sudden Music: Improvisation, Sound, Nature* (Athens, GA: University of Georgia Press, 2016).

Rousseau, Jean-Jacques, *Discourse on the Origin of Languages* (London: Penguin, 1985 [1755]). Translated by Maurice Cranston.

Ruen, Chris, *Freeloading: How Our Insatiable Hunger for Free Music Starves Creativity* (London: Scribe, 2012).

Russolo, Luigi, *The Art of Noises* (New York: Pendragon, 1986 [1913]). Translated by Barclay Brown.

Schaeffer, Pierre, *À la recherche d'une musique concrète* (Paris: Le Seuil, 1952).

Schafer, R. Murray (ed.), *Five Village Soundscapes* (Vancouver, BC: ARC, 1977).

Schafer, R. Murray, *The Soundscape: Our Sonic Environment and the Tuning of the World* (Rochester, VT: Destiny Books, 1993 [1977]).

Schwartz, Hillel, *Making Noise: From Babel to the Big Bang and Beyond* (New York: Zone Books, 2011).

Serres, Michel, *The Parasite* (Baltimore, MD: Johns Hopkins Press, 1982 [1980]). Translated by Lawrence R. Scher.

Shannon, Claude E., *Collected Papers* (New York: IEEE Press, 1993), edited by N.J.A. Sloane and Aaron D. Wyner.

Shannon, Claude E. and Warren Weaver, *The Mathematical Theory of Communication* (Urbana, IL: University of Illinois Press, 1969 [1949]).

Sheffield, Rob, *Love is a Mix Tape: A Memoir* (London: Portrait, 2007).

Siddall, Gillian, and Ellen Waterman (eds), *Negotiated Moments: Improvisation, Sound and Subjectivity* (Durham, NC, Duke University Press, 2016).

Smith, Adam, *The Wealth of Nations, I–III* (London: Penguin, 1982).

Smith, Jacob, *Eco-Sonic Media* (Berkeley: University of California Press, 2015).

Smith, Nick, 'The Splinter in Your Ear', *Culture Theory Critique* 46 (1) (April 2005), 43–59.

Sterne, Jonathan, *The Audible Past: Cultural Origins of Sound Reproduction* (Durham, NC and London: Duke University Press, 2003).

Sterne, Jonathan, *MP3: The Meaning of a Format* (Durham, NC and London: Duke University Press, 2012).

Steyerl, Hito, 'Too Much World: Is the Internet Dead?', in *Too Much World: The Films of Hito Steyerl* (Berlin: Sternberg, 2014), edited by Nick Aikens, 29–40.

Stoever, Jennifer Lynn, *The Sonic Color Line: Race and the Cultural Politics of Listening* (New York: NYU Press, 2016).

Sumner, Bernard, *Chapter and Verse: New Order, Joy Division and Me* (London: Corgi, 2015).

Thacker, Eugene, *Biomedia* (Minneapolis: University of Minnesota Press, 2004).

Thacker, Eugene, 'Sound of the Abyss', in Wilson et al., *Melancology*, 182–94.

Thompson, Marie, *Beyond Unwanted Sound: Noise, Affect and Aesthetic Moralism* (New York: Bloomsbury, 2017).

Thompson, Marie, 'Whiteness and the Ontological Turn in Sound Studies', *Parallax* 23 (3) (2017), 266–82.

Tutti, Cosey Fanni, *Art Sex Music* (London: Faber and Faber, 2017).

van Dijk, Nathanja, Kerstin Ergenzinger, Christian Kassung and Sebastian Schwesinger (eds), *Navigating Noise* (Köln: Walther König, 2017).

Veal, Michael, *Dub: Soundscapes and Shattered Songs in Jamaican Reggae* (Middletown, CT: Wesleyan University Press, 2007).

Voegelin, Salomé, *Listening to Noise and Silence* (New York: Bloomsbury, 2010).

Wallis, Jennifer (ed.), *Fight Your Own War: Power Electronics and Noise Culture* (Truro: Headpress, 2016).

Watson, Ben, *Derek Bailey and the Story of Free Improvisation* (London and New York: Verso, 2004).

Weaver, Warren, 'Recent Contributions to the Mathematical Theory of Communication', in Shannon and Weaver, *The Mathematical Theory of Communication*, 3–28.

Wegener, Alfred, *The Origin of Continents and Oceans* (Mineola, NY: Courier, 1966 [1915]).

Whitesell, Lloyd, 'White Noise: Race and Erasure in the Cultural Avant-Garde', *American Music* 19 (2) (Summer 2001), 168–89.

Wigley, Mark, *The Architecture of Deconstruction* (Cambridge, MA and London: MIT Press, 1995).

Wiley, R. Haven, *Noise Matters: The Evolution of Communication* (Cambridge, MA: Harvard University Press, 2015).

Wilson, Scott et al., *Melancology: Black Metal Theory and Ecology* (Winchester: Zero Books, 2014).

Index